POST-COMMUNIST MAFIA STATE

POST-COMMUNIST MAFIA STATE

The Case of Hungary

BÁLINT MAGYAR

CEU PRESS

in association with
 Noran Libro

© 2016 by Bálint Magyar
© English translation, Bálint Bethlenfalvy, Ágnes Simon,
Steven Nelson, Kata Paulin

Translated by Bálint Bethlenfalvy (Chapters 1-6), Ágnes Simon (Chapter 7), Steven
Nelson (Chapter 8), Kata Paulin (Chapter 9).

Published in 2016 by
Central European University Press in association with Noran Libro Kiadó

CEU Press is imprint of the
Central European University Limited Liability Company
Nádor utca 11, H-1051 Budapest, Hungary
Tel: +36-1-327-3138 or 327-3000
E-mail: ceupress@press.ceu.edu
Website: www.ceupress.com
224 West 57th Street, New York NY 10019, USA
E-mail: meszarosa@press.ceu.edu

Noran Libro Kiadó
Bocskai utca 26, H-1043 Budapest, Hungary
E-mail: kiado@noranlibro.hu
Website: www.noranlibro.hu

ISBN 978-615-5513-54-1

LIBRARY OF CONGRESS CATALOGING-IN-PUBLICATION DATA

Names: Magyar, Bálint, 1952-
  Title: Post-communist mafia state : the case of Hungary / by Bálint Magyar.
  Other titles: A magyar maffiaállam anatómiája.
  English Description: Budapest : Central European University Press, 2016. | Includes
  bibliographical references and index. | Description based on print version record and
  CIP data provided by publisher; resource not viewed.
Identifiers: LCCN 2016001392 (print) | LCCN 2015046331 (ebook) |
ISBN 9786155513558 () | ISBN 9786155513541 (alkaline paper)
Subjects: LCSH: Hungary—Politics and government—1989- | Post-communism—Hun-
gary—History—21st century. | Political corruption—Hungary—History—21st centu-
ry. | Dictatorship—Hungary—History—21st century. | Organized crime—Hungary—
History—21st century.
Classification: LCC DB958.3 (print) | LCC DB958.3 .M3413 2016 (ebook) | DDC
943.905/44—dc23
  LC record available at http://lccn.loc.gov/2016001392

Table of Contents

Timeline of the Past Century of Hungary

1920	The Paris Peace Treaty establishes the current borders of Hungary
1920–1944	Hungary is a kingdom without a king, governed by Admiral Horthy
1941	Hungary enters World War II
1945–1989	Hungary is under Soviet occupation
1949–1989	Hungary is a People's Republic
1956	Revolt against the Soviets and the communist regime
1956–1988	The Kádár-regime, after János Kádár, Hungarian communist leader
1990–1994	First democratically elected (center right) government, Prime Minister József Antall (†1993)
1994–1998	Socialist-liberal coalition government
1998–2002	First Fidesz government (with coalition partners), Prime Minister Viktor Orbán
2002–2010	Socialist government, until 2008 in coalition with liberals
2004	Hungary enters the European Union
2004–2009	Prime Minister Ferenc Gyurcsány
2009–2010	Prime Minister Gordon Bajnai
2010–	Second Fidesz government (re-elected in 2014), Prime Minister Viktor Orbán

Acknowledgements

For his indispensable assistance in the completion of this work—which is a combined, extended and updated reworking of the introductory studies for the Hungarian books *Magyar polip – A posztkommunista maffiaállam 1. és 2.* [Hungarian octopus—The post-communist mafia state, vols. 1 and 2] (Budapest: Noran Libro, 2013 and 2014) I would like to thank Márton Kozák. I am also grateful for critical observations from Mihály Andor, Attila Ara-Kovács, László Békesi, István Csillag, András György Deák, Csaba Gombár, Pál Juhász, Miklós Kárpáti, Júlia Király, János Kornai, Balázs Krémer, Tamás Lattmann, László Lengyel, Ádám C. Nagy, Iván Pető, Eszter Rádai, Ákos Róna-Tas, Károly Attila Soós, Iván Szelényi, Éva Várhegyi, and Imre Vörös.

Bálint Magyar
November 2015

Foreword

Many international observers have been puzzled about Hungary. Hungary was once the star of the post-1989 transition. It was the first in the region to rewrite its constitution to embrace democratic values. It had a steady string of free and fair elections from 1990 through 2010 with regular alternation of governments between left and right. Hungary experienced the largest inward flow of foreign direct investment in post-communist Europe and one of the least chaotic economic transitions. International NGOs put their East-Central European headquarters in Budapest, which was widely regarded as the most stable and sympathetic home for civil society groups in the region. Hungary's 2003 referendum on joining the European Union chalked up 84% for the "yes" camp. The country entered the EU in 2004 after it had sailed through external assessments that showed that it was properly a democracy that respected the rule of law, protected human rights and boasted a stable market economy.

In fact, Hungary became the very model of a "consolidated democracy," defined by Juan Linz and Alfred Stepan (who was himself living in Budapest at the time) as:

> *Behaviorally,* a democratic regime in a territory is consolidated when no significant national, social, economic, political, or institutional actors spend significant resources attempting to achieve their objectives by creating a nondemocratic regime or by seceding from the state.

> *Attitudinally,* a democratic regime is consolidated when a strong majority of public opinion, even in the midst of major economic problems and deep dissatisfaction with incumbents, holds the belief that democratic procedures and institutions are the most appropriate way to govern collective life, and when support for anti-system alternatives is quite small or more-or-less isolated from pro-democratic forces.
>
> *Constitutionally,* a democratic regime is consolidated when governmental and nongovernmental forces alike become subject to, and habituated to, the resolution of conflict within the bounds of the specific laws, procedures, and institutions sanctioned by the new democratic process.[1]

Within a decade after 1989, Hungary seemed like a place where non-democratic or anti-constitutional change was unthinkable. By the time it joined the EU, Hungary was no longer even a "transition" state: the transition was over and Hungary had become a "normal country."

Less than a decade after Hungary entered the EU, however, it has become the model "illiberal state," with constitutional checks and balances in near-total collapse, foreign investment in flight, the independence of the judiciary and independent media no longer guaranteed, civil society groups under attack, political prosecutions and rigged elections the subject of credible allegations, levels of intolerance against minority groups rising, and a single governing party controlling all public institutions in a non-transparent manner and digging itself in for the long haul. The rotation of political power is no longer secure. The left is in complete disarray, leaving far-right Jobbik as the most well-organized opposition party. Constitutional avenues for peaceful political change have been blocked; one now sometimes hears among the demoralized and fragmented "democratic opposition" of the need for revolution in the streets because they see few other choices. In the last five years, more than half a million of Hungary's 10 million citizens have left for a better life elsewhere.

The international community has taken note. The Commission for Democracy through Law of the Council of Europe, the "Venice Commission," blasted the Hungarian government for treating the constitution as a political tool to keep itself in power.[2] Freedom House, which had labelled Hungary a "consolidated democracy," lowered Hungary in 2015 to the status of a "semi-consolidated democracy," the first time that

Freedom House had ever moved a state out of the "consolidated" category.[3] The European Union, Council of Europe, OSCE, United States and others have routinely criticized the Hungarian government—and even used their limited powers to rap Hungary on the knuckles a few times—but these friends of Hungary find themselves without the tools to influence a governing party that vehemently denies the validity of all criticism and demonizes its critics.

What happened?

Those curious about the Hungarian democratic implosion have an excellent guide in Bálint Magyar. With the theoretical sophistication of an academic analyst but with the hands-on experience of someone who has been an important player in Hungary politics for the last several decades, *The Post-Communist Mafia State* is the best analysis yet of the deep reasons why Hungarian constitutional democracy fell apart so fast. It explains what happened in Hungary but it does far more than this: Magyar gives us the tools to understand a new sort of political formation—the post-communist mafia state.

Hungary is not the only example of such a state; many post-communist countries are clearly wrestling with similar tendencies. As I write, Poland is also running off the rails by following the Hungarian model. In a political science literature that has had trouble generating conceptual frameworks to handle the creativity of a new generation of autocrats, Magyar's elaboration of the key features of the new Hungarian political order will be crucial reading for all those struggling to understand the ways that the new authoritarians disguise their power grabs in democratic rhetoric without democratic reality.

Magyar's explanation of Hungary's sudden collapse is partly Tocquevillian: the "ancien régime" was already hollowed out from the inside before it was toppled by revolutionaries.[4] But in Hungary, there was a novel twist: it was also hard to tell the regime players from the revolutionaries before the revolution occurred. Before Viktor Orbán and his Fidesz political party came to power in 2010 with a constitution-making majority, Hungary's public and private spheres were crisscrossed with conflicts of interest, were shadowed by behind-the-scenes deals across the major political parties, and allowed resources and players to float between economy and state in ways that allowed many political actors to use public resources for private gain.

Before the Orbán revolution, economy and politics were deeply intertwined in a novel arrangement that could not be described as state control of the economy (socialism) nor as the economic control of the state (state capture). It certainly was not fully liberal, in which state and economy are separate and the former only lightly regulates the latter. Economic and political tools were used in tandem to hold a governing elite in place in a system of mutual corruption. Economic power corrupted politics and political power corrupted the economy. But because the agreements among allegedly competing players were stable for a number of years, Hungary appeared to have made a model transition. Stability, after all, is reassuring, no matter what its basis.

Not all of the elites were bad guys, of course. But liberals—those who wanted to create a non-corrupt constitutional state and tame a wild market with sensible regulation—were few and far between. In this, Hungary was not alone. Liberal parties across the region rarely gained electoral victories, and when they did, those victories were generally small. At best, liberal parties were junior partners locked in a coalition with parties that were non-liberal. In some countries, Russia for example, liberalism never had a chance.

Why was liberalism so unpopular in post-communist states? Liberalism has different strands that got confused in the public mind. Constitutional liberalism—governing by and according to entrenched rules that create checks on power, respect for the rule of law, and the protection of human rights—was introduced in post-communist Europe as the same time as a particularly virulent strand of economic neo-liberalism mandated radical privatization, slashed social safety nets and insisted on economic austerity in the face of economic contraction. As history would have it, the fall of the Berlin Wall occurred at the height of the Washington Consensus when economic neoliberalism was the only game in town for poor economies needing bailouts from international financial institutions.[5] When the pain of economic dislocation in the 1990s was blamed on liberalism, newly democratic publics couldn't see that constitutional and economic liberalism were separable. As a result, electoral rejection of neo-liberalism, the economic ideology, spilled over into electoral rejection of constitutional liberalism, the political ideology. Liberals now have few friends throughout the former Soviet world.

Before 2010, however, Hungary muddled along in a condition that may not have been enthusiastically liberal but it was not anti-liberal. In 2010, this situation abruptly ended when Orbán's constitutional majority allowed him to rewrite all of the rules in an aggressively anti-liberal direction. With his new powers, he cut all of his cross-party partners-in-corruption out of their various secret joint deals. Orbán, in Magyar's telling of the story, was then able to monopolize the benefits of corruption for himself and his party, using state power to choose his own preferred oligarchs and to provide endlessly ingenious ways of siphoning public assets into private hands. If there were any doubt about the creativity of the Orbán team in privatizing the goodies of governance while collectivizing its costs, this book details precisely how they did it.

But, as Magyar notes, this is not the usual kleptocracy. In a kleptocracy, the hand of the state reaches out to grab whatever resources are coursing their way through the system. In Hungary today, the state invents and entrenches the very business opportunities that it then puts in the hands of the lucky private actors who will benefit, with plentiful resources going to the very political party that uses its resources behind the scenes to perpetuate these arrangements.

Magyar calls this pattern of governance the post-communist mafia state. It is post-communist because the opportunities for corruption were legion as the former state socialist countries rapidly privatized huge swaths of the economy in the 1990s without a regulatory regime in place to oversee and regularize the privatizations. The end result overwhelmingly benefited regime insiders and provided ongoing opportunities for corrupt exchanges. In the second wave of economic dislocation that came in the wake of the financial crisis of 2007, culminating with the change of government in Hungary in 2010, new elites seized the spoils of rapid privatization away from those who initially benefited in the 1990s and they are now redistributing them among their friends. The post-communist economic transition created both the preconditions and the model for the current state.

As Magyar argues, the new political logic through which these economic transfers now occur is also mafia-like. A mafia is an underworld corrupt organization that operates like an "adopted political family." It holds its members in check by the ever-present possibility of blackmail and violence while rewarding loyalists by distributing benefits and opportunities among them. It is run by a single boss, a godfather, who binds others to

him through a combination of affection and fear and who ruthlessly eliminates all competition to his unfettered rule.

When a mafia-like organization goes from underworld to "upperworld"
and controls the state itself, the resulting "mafia state" takes its newly
acquired tools of governance and deploys them with the principles of a
mafia—holding its own loyalists in line with rigorously enforced rules of
discipline while benefiting them with the spoils of power, and threatening
its enemies with criminal prosecutions, libel cases, tax audits, confiscation
of property, denial of employment, surveillance and even veiled threats
of violence. Mafias are expert at providing offers that no one can refuse,
whether friend or foe.

Mafias also have another quality: they do not operate through formal
rules, bureaucratic structures and transparent procedures. Because mafias
have the mentalité of criminal organizations, even when they are part of
the "upperworld," they are accustomed to making their crucial decisions
in the shadows. Like in families on which they are modeled, the political
"relatives" in mafias are rewarded for loyalty, not merit, and divorces occur
on grounds of disloyalty rather than bad performance. The distribution
of available resources within the family rewards solidarity and punishes
improvisational deviation. It is precisely not based on law.

In Hungary, however, this post-communist mafia state has a legal
twist: Viktor Orbán and his circle of insiders are lawyers. Not just lawyers—
but friends who met in law school and who developed a highly legalistic way
of entrenching their powers once they controlled the state. With Fidesz's
constitutional majority, the party could—and did—change the constitution at will. Twelve amendments of the inherited constitution preceded
the rapid enactment of the new Fidesz constitution in 2011. After the constitution came into force in January 2012, it was then amended five times
before the government's first term of office ended in 2014. Anytime the
government hit a constitutional roadblock, they simply moved the roadblock to the side of the road with a constitutional amendment. And then
they sped on.

As Magyar shows, many of the laws passed under the Orbán regime
looked general but were quite specifically targeted at individuals. A law to
lower the highest salaries of public servants was justified as an austerity
measure, but it singled out the head of the national bank for a massive
pay reduction in an effort to get him to quit. A law that set up a minimum
number of years of being a judge in Hungary to qualify as president of the

Supreme Court was justified as a measure to ensure sufficient experience in the job, but it singled out the current independent-minded Supreme Court president for removal. A law that extended the terms and retirement ages of newly appointed constitutional judges was justified as increasing their independence, but it singled out the new Fidesz-loyalist judges so that they could form a working majority through 2022. And so on. Hungary became an obsessively legalistic state as the façade of law was used to cover every action that had a partisan or personal motive.

As Magyar shows, the Orbán government orchestrated a coordinated attack on all of the independent institutions in the country soon after it came into office in 2010. Local governments were neutralized as independent sites of power. Established cultural and educational institutions were battered by accusations of unpatriotic conduct and then defunded, even as new "national" institutes of culture and education were formed. The NGO sector was strangled financially and finally attacked by the public prosecutor and tax office. Churches were used instrumentally to provide ideological cover, but the "official" churches themselves seemed all too willing to go along by trading their support for the regime for material subsidies. Vicious campaigns against the holdouts in each of these categories were conducted by law and law enforcement, by public funding and defunding, and by a public campaign highlighting the disloyalty of those who refused to bend to Orbán's will. Within a few years, there were no major independent bodies of state left standing and the independent civil society organizations outside the state were hanging by a thread.

The media were a particular target of the Orbán regime. While Orbán had a substantial media retinue under his sway before returning to power in 2010, he quickly gained control over the public broadcasting media through a putsch of its most respected journalists. He then brought the private print, digital and broadcast media to heel with a non-independent media council able to issue bankrupting fines against any media outlet that violated vague content standards. Libel actions brought by members of the Orbán inner circle against those who challenged their performance, or raised questions about their private economic dealings, or simply bothered them, helped to chill criticism.

And then there was hostage-taking. Not literally, of course. But in the communist period, the government threatened family members, lovers and friends when a particular target of the regime refused to halt anti-regime activity. If a person wouldn't stop writing samizdat, then he might reconsider when his spouse was fired, his children could not get into university and his friends ran into trouble with the police. Those who grew up under communism understood that the circle around a dissident person could be held hostage to leverage compliance of the dissident. Orbán's Hungary has witnessed a return of hostage-taking, as those who have been particularly outspoken have seen their families barred from public employment and excluded from any public opportunity that the state controls, itself an expanding circle.

If one wants to stay in power for the foreseeable future while pretending to be a democrat, the machinery of elections becomes fascinating. Fidesz's popularity slumped to below 20% in 2012, after the new constitution came into force, and it appeared that there was no way that the party could win another election. The Orbán government's rewriting of the election laws strategically disadvantaged the opposition at every turn while giving the benefit of every new rule to Fidesz. In the end, Fidesz was able to win another term in office with 66% of the seats in the parliament, even though the party won less than 44% of the vote. The drop in Fidesz's vote totals was made up for in significant part by unmonitored votes coming in from ethnic Hungarians in the "near abroad" who had been enfranchised by Orbán. In a vote count reminiscent of dodgy dictatorships, Fidesz got more than 95% of the vote in this group. Without it, Orbán would have lost his two-thirds parliamentary majority and, with it, his ability to change the constitution at will.

Magyar argues that the point of this takeover of the state was economic rather than ideological. But ideology provided a cover for the sheer venality of the governing party. With its "national middle class" (Fidesz voters), its "system of national cooperation" (the party program) and its ethnic exclusionism (summoning ethnic Hungarians as the constituent power behind the new constitution), Orbán and his party could appear to stand for something, even as they failed their own electorate by shoveling resources from the state, through the party and into the waiting hands of the loyalists. Strategically invoked enemies—liberals of course, but also Jews, Roma, bankers, EU institutions and at various times, the governments of the US, Germany and Norway—created a certain solidarity when the slips of the party started to show.

For those of us who dreamed that Hungary would become a constitutional, democratic rule-of-law state that had put its various authoritarian pasts behind it, the years since 2010 have been very painful to watch.

Magyar's analysis isn't cheerful: He documents how the Fidesz money-laundering machine reaches into the nooks and crannies of Hungarian daily life. The capture of the government by the adopted political family—the takeover of state by mafia—is not a routine political rotation of power. It is the rotation of political power designed to eliminate the further rotation of political power.

What can be done? Of course, the answer to democratic failure should lie with democratic organization. In most democracies, when there is a breakdown, a democratic population can rise up and reassert its own self-governing powers. But when a country is no longer a democracy except as a façade without content and when it would be impossible for the people to displace this government and substitute a new one because there are too many mechanisms in place that would punish anyone for trying, then democratic hopes are not enough.

Bálint Magyar has thus written a very brave book. He has exposed the inner workings of the "mafia state." Perhaps now the regime will pass a law banning the word "mafia" the way that they have already told state employees not to use the words "poverty" (because it's increasing), "equal opportunity" (because it doesn't exist) and "stadium" (because the government has built so many of them that the public has started to question the expense).[6] In Orbánistan, as some have started calling it, no criticism goes unnoticed and no deviation is too small to be corrected.

The appearance of this book in English is an outreach to the audience beyond the borders and thus beyond the immediate control of the Orbán government. Given the limited opportunities for democratic renewal within the Hungarian state after a half-decade of Orbánism and its destruction of independent institutions, Hungarians who want to restore democratic self-governance may need the help of others. The failure of a democratic state should be a cause for concern in the international community, especially when anti-liberalism is spreading and new autocrats are looking for models.

Kim Lane Scheppele
Laurance S. Rockefeller Professor of Sociology and International Affairs,
Princeton University

NOTES

[1] Juan Linz and Alfred Stepan, Toward Consolidated Democracies, *Journal of Democracy* 7.2 (1996): 14-33, available at https://muse.jhu.edu/journals/journal_ of_democracy/v007/7.2linz.html. This theory was elaborated in *Problems of Democratic Transition and Consolidation: Southern Europe, South America, and Post-communist Europe* (Baltimore: Johns Hopkins University Press, 1996).

[2] "These measures amount to a threat for constitutional justice and for the supremacy of the basic principles contained in the Fundamental Law of Hungary. . . . The Venice Commission stresses that the Hungarian Fundamental Law should not be seen as a political instrument. The crucial distinction between ordinary and constitutional politics and the subordination of the former to the latter should not be disregarded, lest democracy and the rule of law be undermined in Hungary. In conclusion, the [constitutional change] . . . endangers the constitutional system of checks and balances. . . . [It] is the result of an instrumental view of the Constitution as a political means of the governmental majority and is a sign of the abolition of the essential difference between constitution-making and ordinary politics." Venice Commission, Opinion on the Fourth Amendment to the Fundamental Law of Hungary, Adopted by the Venice Commission at its 95th Plenary Session, 14–15 June 2013, Opinion 720/2013, CDL-AD(2013)012 http://www.venice.coe.int/webforms/documents/default.aspx?pdffile=CDL-AD(2013)012-e at para. 145–147.

[3] Freedom House, Nations in Transit: Hungary 2015, available at https://freedom-house.org/report/nations-transit/2015/hungary .

[4] Alexis de Tocqueville, The Old Regime and the Revolution (trans. Alan Kahan) (Chicago: University of Chicago Press, 1998). In two volumes.

[5] For an explanation of the Washington consensus during these years, see Joseph Stiglitz, *Globalization and its Discontents* (2002). Neoliberalism is obviously still pressing on EU Member States who must live in often bone-crushing austerity. See Michael Wilkinson, "Authoritarian Liberalism in the European Constitutional Imagination: Second Time as Farce?," *European Law Journal* 21:3 (2015): 313–339.

[6] Zoltán Szécsi, "'Poverty,' 'Stadium' on List of Words Ministry Employees Urged to Avoid," Politics.hu, 15 February 2015, available at http://www.politics.hu/20150223/poverty-stadium-on-list-of-words-ministy-employees-urged-to-avoid/.

1. The system we live under

People cannot relate personally, let alone politically to a no-name regime. If we are unable to capture our own reality in conceptual terms, we will become captives of other people's realities. As Stephen Hawking wrote in *The Grand Design*, co-written with the scientist Leonard Mlodinow, "there is no picture- or theory-independent concept of reality. Instead we will adopt a view that we will call model-dependent realism."[1] At another point the book also proposes, "an independently verifiable model of reality does not exist. Consequently, a well-constructed model creates its own reality. [...] Model-dependent realism applies not only to scientific models but also to the conscious and subconscious mental models we all create in order to interpret and understand the everyday world."[2]

If this is the case with nature, then it must be even more so in human societies. If we take a look at something, it is given meaning by the cognitive processes of our mind. Without an adequate linguistic and conceptual framework we are forced to merely suffer a reality contradictory to our values, formed and imposed upon us by a language that others speak. The very first, unavoidable step towards the formation of personal identity and freedom is a language based on our own values. This is a core requirement in order for an individual or community not to be swept along by an alien, unintelligible reality constructed from a language dictated by others.

During the regime change following the collapse of East European communist regimes at the turn of 1989–1990 the formula seemed clear: a step was taken from ***one-party dictatorship*** with a state monopoly of property into a multi-party parliamentary democracy based on private ownership of property and a market economy. This model, established by the western democracies, is called liberal democracy, whether presidential or parliamentary. The institutional guarantees at the heart of both systems are, in political terms the separation of powers, provisions to allow for the removal of reigning powers, and conditions for proper competition for taking government, while in the economic sphere, guarantees for the pre-eminence of private property, clean market competition, and security of ownership.

When the norms of the legal system are violated in a *liberal democracy*, mechanisms of institutional control and the division of powers will—more or less—correct such deviations. In their case these deviations do not achieve a critical mass, and do not thereby pose a threat to the system. However, if the deviations undermining the legal standards of liberal democracies are not only present in great numbers, but form the mainstream goals and values of government, thereon the dominant characteristics can be said to constitute a new system. New phenomena call for new narratives, which are usually offered by metaphors or analogies, based on previously experienced patterns. This is how the Orbán regime was likened, for example, to the autocratic, corporativist regimes of Spain, Portugal, and Italy of the twenties and thirties, or Hungary of the interwar Horthy era, with its many related traits. Their experience of events in Hungary since 2010 reminded others of South American dictatorships, quasi or real, or even a softer version of the communist regimes. Yet these historical analogies are sharply limited in their validity: while they may evoke a sense of one or another individual phenomenon within the system, they nevertheless fail to give a comprehensive description of the system as a whole.

Hungary is currently a *post-communist mafia state*. The term post-communist is descriptive of the mafia state, pointing to the circumstances of its formation, the conditions of its germination, that is, to the fact that this is a system that came about—though with some delay—in the wake of the one-party dictatorship that went hand-in-hand with a monopoly on state owned property. The words mafia state are definitive of the way in which this state functions. All that had begun in Hungary between 1998 and 2002—the first time Fidesz had come to power—and has been fully realized since 2010 is best compared with what has happened in most of the countries of the former Soviet Union: Russia under Putin, Azerbaijan, or other Central Asian former member republics of the Soviet Union. The difference in the case of Hungary is merely in the path of political evolution taken since the regime change. It is not merely a matter of a distorted, truncated democracy or a deficit of democracy where Hungary is concerned, since that would still actually mean there is democracy, though limited. Rather, this system aptly described as a mafia state fits no traditional framework of interpretation dealing with the relationship between democracy and dictatorship. Nor does it have a place on the kind of corruption rankings normally produced by international organizations about the countries of the world, since these usually presume that different gradations of an identical quality is at issue, as if all that needed to be measured would be how widespread a homogeneous phenomenon is. As opposed to this, the current Hungarian political system has become a phenomenon of a different brand, and these rankings only obscure its essence. This new brand can only be described by clear citation of the specifics of the system set in a new framework of understanding.

This explanatory model of the post-communist mafia state aims to focus on the system as whole, rather than mere individual phenomena that may have occurred in other systems, yet whose historical antecedents differ fundamentally from the established mafia state. The fundamental feature of the mafia state is the intrinsic logic of the accumulation of power and wealth which primarily determines all its actions, and which realizes a combination of political power concentration and the growth of fortunes in the hands of the adopted political family by means of mafia culture elevated on the rank of central politics, operating a state monopoly on coercion.

1.2. Evolutionary forms of corruption

Where *day-to-day corruption* is concerned, private interests hold an illegitimate sway in state and local government decisions concerning allocation of resources, procurements, concessions, and entitlements. As a result, illegal barter deals are concluded between discrete economic actors and state officials or bureaucrats at various levels of seniority. Day-to-day corruption consists of a series of individual phenomena: an official responsible for a decision accepts or requests financial or other benefits for handling a case in a manner advantageous to the dispenser of the bribe. A system is considered corrupt if there is a high occurrence of such incidents, or if civil administrative or business matters can only be managed through *bribes*. Hungarian citizens were not assured of civil servants being above accepting bribes by the experience of the transformation years following the regime change. Political connections were a means to acquire property, or loans that never had to be repaid, and an array of other advantages. Nevertheless, irrespective of the endless incidences of such corruption, it never coalesced to become a force structuring the system. An administrator having to be paid off in order for a contract to go through may poison public life in general, but as a private action of the parties involved, it does not undermine the foundations of the democratic establishment or impinge on the essence of the system, for it is still clear that the incident goes against the expected, legitimate behavioral norms. (Corruption related to party funding—which is widespread even in well-tried democracies—is qualified as a deviancy, similarly to corruption in public office.) Beyond state deterrence and penalties, anti-corruption watchdog organizations operate so as to inhibit the spread of corruption. Their means are investigative journalism and any other tool to draw the veil from incidents of corruption, lifting it from a private into the public sphere on the assumption that the offender will be subject to their due desserts subsequent to exposure.

Though not a constituent building block of the **communist system preceding the regime change**, corruption was a typical byproduct of the system. Under command economy, three economic modes coexisted:

- State ownership was the basis of the *"first economy,"* which was a determining force of the economy following the wave of nationalizations in the late 1940s.
- The private businesses linked to the state sector meant the *"second economy"* which filled in the market gaps of the general shortage stemming from the centrally planned economy in a rather surprising bounty of forms: in retail, retail services and the family farms, so called backyard farmsteads (*háztáji*).
- The category of the *"third economy"* used to designate the myriad market maneuvers oiled by corrupt transactions, also in the context of the consumer bottlenecks of the shortage economy. The great variety of forms of corruption, both solicited and expected, permeated the gamut of society—from the reception desk to the party chairs—rather evenly. At virtually all points of economic contact across the shortage economy that accompanied state monopoly, individuals would find themselves equipped with some stock, service, or compe-

tency in a discretional decision to sell, for which they could pocket a tip, gratuity or corrupt allowance. The everyday Hungarian terms, such as *"kenőpénz"* meaning grease-money, or *"csúszópénz"* sliding-money, were indicative of the fact that without oiling the machinery, the planned economic system itself would have in fact been paralyzed. The unavoidable, system-preserving character of these mutual reciprocities that could be placed anywhere on the scale of legitimacy and illegitimacy made this web of corrupt transactions a morally accepted convention. For this system worked in a quasi egalitarian manner, after all the opportunities for illegitimate ways of accumulating wealth were greatly limited even for leaders in the economy built on state monopoly, while by means of their mini-monopolies the hundreds of thousands people in the lower strata of the system could also impose their "allowances."

However, **the regime change** resulted in unprecedented inequalities not only in wealth, but in terms of corruption prone positions as well. Since the shortage economy dissolved in the interactions of the participants of the private sector, the arena of corruption was driven back into the channels of business established between the private and public sectors. Yet in this new barter economy the client was no longer the small customer of the old communist regime under János Kádár, but increasingly the ever-wealthier circle of entrepreneurs, from the small lessees of local government commercial premises to the moguls commissioning legislative regulations. Changes in everyday corruption following the regime change included

- first, a narrowing of the circle of those to be corrupted and an end to its mass aspect, as well as its basically becoming linked to the participants of the public administration and the broadly considered political class;
- secondly, a transformation of the structure of decision-making in areas affected by corruption: displacing advantages tied to everyday consumption, state assistance that offered advantages in the competition for accumulation of wealth came into the foreground, e.g., privatization, state and local government procurement, tenders, real-estate reclassifications, permits issued by the authorities;
- thirdly, the profit margin to be achieved through individual corrupt decisions grew significantly: it was no longer the one white porcelain

toilet bowl one could acquire under the counter of the state owned shop by greasing palms, but the entire factory that made it, along with the retail chain that distributed it, purchasing it on a loan from the state;

- fourthly, the roles in corrupt transactions had permanently diverged: no longer was "everyone" simultaneously corruptor and corrupt as they participated in the widely strewn social fabric of scarcity; while the initiators of the corrupt transactions, who approached actors in the public sector now came from the business or civil sphere.

The anomalies of party financing and its openness to corrupt deals were caused by misguided and unfounded presuppositions. At the time of the regime change, it was believed on the basis of western models that parties would have a significant income from *membership fees* and *legal donations*. Though it was obvious that even the total membership—and the fees they paid—of all the parties following the regime change would remain below the eight hundred thousand Hungarian Socialist Workers' Party peak membership under communism, it was not anticipated that in 1990–91 the combined membership of the new parties would be around the tenth of the same figure of the former communist party. Which rate continued to decrease thereon. Moreover, due to the slowing down of public life outside of campaign periods, worsening income levels, rising unemployment and inflation only a symbolic sum could be charged as membership fees, or else non-paying members would have been expelled from the parties. The losses of such a strategy on an organizational and communications level would have far outstripped the gains of overstraining people's ability to pay membership fees. Naturally, the later slump in membership of the new political parties went along with a decrease in income from membership fees, resulting in difficulties with supporting even the most minimal organizational infrastructure.

The annual budget for the state system of party financing did not however take into account the demands of the *election campaigns*, and the fraction of the campaign costs that could be met from the state allocation was negligible from as early as 1994. Party spending on election campaigns was not capped in the beginning. This action was only taken in 1996, when the limit—valid until 2013—was set at one million forint (about $9,000 at that time) per candidate. This was not only problematic because the figure did not follow a then double-digit inflation, but also because expenditures related to the election campaign in one way or the other, reached beyond both the time-frame of the election period established by law and the narrowly defined circle of campaign events. This resulted in the escalation of campaign expenditures and made the enforcement of accountability impossible. To add to all of this, the State Court of Auditors only had the right to check the declared campaign expenditure of parties, in other words, to examine if the items declared by the parties had been added up correctly.

Due to the tight allowance of official party financing the nationwide parties would have been unable to function had they operated on membership fees and state allocation alone—while the mayoral office of a smaller city had more employees working in it than the national apparatus of major parties involved in the regime change. Since they were necessarily dependent on additional resources, and their financial matters beyond the official budget funds had become practically unaccountable, the budgetary limitations on party income and expenditure became loosened. Only the actual and expected political clout, and aggressive ambition of a given party—in fact virtually its self-control alone—could limit or spur on the measure of resources it could tap.

The party revenue from fees and state budget did not cover anything beyond basic operation costs. Apart from the invisible income presumable on the basis of the massive election spending parties indulged in, substantial loans also became a part of the system of financing. The loans were taken out on the presumption that they would be paid either through sale of the real-estate the parties had received free or at huge discount, or revenues from social capital—in the event of taking power. While party support based merely on sympathy, offered without expectation of recompense fizzled out, the indebtedness of parties grew and corruption attendant on the financing of parties inevitably became more widespread. The focus of income from sources other than the state budget shifted away not only from the membership fees to other sources in the economic sector, but within that field in increasing measure to immediate business interests and reciprocities wholly irrespective of political sympathies.

Both sides now court one another: not only was business looking for contact with members of the new political class, but also the reverse. Reciprocal favors were traded at various levels on the scale of legitimacy and illegitimacy. Such relations carried the inherent possibility not only of parties working their budgets around the law, but the personal corruption of members of the political class.

The threat of such illegitimate intertwining of interests was even greater outside the range of central party financing. Since the election campaigns of local governments and mayors also required significant budgets, the anomalies of central party financing fanned out in waves across the country. Moreover the overlap between possible supporters and those benefited on a reciprocal basis was even more immediate in the use of local funds. Though the spread of corruption had a major role in the political elite falling into disrepute, its *routine operational role* did not become a *systemic operational role*, fundamentally determining political goals. Rather it merely constituted a world loosely controlled from the center, profiting from its positions with chaotic autonomy, often competitive in itself. The Hungarian political parties—with the exception of the Alliance of Young Democrats (*Fiatal Demokraták Szövetsége, Fidesz*)—did not establish their own business ventures to generate income, but pressed businesses for allowances and contributions episodically. Though doing so with great regularity.

The emergence of the *organized underworld, the mafia* represents a new stage as compared to the world of "free enterprise" corruption. Thereon organized criminal groups try methodically to draw the figures of public power into their sphere of influence. When they succeed, we can say that the organized underworld has found its way into the topmost, political sphere of politics, and seeks to influence not only individual decisions—about access or distribution—but the system by which the rules are established and legislation as well. In such cases it is difficult to draw a clear line between legitimate lobbying and the advance of the organized underworld involving bribery and blackmail. Its actions are based not necessarily on the voluntary acquiescence of both parties and the reciprocity of illegal advantages—as in the case of ordinary corruption—but the will of the underworld is carried through even by means of threats and violence: blackmail and *protection money*, as well as oversight of branches of business promising great returns. While attempting to monopolize a given area of illegitimate economic activity, in geographic terms and where branches of activity are concerned it operates in a segmented market, that is, it is not capable of extending its authority to control the whole economy or the country as a whole. The fact that the hard fought contract between mafia families composes the distribution of the markets, at times taking institutional shape as the council of the heads of the families, does not contradict the hierarchical nature of relationships within each family or clan. (The renewed forms of mafia and the organized underworld across the ocean increasingly dismiss traditional ways and their "communal" functions and forms of behavior.)

Besides creating illegitimate profitable economic opportunities for itself through bribes, the mafia also draws taxes through forced payments of protection money. It motivates figures in public office through bribes and forces the participants of the business sector to pay for protection. The classical model for this is the Sicilian mafia, where the tentacles of the polyp rise from below to weave around the world of politics. The organized underworld is already a dangerous phenomenon that is difficult to eliminate, but it only causes a shift in the fundamental situation typical of the rule of law when its representatives gain political power. In spite of officials and politicians—even in vast numbers—who can be bought, the faith that the state is at war with the mafia can remain unbroken. In other words some individuals may go astray, but the institutions are in combat with the criminal groups of the organized underworld. At this point the formula is still easily expressed: the methods of the organized underworld, the mafia, do not offer the political figures of public power a model to be emulated systemically. However if the infiltration oversteps certain boundaries in the long term, and the business mafia—which does not accept public political roles—recruits a number of political decision makers, the accepted term that comes to apply will be state capture. In such cases a series of laws, regulation and decisions are brought in the service of illegitimate private interests.

Though after the regime change in Hungary criminal groups from the organized underworld did come to the fore with the intention of gaining influence in politics, their progress could not be described as state capture. Vast fortunes nevertheless were built—exploiting legal loopholes that were at times artificially left open—on the "oil-bleaching" scam, that is, the illegal oil trade, the world of nightclubs, or even the security guard services in the early 1990s. Yet the organized underworld was not seeking a primary, political role. One reason was the considerable penetration of the fresh Hungarian market by foreign (mainly Russian and Ukrainian) organized criminal groups in the 1990s. The organized underworld was merely intent upon expanding and carrying on its illegal activities unharmed. By the turn of the millennium, the new political elite had in part eliminated this factor, and partly confined it to certain limits, domesticated it. The fountain of fortunes from oil bleaching had been shut by legislature in 1995. Meanwhile, following the drawn-out turf wars and liquidations between security services companies made up of veteran secret service men and ex-law enforcement personnel, a representative could be jailed, become a minister.

The organized upperworld, the mafia state nevertheless goes far beyond both the mentioned anomalies in party financing and the underworld's ambitions for political influence. In fact the relationship is turned around in both cases. It is not, after all, the party financing needs that generate the illegitimate resources which are then pocketed: meaning that the potential of a party in decision-making is not incidentally, but systematically exploited in advance, to lay the foundations of private fortunes. On the other hand, the decisions are not distorted by the hidden meddling hand of the underworld from "below" and "outside," but rather government and the regulations are deliberately adjusted in advance, from "above" and "inside" to illegitimate and particular interests. In the mafia state, the duality typical of the practices of the organized underworld, where bribes are offered to those in higher positions and protection money squeezed out of those below, ceases to exist, because in possession of public authority, the organized upperworld simply taxes and takes an allowance from those below in the form of "protection money."

The classical world of proliferating corruption is typified by the chaotic weave of competing illegal transactions both great and small, which take increasingly structured forms rising incrementally from one evolutionary stage to the next.

- The first stage of evolution is the world of free enterprise corruption. The bribe as its most widespread tool, an expression of the fact that the client is representative of the business sector, while the provider of the corrupt services is a representative of the public sector. The corrupt transaction is incidental, and has not been organized as a group function on either side.
- The second evolutionary stage of corruption is built on the first, with the local-partial monopolies making up the oligopolistic provinces of the underworld mafia groups (organized underworld), enforced through never-ending wars and liquidations. This simply mirrored in the sphere of the public authorities when a considerable political force is also able to form its own oligopolistic mechanism for coerced corruption with which to pressure actors in the private economy. In this phase the players of the economy and politics seek each other out along established paths, mutually.

- On the third evolutionary level the mafia state (the organized upper-world) already restrains, squeezes out the organized underworld, elimi-nating the anarchistic, partially autonomous world of the oligarchs, while reorganizing corruption in practice into a single chain of order, nationally centralizing and monopolizing it. It fights not corruption at large, but against partisan acts of corruption that it is not carried out by its express permission. It acts in the way the classical mafia would within the scope of its interests, but on a national level: it eliminates the "private thief."[3] The American bon mot, "Don't steal! The govern-ment hates competition," finds its literal meaning here.

It may be worthwhile to illustrate the difference between the three phases by means of a simple example—that of the real estate racket in a district of Budapest.[4] If a business that rents a local government owned premises and attempts to acquire possession of the same premises with a bribe to the local government official, this would be an example of *day-to-day cor-ruption*. This would be the case irrespective of how widespread the practice was, if the owners of the business attempting the transfer were not related or friends either with each other or the official, and it is the official's rogue operation. The corrupt transaction is *single tier*, bribe money changes hand in exchange for the illegitimate, or scantly accessible permit for ownership of the property. If the *organized underworld* forces a significant number of those renting such premises by means of a variety of violent means at its disposal, to sell or handover their right to rent, so that after the fact, in col-lusion with the local government officials they can buy them at the discount price at which they are sold to the rent holders, this belongs in the second evolutionary phase of corruption. In this set up however, those favored by the deal acquire their properties as members of a network and are no longer isolated beneficiaries, but members of the adopted—underworld—family. In this instance the corrupt transaction is *double tier*: in its dealings with the less strong—the original businesses holding the rent permits—it black-mails, threatens, coerces, while bribing those with power—the local govern-ment officials. And if amendments of the law are required for the transac-tion to be secured, as well as stable partnerships for cooperation at all levels of local government, this would mean a case of local state capture. Yet *the form in which the organized upperworld exists* is on a new level altogether. Even if relations with the underworld have not been cut, local govern-ment heads would themselves manage the eviction and replacement of the businesses renting the premises with their clients, members of their own adopted political family. After a few days of renting the premises the new individuals with the rental status can become the owners at a discount price. The right to a preferential rate those renting premises to become owners of the property has thereby opened an institutional course by which individual "scams" can be replaced by organized crime, which is neither owned nor driven by the underworld, but rather the local elite with a grip on public authority.[5] The deal has once again become *single tier*: it employs the tools of deceit, coercion towards those with less power. Yet it becomes difficult to speak of the case outlined as corrupt, because the beneficiaries favored illegitimately and those managing the transaction are not separate groups on two sides of the transaction, but equally members of the adopted political family. It is not an outside force that seizes hold over the local authorities, but the public administrative office itself that acts like the mafia through the tools of public administration and enforcement at its disposal.

The systemic corruption of the mafia state on a national level is therefore no longer an ordinary or underworld instance of corruption, for at this "stage of evolution" corruption has suddenly been elevated from a deviancy to be kept hidden, to the rank of state politics, of a general practice overseen centrally. Oligarchs no longer draw the state under their control. Instead, a political venture creates itself the right to appoint oligarchs. In other words it is not an economic interest group that takes over supervision of certain segments of a politics that is otherwise personally and organizationally detached from it, but *the political venture, which itself simultaneously becomes an economic venture also*, capturing both the worlds of politics and the economy, and establishing its mafia type culture and influence by means of the whole arsenal of the powers of the state. During the first period of Fidesz government from 1998–2002, the progress of this model had tough institutional constraints. Though the democratic institutional system had been eroded, it was nevertheless upheld—more or less—by the laws requiring a two-thirds parliamentary majority. With less than a two-thirds majority the conditions fundamental to the formation of a mafia state, a monopoly on power and the elimination of a separation of the powers of state could not be brought to pass. Since 2010 however—with this barrier gone—the entrenchment of the mafia state has been carried out at the highest possible intensity.

Under the mafia state private interest takes the rightful place of public interest systemically and permanently, rather than by chance and on occasion. There is virtually no field of activity that is not subject to the concentrated demands of power and wealth accumulation. *The mafia state is the privatized form of the parasitic state.*

NOTES

[1] Stephen Hawking and Leonard Mlodinow, *The Grand Design* (New York: Bantam Books, 2010), 42.

[2] Ibid., 46.

[3] Eric J. Hobsbawm, *Primitive Rebels* (Manchester: Manchester University Press, 1959), 40.

[4] "Fifth district local government delegate for the party Együtt, Péter Juhász held an anti-corruption scenic walk, alternative city tour yesterday evening, drawing public attention to the real estate affairs of the district authorities that are suspicious, to say the least. The demonstration targeted the 'inner city Rogán–Szentgyörgyvölgyi-real estate mafia,' which has already succeeded in spiriting away one-third of the real estate holdings of the district government." Dorka Czenkli, "És tőled mennyit lopott el a Fidesz?" [And how much has Fidesz stolen from you?], *Magyar Narancs*, 15 January 2015. http://magyarnarancs.hu/belpol/es-toled-mennyit-lopott-el-a-fidesz-belvarosi-antikorrupcios-seta-93364; Antal Rogán was earlier mayor of the district, now leader of the parliamentary faction of Fidesz; Péter Szentgyörgyvölgyi is the current mayor of the district representing Fidesz.

[5] http://atlatszo.hu/2015/03/02/ennel-a-nagysagrendu-penznel-nincsenek-partszinek-portik-tamas-ingatlanokrol-olajos-alvilagrol-politikai-kapcsolatokrol/.

2. The disintegration of the Third Hungarian Republic[1] in 2010

In East and Central Europe the regime change brought about political institutional systems modeled on western democracy—truly exemplary in Hungary. Yet the eastern forms of behavior that are, so to speak, foreign to the system in a liberal democracy continued to thrive. In the "two troubled decades" between 1990–2010, as the Fidesz stigmatized the period that had passed since the regime change in retrospect, *a western political establishment struggled with an eastern pattern of wealth and property accumulation.* Thereby the elections and changes of government were not merely the routine stations of a process of adjustment within a single value system—along the lines of a social model otherwise based on consensus—but the bitter battles of a war to secure property and the new positions generating wealth. The eastern patterns of nepotism emerging in this battle—escalated by the political elite and causing continuous social and political turbulence—ate away, and finally largely devoured the western political institutional system established during the regime change. Of course, it makes sense to ask why in the struggle between the western institutional system and eastern cultural patterns the latter came out victorious.

In order to explain the disintegration and two-thirds victory of Fidesz at the polls it is necessary to delineate, first the responsibility of individual political figures (the crimes, mistakes, inertia, etc. of the governing parties, and Fidesz's deliberate strategic war on the institutional system of liberal democracy) and second, the sociological causes following from the structural and mental state of Hungarian society that a right-wing political force on the offensive could prey on. Nonetheless, the unfortunate simultaneity of causes was required for the Third Hungarian Republic to meet the fate of becoming a mafia state. The same directly befell most of the republics emerging from the Soviet Union, while Hungary took a circuitous route. So in fact **what unfolded in Hungary was not necessarily its fate.**

2.1. The value system of the Hungarian society

"In 1989 it may still have seemed as if" Péter Tölgyessy[2] writes "all we Hungarians had to do would be to follow the practices of building a social market economy and rule of law grounded in Germany by the *Grundgesetz* (the Basic Law of Bonn), and well tried in the following by a row of nations. Then, having developed the new Hungarian model of progress based on our own traditions, a convergence with the west becoming possible within the foreseeable future if consistent efforts were made. Except that rather than a few decades of successful European convergence with a broadening of the middle strata of society, what followed the turn of 1989 was a prolonged period of crisis. The legacy of communism proved far more cumbersome than expected at the time. It soon became clear: there was no direct transition from the half-baked petit embourgeoisement of the Kádár period to real market capitalism. It was more difficult for people socialized in Kádár's world of bargaining and circumvention of rules to adapt to the competition of the world market than it was for other citizens of Central Europe. All at once in the free country it became apparent: Hungarian instincts, desires and hopes, culture and codes of behavior were seriously scarred, and had far more in common with East European and Balkan patterns than those of Central Europe."

A research project[3] placing the value system of Hungarian society in international context gives an outline of the firm obstacles to a consistent commitment to liberal democracy and a market economy based on free competition. The traits described by the research findings barely changed from the beginning of the eighties until the fifth survey in 2009. The study delivers a sobering message to those expecting the western value-set of liberal democracies, showing that the closest value-neighbors of the Hungarians on the map of value systems are the countries with an Eastern Orthodox culture, the Republic of Moldova and Bulgaria, as well as Ukraine and Russia. Not only the countries beyond the Leitha (the river that historically separated Hungary from Austria), but the Central European countries belonging—just like Hungary—to the western Judeo-Christian cultures, are also placed at a much greater distance from Hungary on the value map. The value system typical of Hungarian society falls far even from the periphery of the West. The study shows that the otherwise secularized Hungary is pushed a long way into the East by a closed way of thinking: Hungarian citizens are only characterized by a commitment to freedom of speech, the need to participate in public issues, the practice of freedom of rights and trust in other people, tolerance of those who think differently or their ability to influence their own fates to the same degree as that of Moldavia, and nowhere near that of their Slovak or Slovenian neighbors. A pithy comment by Péter Esterházy in his comedy titled *Búcsúszimfónia* [Farewell symphony] simply states: "The Russian are gone, and we are left here."[4]

According to a survey in 1991, only 5 percent of the 30 thousand membership of even the most western oriented, liberal party to have emerged from the anti-communist dissident movement, the Alliance of Free Democrats (*Szabad Demokraták Szövetsége—SZDSZ*) revealed a value system that could be considered consistently liberal in matters concerning human rights and economics—though the party leadership proclaimed such a stance with full determination.[5] A value analysis of liberalism in 2013 on the other hand showed that though the proportion of those considering themselves liberal in Hungary was 14 percent, and 18 percent categorized themselves as liberals in matters of human rights, the percentage of those committed to capitalism was a mere 5 percent. Among the three dimensions of the liberal value system examined by the survey, the number of those who believed in at least two of the three did not even reach 5 percent. Yet the condition of the stability of western liberal democracy is a broad and cohesive sense of commitment to the values of human rights, the free market and respect for private property, and awareness of this commitment.

2.2. The political right and left: Two competing anachronisms

János Kis, the early leader of the anti-communist dissident movement both intellectually and personally as a figurehead in the 1980s, presents the situation in a recent essay as follows:[6]

[In the] twenty years following the regime change *two* anachronisms battled it out and at the same time kept each other alive: the right-wing approach yearning for the Horthy period [between the two World Wars] and the leftist approach unable to wean itself from the Kádár period [following 1956].

Hungarian history of the "short 20th century" was dominated by a state of war between the right- and left-wing. Either this or that one would triumph periodically; either this or the other would smash its opponent to bits. [...] The system that followed 1989 was the first to force the political sides once engaged in a life and death struggle into peaceful competition based on periodic elections. This was the first time the loser had to acknowledge that its opponent was forming government on legitimate grounds. [...] This external pressure was meant to get translated into an internal stimulus.

It was only to be expected that the constitutional guarantees of rights to political freedom would help unspoken grievances rise to the surface. The opening of the wounds could however also have brought purification and reconciliation; after all, the enmity belonged to a passed epoch, and the democratic rules of the game ultimately favored an eventual accommodation of the other. However, with the reanimation of the past mutually harbored, age-old fears also sprung into action and rather than extinguishing one another, these only perpetuated the mutually exclusive anachronisms on both sides. Upon seeing the right-wing behavior that accorded admiral Horthy a reburial with government support and erected statues to Pál Teleki,[7] and Albert Wass,[8] the left saw its post-World War past as being justified. Seeing the behavior of the left lost in its reverie of "goulash socialism" the political right thought its past prior to the war as justified.

The apologetic attitude of both the right and the left wings to their own past took a major toll on the advancement of a democratic public morale in the first place, because it idealized anti-democratic conditions. They also caused further damage however, as the two approaches to the past cannot be soldered into the common tradition of a single political community. [...]

Meanwhile [...] the norms and operational rules of the democratic establishment went against the mutually exclusive anachronisms, which kept each other alive precisely by virtue of this characteristic. The outcome of the story was not decided in advance. The political right- and left-wing of the past were equally antidemocratic; after 1989 they were simultaneously engaged in a nostalgic longing for the—undemocratic—past while learning the strings of democratic politics. Both time and occasion were afforded to straighten out the anachronisms. [...]

The relationship between the Hungarian post-regime change right and left was steeped in mutual suspicion that the other was *preparing* to overpower the constitutional framework. In the autumn of 2006 [in the aftermath to the anti-government disturbances and a response from law-enforcement] it became the firm conviction on both sides that the other had in fact *already overpowered* the constitutional framework. According to the right-wing mythologem the left-wing government showed its true colors as a police state. According to the left-wing mythologem, the right-wing opposition had showed its true, putschist face. Nothing stood in the way of the "cold civil war" from this point onwards.

At the same time the legitimacy of the conflicting mythologems within the opposed camps was not determined by the extent to which they were justified or baseless, or whether they were honest sentiments of their leaders or mere sham. It is a fact however that the socialist-liberal government with a two-thirds majority in parliament between 1994 and 1998 practiced self-restraint, and did not make use of its constituent powers while after 2010 Fidesz carried out its constitutional coup d'état claiming a "two-thirds revolution in the voting booth."

2.3. Spaces of rational public discourse in demise

No social integration is possible without linguistic integration grounded in a general consensus on public discourse. By the 1980s, a secular, rational, western discourse had developed under the conditions of the soft communist dictatorship, which only carried a glazing of that official, apparatchik language dictated by the communist regime, which was taken less and less seriously. The language used by the liberal intelligentsia and anti-communist dissident movement incrementally pushed the language of authority into a defensive position, and in the course of the peaceful regime change the reformer communists made the partial switch from one language to the other. The liberated press relayed the process to a wide public. Yet the homogeneity of the westernized, rational vocabulary masked the great divide in the value system of the society, with its stridently eastern character. This is the period of illusions, of disappointments in political perceptions. The language of the fallen regime was worn away. The socialists do not have a language of their own even today, while having more or less adopted the secular, rational, westernized discourse. To begin with, the language of the outdated—or even evil—ideas remained repressed in political subcultures, and broke to the surface during election campaigns at most. Later it was unbound from those confines by the bitter struggle within the political elite, which employed verbal aggression as an instrument of extreme political and social polarization.

This brought into being the **multilingual nation** incapable of dialogue between value systems. When the two languages serving disparate functions have become the languages of two political camps, the political struggle is conducted on the linguistic front.

Interpretation and debate are the functions of the **language of the liberal, left-wing camp**. By means of its descriptive, analytical, critical and argumentative tools **it forms an identity rationally**. It actually has no set of symbols it could reflect upon apart from the rational message of the language. Yet this idiom of rational public discourse was gradually limited to an intellectual subculture.

Cohesion and recruitment are the functions of the **language of the right-wing camp**. By means of its indicative, enunciative, labeling and stigmatizing tools **it forms an identity symbolically and emotionally**. By these means this language was capable of reflecting on the visual, ritual, and emotional world of the ideology beyond the language itself, and began to take over as the dominant language by providing it with, so to speak, a consistent order.

The erosion of liberal democracy began with the squeezing out of its language. This is the **twilight of rational public discourse and dialogue**, when an argumentative, intellectually consistent form of speech is replaced by a fragmented, narrative-centered, stigmatizing language, which is an effective tool in bolstering ideologies that simplify and create an emotional consistency. Rather than argument and acknowledgement, this language calls for belief, mediates struggle rather than comparability.

Fidesz grounded its cold civil war in linguistic militancy, in the course of which the liberal and left wing suffered defeat after defeat daily without even realizing it.

Of course it is the rationale of the political struggle's vote maximization that helps to cleave liberal democracy apart and also promotes the *derationalization of public discourse*. Since the results of the elections in post-communist states affect conditions of all spheres of life much deeper than in the established western democracies, the electoral battles were marked by a sort of escalating "tsunami of promises," which did away with the political basis of rational responses to economic-social challenges.

The economic crises—that had first led up to and become apparent through the regime change, later to return in the crash of 2008—was not Hungary's only affliction, it had also run into *the pitfall of populism*. A pitfall encapsulated in the fact that barely one and a half million of the nearly eight million citizens eligible to vote in Hungary paid eighty percent of the state's revenues from personal income tax. The main question of the three parliamentary elections following 1998 was what share of the tax-payers' money the main parties offered those who were not paying taxes. The two forces with a chance to win, Fidesz and the Hungarian Socialist Party (MSZP) both employed populist rhetoric, while carrying on a give-and-take politics when in government ("distributive" on the one hand, and "plundering" on the other).

Fidesz's marching from a set of liberal values to the right-wing value system meant at the same time a systematic traversal of the path that lead from a political discourse based on rational arguments to one based on populism. It first separated itself from the set of values and arguments of liberal democracy and free market society by adding the adjective of national to liberalism, symbolically reinforcing the nationalist rhetoric. With mixed results: though populist nationalism—in combination with the application of Fidesz's internal techniques for power to the whole of right-wing politics and the grinding down of any people or organization wishing to uphold the divisions on the right—was sufficient to bring about the broadest unified political block, it was not enough to achieve an absolute electoral majority. As evidenced by Fidesz's 2002 defeat, "their support was large in numbers, but not large enough." The experience was repeated in the referendum of 2004, which—in seeking to offer dual citizenship to people of Hungarian origins abroad, and with it, the right to vote—could be described as a conflict between national and socialist populism. While Fidesz still lost out on this contest, from then onwards it consciously strove to also win over voters who felt a nostalgia for the sense of security in the Kádár period (and had until then remained immune to the right-wing and voted for the left), by uninhibitedly *molding national populism with social populism*. Fidesz's crossover into social populism which had been considered an exclusive privilege of the socialist party until then was not only marked by the demagogy of the 2006 elections' slogan, "we live worse than four years ago," but also a switch from the elegant, dark suite to the purple-striped shirt without a tie and the grey-checked polyester coat. The target audience was no longer the autonomous "citizen" representing the deliberative world of rational public discourse, but those who wished to believe in populist promises, the "simple masses."

The common denominator between nationalist and social populism is a diversion of a sense of responsibility for our own fates: *the "long suffering" Hungarian nation and the existentially vulnerable little man joined in one.* In the long run of course it came down to a systematic expulsion of responsibility and self-reflection from the culture of Hungarian politics. Clearly however, an individual or a nation that is incapable of equitable consideration, rational argument, self-reflection and even self-irony is underage. The inability for learning and renewal means an insurmountable obstacle to either an individual or a community in our world, built as it is, on competition. A fairytale narrative about who and why destroyed their life and stole their good fortune is indispensable for a nation or individual who has shed its responsibility for itself and delivered itself into the care of the state. Next the path from unrestrained self-acquittal leads directly to emotional scapegoating: foreign-hearted people, commies, bankers, oligarchs, offshore-riders, liberals, Jews, gays, gypsies, and just about anyone, even the inexistent Piréz (a fictional people invented by the Hungarian polling company Tárki, who are disliked by two-thirds of the population).[9] They are all liable for the misfortunes of the Hungarian people. And if the political elite does not consciously take up a stance in opposition to this self-acquitting instinct, but rather reinforce it—at times stridently, and at others with a nod and a wink—the culture of sensible discussion and a critical, yet still equitable behavior towards each other will be extinguished in both politics and public life.

Fidesz recognized the potential in the psychological force behind self-acquittal and scapegoating others for one's own fate, which could be converted into a political one, and deliberately based their politics on this. If the path to victory was to be paved with such stones, so be it. The character assassination and scapegoating (i.e., the stigmatization and criminalization of political opponents), which has been the rule rather than an occasional tool, determining Fidesz's communications since 2002 is no more than the use of populism for the elimination of obstacles in Fidesz's way. Verbal aggression has become the day-to-day routine of political communication. While they played on negative instincts and base emotions in their communications with the political advantages in mind and in cold calculation, the extreme right was racist and antisemitic with full self-abandon in a candid way, straight from the heart. Fidesz made these feelings acceptable in society at large, while the extreme-right verbalized it under the mantle of naivety. Since the expectation raised by social populism cannot be satisfied, scapegoating and stigmatization become the indispensable prop of government after 2010. The tools to keep the potential voter base together are existential liquidations and hate-campaigns directed from above: they form the audience at séances of ritual and verbal lynching directed from the center. If the lives of the people cannot be made easier, let their chains rattle at least—both literally and virtually (as heckle-campaigns threaten and end in criminalization).

2.4. The actors and the instability of the new ownership structure

At the time of the regime change, in the course of privatizations, it was only natural that there could be two types of new owners. On the one hand there were those new owners who had capital at their disposal and joined a business by buying up a company or increasing its capital. These were generally foreign owners: mostly **multinational companies**. On the other hand, in cases where such buyers were not found, or if those who showed interest had been excluded from the competition on various accounts, the management in charge at the time could take possession—at times by underhand means—of the company once operated by the state. In general the management would then come from the strata of technocrats loyal to the previous regime, embedded in it, and adaptable to it, even if they were not particularly engaged actually by its ideological patterns. It was nevertheless easy to brand them as **commies**. (Though in the given financial and market conditions a significant majority of the companies did not have a chance of survival without a competent management.)

Yet—irrespective of its level of efficiency—this form of privatization had **serious collateral consequences for society**. First of all, the fact that the "people" were left out of the property acquisition gave rise to a general feeling of having been cheated out of the common property—which it never was in actual fact. Though only a few people became wealthy by means of the mass "coupon" privatization employed in some other countries, or the compensation vouchers used for the re-privatization of agricultural land, it must nevertheless have allowed for the illusion of a share. Furthermore, the rushed privatization was by no means helpful towards supporting small and middle-sized businesses. And finally, the social legitimacy of newly acquired property was weak, especially when it was acquired through state largess.

For those, on the other hand, who were directly affected by unemployment or fear of unemployment in the aftermath of the regime change, facing the negative consequences of a growing social gap, the need for a redistribution of wealth could be drummed up over and over again, since the property that had come about through "common sacrifice" had been taken over by "commies" on the one hand, and "alien multinationals" on the other. Compensation, re-privatization, a national middle-class, a strong Hungary— these are all buzzwords for the proclamation of a demand for a share in the property, ensured by forcible means, outside the world of economics. The small shareholder and the oligarch of the future shared a common expectation in that both expected state assistance to realize their dreams of accumulating wealth. The reason why the elections in Hungary took on the semblance of a live or die struggle was, because they indirectly concerned a *redistribution of wealth*. Moreover, nothing stood in the way of calling upon these impulses, because the Hungarian history of the past century could be described as a series of confiscating and redistributing people's property with state assistance. The dissolution of the Austro-Hungarian Monarchy after World War One had consequences of dispossession in the successor states; the anti-Jewish laws prior to, and during World War Two and the Hungarian Holocaust stripped Hungarian Jewry en-mass not only of their property, but of their lives; then the communist nationalization wrested property from owners, and land from the peasants. An ideology for why property should be taken away from certain people and given to others was always ready at hand.

It was self-evident to the liberal elite with a background and knowledge in sociology and history that the first generation of a propertied class in a newly established capitalism would not be the moral heroes out of fairytales. Since they themselves were not driven by personal ambition to join the competition for the properties being privatized, they were likely to consider only aspects of wider economic effectiveness in ensuring the

regulatory framework for the process. One such concern was that property should be acquired by way of a real purchase. This was a rational stance
from an economic point of view, since it generated significant injections of
new capital, but naturally favored foreign investors with ample resources.
The other consideration was to assure some expertise in company management—in lieu of capital that could be drawn upon—which as mentioned
previously resulted in the empowerment of the earlier management, who
did not necessarily have any communist leanings in ideological terms, but
were certainly embedded in the earlier regime after having acknowledged
its premises. This macro-economically reasonable and quite acceptable
approach also came into conflict, so far as the terms of the rule of law were
concerned, with a need for justice, a rather difficult notion to define within
the confines of this issue. Of course in general everyone may benefit from
a prosperous economy, while the fundamentally economic reasons for the
collapse of the communist system are not evident to a vast majority of the
public, nor did they have to face the consequences until the regime change.
The brutal impact of economic disintegration fused with the political shift
of 1989–90. The appearance and explosion of unemployment, a high rate of
inflation and the growing abyss between various social groups were simply
blamed upon the new regime by a significant part of society, without recognition of the fact that the economic difficulties were not triggered by
democracy and the market economy, but rather these problems had actually
led to the change of regimes. This social shortsightedness led to the formation of the politically utilizable emotions justified by the ideology of the
"stolen regime change," while the elite that had handled the dismantling of
state-owned property were accorded the labels of *"servants of international
capital"* and the *"supporters of the conversion of commie power."* Attached
to the regime change, irrespectively of their validity, these sentiments have
served as fuel to a vast variety of populist politics over the decades since,
fixed firmly as social-political factors with immense power.

2.5. The responsibility borne by the coalition government of the socialists and liberals

No doubt, by 2010 the situation was indeed ripe for a "revolution in the
voting booth": the ruling forces were no longer able to govern in the old
way, and the electorate no longer wanted to live the old way.

The unscrupulous, cold civil war politics of the opposition forces was instrumental in the opening of the floodgates: they did not acknowledge the elections' results; denied the legitimacy of the governments between 2002 and 2010; they used the institutions of power under their control to constrain the government, and kept it under siege with nationalist and social populism. They were successful. The temptation to blame all of the disintegration squarely upon the utterly confrontational politics practiced by Fidesz is strong, however, one cannot spare the examination of the responsibility of the socialist-liberal coalition in clearing the path to the building of an autocratic regime. The reason why Hungarian history has taken such a turn could be interpreted with the often quoted historically doomed dead-end course, or the broader trends in Eastern Europe, but it would be self-exoneration not to take account of the measure in which responsibility for the situation that had come about is borne by the socialist-liberal coalition.

Indeed, though the Third Hungarian Republic was not actually stabbed by the left and the liberals, they had no small role in it becoming mortally vulnerable. One could also say, without their performance in government, Fidesz could not have acquired a two-thirds—i.e., constituent—parliamentary majority. Political science explains the defeat of the socialist-liberal coalition with a loss of moral credibility, a series of tactical mistakes in political strategy: the widely experienced corruption that could be tied to the coalition; the repeated austerity measures that stemmed in unsustainable budget overspending, and were announced, honestly as it were, but with a threatening tone; the mixed messages sent by conflicting government initiatives and programs; the stuttering and discontinued reforms of the major distributive systems (health care, education, pension and welfare, public administration, etc.); the tragically discrediting impact of the socialist prime minister's speech at Őszöd;[10] the state of cold civil war that had become a constant; the international economic crisis of 2008 that only compounded an already difficult situation; and the all-round sense of hopelessness and despair that followed from all of the above.

All of these would have been enough to bring defeat in themselves. We should in addition recall the deeper sociological reasons, which also take account of the socialist-liberal responsibility in the defeat and in the growing exposure of the electorate to populism. This is also why further causes of the right-wing advance to be found in the role of the government must also be discussed: the deprival of identity that came from a lack of symbols in their politics; a loss of perspective as sources for distribution ran dry and reforms were either put off or failed; the lack of efficient public policies that gave effective answers to the social problems generated by the regime change; and the managerial-administrative incompetence of the governing elite. All of these are merely important symptoms of the fact that the *democratic forces that could have stood up to emerging autocratic tendencies had no shared ethos or a modern social vision, nor an institutional background, and finally were left without capable political players too.*

2.5.1. Lack in symbolic, community-building politics

The Hungarian Socialist Party and the liberal Alliance of Free Democrats never spoke the same language in terms of shaping symbols and community building, so their governing coalition was in itself an obstacle to any outlooks of collectively creating new symbols. The truism "man lives not on bread only" could not become a factor that would generate a common symbolic space in left-wing politics. The distributive politics of the socialists created temporary alliances of interest at most, rather than long-term spiritual communities, and in more difficult times, when the "supplies" were scarce, the lack of such ties only became more apparent. The political right only had to invoke the ideological props of memories from the past (God, motherland, family), to provide points of fixture for people who were also looking for a symbolic community and a livable value system, while the left should have creatively brought new patterns into play for community cohesion. However, the latter was not to be.

The approach to faith and religion could have meant one of the least conflicting points of connection between the socialists and the liberals. The struggle of the liberals who were once the anti-communist dissident movement was directed at abolishing state monopolies on any form of ideology, and following the regime change the socialists could also not have hoped that the ideology that they represented could find its way into a monopolistic position secured by the state. Under the terms of the 1989–90 constitutional establishment a liberal vision of faith treated as personal matter based on the *strict separation of the state and the Church* was reflected. The worldview built around citizens free to choose their own values until they do not offend others could have achieved long-term popularity in Hungary, where the charisma of the Church did not carry much weight.

The cautious politics that led to the 1998 Agreement with the Vatican as proposed by the socialist Prime Minister Gyula Horn and fears to renegotiate it later, liquidated this chance. The socialists still looked upon the Church—as they used to under the communist regime—as a world of "peace priests" who could be kept under their influence or bought. In fact, ever since the regime change the Church had been fighting, not for its existence and survival, but for a new, assertive role both in politics and society. The Church also wanted to be rid of the socialists—and partly of its own compromised past. As the Church grew both in self-assurance and ambitions, the socialists were forced into a constant defensiveness, while the liberals were cornered with the role of stubborn anti-clericals. The religious faction within the MSZP—which can only be counted in the category of socialist kitsch—droned their repentant excuses, saying: "there are some decent people even among us." Both parties watched impotently as the spaces of public life were filled with Church symbols and rituals, intimating that there can be no morality without faith. As a result, they symbolically exiled themselves to a world outside of morality.

Followers of the camp that adhered to a secular-rational language in politics suffered their first defeat in the matter of how to interpret the concept of *nation*, another symbolic debate of great significance in 1990. By the decision of the National Assembly 20 August, (the feast day of St Stephen, first king and founder of the Hungarian state, the converter of the country to Christianity a thousand years ago) became the primary national holiday, and not 15 March (the day celebrated as the beginning of the 1848 national freedom fight against the Habsburg), while the coat of arms with the crown was chosen as the symbol of the nation, over the "*Kossuth-címer*," the coat of arms tied to the revolutions in 1848 and 1956. The reference of association to be considered the symbolic legitimization of the Hungarian nation following the regime change was at stake here: whether the series of events depicted in the foundation of the country a thousand years ago, with the Magyar conquest, the establishment of the state and the acceptance of the Christian faith; or the nation reaching its adulthood through the liberal revolution and freedom fight of 1848 that legislated the freedom of the press, equality before the law and taxation and the sharing of public burdens. A debate on value of this kind clearly cannot be won without linguistic and visual symbols, and the ethos of the republic was inhibited from touching the souls of the people. The socialists and liberals let the symbol of the 1956 revolution also slip out of their hands, leaving the surviving, once central leftist figures of those days to their own, while the now ritualized national remembrance suggests that right-wing radicals had dominated the revolution.

Paradoxically another opportunity for the citizens to reinterpret the national symbols sprung open in the early 2000s, when Fidesz in opposition placed the interpretation of national identity in a new radical, even extreme right-wing referential framework by presenting the Hungarian national tricolor and the historical Árpád-striped flag: it was the flag used by the Hungarian Nazis, the Arrow-Cross before 1945 and wore the colors of the House of Árpád, the 9th century Hungarian conqueror of the Carpathian Basin. This was the moment when the groups of symbols representing the nation and the European Union could have demonstratively been presented against the duality of the national and Árpád-striped flags. The imagery would have formulated a clear, modern view of the nation, which defines the Hungarian identity as simultaneously Hungarian and European, a community of free citizens of a broader and a more narrow community at the same time. For no path can lead to Europe against the national identity, the only way is through its regeneration.

The constant Fidesz refrain with which it calls upon the nation, Klára Sándor writes, is a wholly rational, well prepared strategy. By attempting in every possible way to overlap the meaning of the phrases "nation" and "Fidesz supporter"—even by appropriation of the national symbols, or the constant emphasis on the notion that they are the nation, meaning by implication that anyone not on their side is not a part of the nation—*Fidesz positions the divide which normally serves to define ourselves in comparison to other nations within the nation itself*. With this act it appropriates all our common values that we can associate with the concept of nation—such as patriotism, our shared culture and history—, and tries to divest all those who do not belong under what they call "the only banner" or "the only camp" of their Hungarian identities, and declare all of their political opponents illegitimate. [...]

Therefore the issue here is not only that of division, but a complete despoilment of those holding to different views. In this case Fidesz *strips its opponents of intellectual and moral property in a symbolic space*. The case is hugely troubling as it is. However, it is even more tragic that many of the political opponents of Fidesz fall for this trick of language and symbol use, accepting the Fidesz narrative, and then either try to evade exclusion through adoption [...], or by voluntarily renouncing the national symbols, because they associate them more closely with Fidesz than with Hungarian national identity. In the process they themselves supply the demonstrable "evidence" that indeed, they are emotionally not bound to the national symbols—in other words, to the nation.[11]

Never having found a new interpretation for community of these levels or framed a modern symbolism for it, the left, on the permanent defensive, could merely reflect on the exclusionist ideological bias of this use of the traditional national symbols. The liberals were also insensitive to the political use of symbols. Having been socialized under a totalitarian regime, the anti-communist dissident movement was wary of anything that would even symbolically subordinate the freedom and autonomy of the individual to any type of community (class, denomination, ethnic group, nation). The confidence and strong internal poise of the secularized intellectual— seeking no communal footholds—came across as the arrogance of the "rootless" in the perceptions of people who were not open to liberal values. With these steps, a nationalism that was a bare cold comfort after the disappointment of the regime change, swept away the chances of a rational, yet also sympathetic concept of the nation.

The left was not even capable of building on the potential of an issue most easily traceable to its traditions, the politics of equal opportunity for women. Doing so may even have led to a *modern family policy*, which puts dignity and equal opportunities for women in the focus, unlike the traditional family model. This family policy—as international examples show— is far more effective in alleviating problems with population decrease than the conservative pattern of strongly contrasting roles in career-building and motherhood attached to the slogan "Hungarians are fewer and fewer," raising with it a vision of the death-knell of the nation.

Since left and liberal political actors failed to reinterpret these three levels of community—*spiritual community of values, national community, community within the family*—an easy path to advance the systems of elusion and prejudice framed in large part by national populism was opeed. This was the price to be paid for failing to recognize how these public spaces around which life is organized play on people's daily feelings, sense of security and comfort. Neither material goods (political left), nor the supranationality and superrationality of the world citizen (liberal) can replace these spiritually and materially bound communities. Left to their own devices, people could satisfy their emotional needs only with supply that ranged from national kitsch to the evil ideas of the past available in the second hand consumer store of ideologies.

2.5.2. Distributive politics and its exhaustion

In grounding the legitimacy of their relationship with their electorate, the socialists followed (with exception perhaps for their approach to the issues of freedom rights, democratic establishment, and market economy) the usual pattern for communist successor parties: they believed that their popularity was assured by the "relentless rise in living standards," and that it would be sufficient. In the program of the *"welfare regime change"* a legitimation of the soft communist dictatorship of the Kádár period was reincarnated: it set no store by the market mechanisms that raised efficiency, preferring the caretaker, distributive politics of the state. Their aversion to reforms was not merely based on a lack of creativity, but also the fact that the Hungarian Socialist Party remained basically the party of public servants, the people in the administration, education and social welfare, and the growing petit bourgeoisie of the Kádár era. The reforms that would have made a rise in the standard of living possible—as well as growth sustainable—would have shifted precisely these strata into a state of discomfort. This was a real trap: leaving the structural make-up the way it was would shut the sources of distribution off, on the other hand structural reforms would shrink the support base of the socialists. This unresolvable dilemma caused the wavering between the extremes of painful inertia and neoliberal thrusts of zeal. This is an identity crisis that has not found resolution until today, between the value systems of a reform-communist successor party and a center-left party peppered with liberal notions. In the course of the two cycles in government of the socialist-liberal coalition (2002–2010) the country dropped into a crisis resulting from overspending.

The use of distributive politics also elicited the disdain of supporters. An attitude of "I will buy your loyalty"—over time, lacking finances—dispersed the members of the nonexistent community. Naturally, since no sense of a left-wing community had formed, which would have allowed the call for "blood, sweat and tears" to pass. The 50 percent wage increase for public servants, the doubled month's pay and pension at the end of the year, as well as other benefits promised by the socialist-liberal coalition taking government in 2002 could not create a community for the formation of an identity. And when they were all canceled upon the 2008 worldwide financial crisis, the support for the center-left evaporated. The reduction of the relationship with the populace to a cry of "To the trough!" proved too feeble to build an identity for the community, when the trough was empty. And ultimately the coalition had "cried wolf" all three times in vain, proclaiming an "antifascist battle" against the right-wing that had been operating with the conservative symbols from between the world wars with increasing openness, when it no longer had either any credibility, or community-building force. Following the economic crisis, no room was left in the hearts of people, to which they could have returned. The souls thus left abandoned were gathered in by the *social populism* of the opposition forces of the political right-wing, which was not bogged down by the pressures of government, and duly delivered into the arms of their *national populism*. By then the socialists could only watch with offended impotence as Fidesz fished away what they had until then considered their monopoly: social demagogy.

2.5.3. The shoddiness of freedom and hopelessness of the dispossessed

At the time of the collapse of the communist system a significant proportion of society expected that upon adopting a western type establishment the standard of living would also shortly be on a par with the west. In bitter fact, although the large monolithic systems of repression (political dictatorship and state monopoly on ownership) came down, unprecedented new forms of personal day-to-day vulnerability appeared as a consequence of the transition crisis.

- Whole branches of industry dissolved with the loss of the traditional markets of the Soviet bloc, and after a virtually full employment came waves of *unemployment* in the hundreds of thousands. The transformation of the industrial structure drove the *untrained labor*, most of the *commuters* from the countryside, as well as the more *backward regions*, especially the *Roma* into a state of permanent lack of prospects. By the nineties, the light industry that had given employment to masses of untrained women completely collapsed. The decrease in opportunities for employment as menial assistants in industrial and construction work forced the Roma back into the backward settlements where work was not available. Along with the agricultural cooperatives their adjunct industrial branches were also liquidated, and people who could not be employed as commuters to the cities were forced to remain in districts overtaken by poverty. In such regions permanent poverty and merciless unemployment were further exacerbated by the rise of ethnic conflicts between the Roma and non-Roma populations with different patterns of socialization and culture. The existential uncertainty was largely transformed into challenges of public safety in a number of dimensions. The Roma and non-Roma populations of depression regions, exposed to forces they could hardly influence and shut in together with their hopeless situations, simultaneously became the victims and perpetrators in mutually felt fear and aggression.

Lacking life strategies that would offer any prospects those in hopeless situation escaped into an easily digested, prejudiced, intolerant, largely racist worldview, in which the impersonal powers that were the cause of their squalor could be personified in the scapegoated "slacker," the Gipsy. The lack of intellectual conceptualization in the socialist ranks and the blinkered liberal approach only focusing on the macro-economy drove the majority of the population of the poverty-stricken regions, which had till then been committed to the left, into the right- and extreme right-wing camps—paradoxically not only the non-Roma population that had been left stranded, but a large segment of the Roma people as well. The implemented bits of public policy attempts to address the tragic situation of the Roma also achieved very little in terms of results. The chances of more strident, more creative solutions would also have been limited, since Hungarian society at large and the institutional system were not suitable for a more tolerant policy of integration. Due to the uncertainty that took the place of the humble, yet predictable standard of living in the Kádár era, the bankruptcy of the emerging groups of society, the repeated budget cuts framed by the shock of transition, the "people's majority" looked with hostility upon the—in fact rather ineffective—redistribution in favor of the even less fortunate and the prejudiced perspective advanced. As a result, on the settlements, rather than locally alleviating the ethnic tensions, the local governance often even reinforced ethnic antagonism and segregation.

- Though under the conditions of all-round employment the communist command economy leveled pay scales and kept them low, it also kept rent prices, public utility costs and public transport expenses at bay—until the final decade of the regime. With the reorganization of the state system of redistribution the price of these services gradually approached their market value. *The low income of the people of the housing estates, the urban dwellers of humble means and villagers trying to get further on the social ladder,* along with the slowly advancing, consumer rather than entrepreneur *petit bourgeoisie of the Kádár period* (labeled "frigidaire socialism" upon the fascination of consumerism) could not keep up with this rise in prices. The euphoria of the turn of the 1980s and 1990s that came from the privatization of local government housing in favor of the tenants (affecting millions of citizens) soon declined. The increasing available supply on the retail credit market at a time of a brutal downward turn in the value of the forint on the one hand, and the shrinking real value of wages and growing unemployment on the other generated such a high rate of *indebtedness of families* which did not even stop at a sustainable poverty, but slid into a complete existential bankruptcy for many.

While the liberals appealed to the responsibility of the individual and defended the principle of a market free from interventions by the patrimonial state, they did not notice that they were unintentionally ensuring the dominance of large credit institutions against the fragmented and defenseless clients subject to one-sided modification of contracts. Emphasis on the territorial value-neutrality of the large banks masked the fact that the international credit institutions—especially after the explosion of the 2008 crisis—applied varying norms of sympathy with debtors—especially those in foreign currencies—, in the banks at home and abroad. (Though loans in Swiss francs were significant throughout the eurozone due to the low interest rates, but since the euro had depreciated much less in comparison to the franc, and the unemployment benefits in many countries remained rather generous, this made the credit liabilities of the citizens of these countries much less dramatic.) The socialist financial governance in Hungary did not in the beginning consider the problem a matter of competency for the sector, and then began to fiddle with ethical codices that did not oblige the banks to take any sort of action. Government was not willing to face the impact of the financial crisis of 2008 as an "economic disaster." Not only growing unemployment resulting from the global crisis was at issue here, but also the fact that a drastic depreciation of the national currency against the euro, and especially against the Swiss franc raised the monthly installments drastically, without reducing their base debt, which on the contrary had increased enormously. In the absence of the institution of personal bankruptcy debtors could have been locked in a debt spiral after even a loss of all their belongings. Government was still not willing to apply the policy of fair burden sharing—usually followed in the case of natural disasters. This doctrinarian (liberal) and impotent (socialist) approach made those in a hard-pressed situation—and unable to find any concrete support—increasingly susceptible to ideologies that attacked bankers, capital and foreigners in general, sentiments that were often also openly antisemitic.

- Just as citizens felt vulnerable to large institutions, so *small entrepreneurs* felt vulnerable as competitors and suppliers to the bureaucracy, the multinational corporations, and the banks. Late payments from the state, depressed supplier prices and *debt chains* often made market success or failure have troublingly little to do with actual performance.

  While domestically the debts and withheld payments between companies caused huge difficulties, the governing coalition's incompetence in establishing a fair entrepreneurial environment only swelled the audience—lacking any alternative handle on affairs—with an openness to the demagogy aimed at foreign capital and multinational companies.

A resolution of the dramatic social tensions and pitfalls created by the regime change would have required *effective public policy programs* based on creative intellectual approaches, absolute determination, and cooperation between sectors. All these were lacking. The government apparatus proved incapable of developing complex, multifaceted programs, and implementing them while neutralizing the resistance of sectors to cooperate.

2.5.4. Inefficacy in government, the incompatible attitudes of the two coalition parties

The socialists—trapped by their history—could only think in terms of paternalistic solutions that increased the budgetary expenditures of the social services without helping people get out from their hopeless situation.

The liberals on the other hand—trapped by their ideology—in defending the mechanisms of the market from the intervention of the state, and emphasizing the responsibility of individuals for their own decisions, showed insensitivity to the hopeless existential situation that masses of people encountered, where responsibility cannot be fully transferred to the individual. With the exhaustion of resources for government distribution and without long-term public policies to resolve the situation they were locked in, people were virtually driven to set their hopes upon the arrival of a heavy-handed savior. While demanding that individuals be prudent and rational in their economic decisions, the liberals did not create the predictable, stable macro-environment required for this. Criticism of the self-acquitting, responsibility-transferring, scapegoating instincts of the populace may be raised, but the responsibility of those in government cannot be dismissed based solely upon it, even as it—together with the populism Fidesz had adopted as the core of its politics—drove citizens towards populism, even close to the extreme right.

The *coalition of the socialists and liberals* always carried the marks of a *marriage "for the lack of a better choice"*: the liberals had come from the anti-communist dissident movement, while the socialists formed the successor party of the earlier reformer communists. Their coalition was not about what they wanted to do together and how they could go about it, but what they wanted to avert among the endeavors of others. Their common allegiance was basically confined to upholding the institutional system of liberal democracy established in the course of the transition. Their disparate socialization, values and social vision formed an obstacle to their realization of a common approachable, coherent socio-political program, which is why the coalition was seen by the parties and their supporters as representative of themselves only in its opposition to the political right. The regularly reappearing tensions—facing off in opinions such as "it is the tail wagging the dog again," (i.e., SZDSZ, the smaller coalition partner is dictating terms again), or the often deserved cry "look at what these 'commies' are doing again"—along with expressions of a continuous sense of frustration on both sides indicated a desire to validate the dominance of either a liberal set of values, or one that rested largely on the Kádárian traditions across the entire range of activities of the government. The parties of the coalition exhausted their energies in this struggle. Their public communications at the service of their own supporters turned the cooperation of the coalition partners into a candid camera reality show exposing the government. The state of the coalition or its denunciation, and the constant internal strife within the parties made the mutually frustrated, failure-ridden world of the coalition partners lacking all vision disenchantingly transparent.

The government apparatus was even less capable of finding its place in this coalition of contradictory values and ambitions that extinguished one another.

As a result of the consolidation of the soft communist dictatorship beginning in the mid-1960s, the bureaucratic-managerial performance of those working in the **administration** could have been said to be good in an East-European comparison. Public administration, as one of the fields particularly open to social advancement offered careers to those talented people who could consent to the communist ideological barriers. Justified criticism of the bureaucracy of the times is aimed at the system, rather than the abilities of those working in it. It is no coincidence that the socialist come-back in 1994 was grounded not only in the nostalgia for a 3.6 forint loaf of bread, but also the expectations of the voters to get "expertise back into the government."[12]

The regime change might have offered an opportunity for following the example of western democracies in mostly leaving the administration untouched when government changes. However, as political paranoia took over, a growing distance from this model could be seen, where eventually even within an electoral cycle, a change of ministers would mean *the decapitation of the administration*. Downsizing of state administration was the easiest to implement from the consecutive austerity packages. With the waves of layoffs and a simultaneous escalation of the number of political appointees the administrative apparatus had gone through a massive process of negative selection by the mid-2000s. The so-called "administrative career paths" then only served as a euphemistic formulation of how the regime, after removing the specialists of previous governments, would try to install its own people for ever, or press the apparatus into its own unconditional service. This situation was further exacerbated by the fact that while prior to 1989, in times when life was defined by state monopolies, the administration and affiliated offices (such as the elite research centers, background institutions of ministries) attracted talent, by the 2000s young people could choose from plenty of career opportunities unconnected to the state administration, or to the country for that matter. Justified politically with claims of electoral authorization the waves of purges and layoffs reached lower and lower levels of the administration. Even the pool of experts that had deliberately tried to steer clear of politics suffered serious repercussions, though by this time a trend of demotions rather than layoffs had come to dominate.

This process, rooted in instincts of power difficult to control, was only compounded by the radical reorganizations carried through every four years, comparable in effect to natural disasters, and singular catastrophes such as the *removal of the state secretaries of public administration*—i.e., undersecretaries in charge of the everyday running of the ministry—in 2006. The last mentioned action, carried through by the socialist prime minister for the sake of a communications blip lasting a single day while brushing aside strong dissent even within the governing parties paralyzed the administration and left it without its top tier. The grey eminence of the state secretaries of public administration was replaced by the simply grey political state secretaries, who lacked the administrative routine and specialized knowhow of the former. The public administration could no longer recover from such a blow.

The *relocation of the police directorate* from the ministry of interior to the ministry of justice also proved catastrophic. Of course the move was also favored by the liberal doctrinarians, as it appeared to fulfill the promise of civil control over the police. Indeed—in the course of the disturbance that was prompted by the prime minister's before mentioned speech to the socialist faction at the government resort in Őszöd—the ministers with backgrounds as professors of law were not capable of directing law enforcement authorities used to a hard-handed leadership. The police, subjected to budget cuts, lacking experience in action and without government leadership lost its professional credibility and standing even as it could not find a clear point of orientation, and reacted to the aggression from demonstrators either ineffectually or violently, overstepping legal authorizations.

It became clear in the course of the irresolvable arguments within the coalition, the budget crisis brought forth by the distributive politics, the civil disobedience actions initiated and supported by the opposition, which had never recognized the legitimacy of the government, and then in the aftermath of the street demonstrations turned violent: the government could not hold up to the professional demands needed whether in times of peace or cold civil war.

2.6. Frailty of the institutions guaranteeing the system of checks and balances

Political life—following from the principle of the separation of powers—is directed not only by the party political elite, but also the various figures in charge within the branches of power. Liberal democracy consciously developed the institutions guaranteeing checks and balances, and these can form a barrier to the surges of populist instincts. The way the individuals composing these institutions are selected is purposely kept at a distance from political campaigns that are open to demagogy: the objective is to ensure that—to protect democratic values—these institutions are not exposed to **pressures for popularity**. Every single transposal applied in the process of their selection is intended to decrease the impact of the populist instincts of mediatized democracy. The long periods of office lasting across election cycles also serves the same purpose: so in their decisions the officials of these institutions do not have to become subservient to the likely victors of the following elections. The party-political elite however tried to fill up these positions with their own cadres, thus eroding the integrity of the people who compose these institutions. Therefore the role of this elite in the spread of populist ideologies across Hungary to finally achieve social acceptability also cannot be denied. The role of legal-institutional guarantees is held up in vain if those who operate them frequently do not act according to the democratic ethos they represent. Thereby they also void their roles as examples in holding back the anti-humane and anti-democratic instincts represented by certain segments of the party elite.

How could the **President of the Republic** not have a role in the social acceptance of **racist speech and racist actions** if he declines to comment on the formation of the extreme-right paramilitary organization, *Magyar Gárda* (Hungarian Guard) under the windows of the presidential palace (2007), and reacts belatedly to the horror of the racism-motivated serial murders committed against Roma people (2008–2009); or the **courts**, if sitting it out while the Hungarian Guard gained strength and only ordering its dissolution after a multiple-year-long legal tug of war, and then only to practice leniency at the appearance of its clones, and turning the legislation for protection of the minorities against the same minorities, and "serving justice" without actually meting out penalties or compensations for damages to the victims of ethnic segregation; the **ombudsman**, if he speaks about the "profile of gipsy crime";

the *prosecutor's Office*, if it is not willing to assume racist motivation even in the case of the most obviously anti-Roma atrocities, and observes the spread of hate-speech (incitement against minorities), violent disturbances at minority (for example gay) demonstrations unmoved; or the *National Bureau of Investigations* and the *police*, if evidence of racist motivations disappear and they apply double standards in regards to the victims?

By representing the legal norms, the *Constitutional Court* advocates fundamental values. Yet it ruled out politics based on an equitable and rational public discourse—which would have been capable of leveling populism—already in 1995, by using various pretexts to turn against a large number of severe austerity measures included in the so-called Bokros package (named after Lajos Bokros, the finance minister who introduced it), a response to the transition crisis; then in 2008, by giving way to the initiative of a national referendum—affecting the budget against constitutional regulations—on the annulment of higher-education fees and a nominal fee for visiting the doctor, thereby legitimating and reinforcing the unrealistic expectations of the voters as well as disabling the operational ability of the government. The responsibility of the constitutional judges is therefore beyond question—on account of a number of their decisions—in the erosion of the liberal laws of the republic and in bringing down the socialist-liberal government as this attempted to carry through unpopular but necessary reforms.

The concerted surges of nationalist and socialist populisms not only brought to power an autocratic government by sweeping the socialists out to the periphery of political existence and the liberals even further, but also buried the institutional system of checks and balances.

2.7. Fidesz as political apex predator

The downfall of the Third Hungarian Republic naturally could not have happened without the sort of political apex predator that first stalks and then chases down its wounded prey. This was Fidesz.

2.7.1. From the close college fraternity to the adopted political family, an alternative rebel turned godfather

The organizations forming the opposition at the time of regime change grew out of informal communities of various sizes: the liberal Alliance of Free

Democrats (SZDSZ) had come from the anti-communist dissident movement and a number of critical groups of urban intellectuals who were
linked to it. The populist-nationalist Magyar Demokrata Fórum (Hungarian
Democratic Forum—MDF) came from a more loose circle of populist or
folk writers ("*népi írók*"), and people who looked upon the more risk-taking,
conspirative culture of the dissident movement with suspicion. While the
so called historical parties (Kisgazda [Smallholders'], Social Democrats)
formed along the labels of non-communist parties that had existed before
1948, essentially loose agglomerates of personalities who had not necessarily been in touch with each other before. **Fidesz**, on the other hand,
was formed from a *small, very close and tightly knit college community* of
friends who had found their social bearings together—through the literature of the anti-communist dissident movement and reform communist
lecturers—in virtually the same dormitory room. When it was formed in
the spring of 1988 as an adversary of the Communist Youth Association, it
defined itself as a *liberal, radical, alternative*—indeed youth[13]—*movement*.

    Western oriented political party. This is how Fidesz perceived itself at
the 1990 national assembly elections, but its internal formal organization
carried on the ethos of a movement: the party still does not have a president at this stage, though the question of who heads the nation-wide electoral party list does explicitly point to the matter of leadership.

    Centralized party. The disciplining of the membership began in the
early 1990s. The nostalgia for stability broadly felt by the populace and
associated with the socialists, as well as the presence of the strong liberal
party made it clear to Viktor Orbán, elected president of Fidesz in 1993,
that the party could not grow to become a mass party positioned in the
political center-left. Having observed the erosion of the first right-wing
government after the regime change, the party was steered towards the
gradually emptying field on the political right and re-profiled their party
step-by-step. The first motions were to get rid of representatives of the
alternative liberal line within the party, who opposed the turn to the right,
unseating them from the leading bodies and then forcing them out of the
party. Concomitantly, a motion as candidate for presidency of the party
that did not take account of the realities of the situation already counted as
an unforgivable disloyalty: this is why Tamás Wachsler—the first, and ever
since only challenger of Viktor Orbán for the leadership of the party—disappeared from politics for a while in the mid-1990s. (A return following due
penance and pardon saw him not in a political role, but as project director

of the reconstruction of the Budapest Sport Arena and then the renovation of *Kossuth tér*, the square outside the Parliament.) In selecting the new candidates for members of parliament in 1994 a psychological test was introduced to filter out the autonomous personalities not deemed suitable by the leadership.

In the time of the first period of governance of Fidesz (1998–2002), the highly respected weekly journal of economics *Heti Világgazdaság*, a memorable cover picture[14]—"*Csapatszellem*" [Team spirit]—showed soft hatted gentlemen in suits standing around an eighth gentleman seated in an armchair, the Boss, also wearing a suit and soft hat. We see a team by the intent of the designer, resembling the type found in Chicago in the thirties, where the figure of Viktor Orbán is definitive, though all of the others are also members of the team. At this time, next to the leader, there still existed the leadership.

With the passing of a decade, of the whole team only the Boss has remained. The rest have almost all been exiled from the innermost circle of power: some have been sent to the European Parliament: József Szájer, Tamás Deutsch, and János Áder, to Brussels, though later the place of service for the latter was relocated, and he was reactivated as President of the Republic; Zoltán Pokorni became a mayor of one of the districts of the capital, while István Stumpf was made Constitutional Judge, László Kövér Speaker of Parliament, and Attila Várhegyi joined the private sector affiliated with Fidesz. The locations of the Goulash Archipelago—Brussels, the presidential Sándor Palace in Buda Castle, the local government of the Buda hills (12th District, Budapest) or the Constitutional Court—are unarguably sweeter destinations for political exile than the labor camps of classic communist dictatorships decades ago. Those concerned cannot complain. Indeed, they do not.

Vassal party. Following the electoral defeat of 2002, the organizational remodeling of Fidesz was carried out to reflect the electoral constituencies. Since then the key figures of the ruling elite in each field are designated by the president of the party, that is, he alone decides about the selection of the candidates for the national assembly both for the individual constituencies as well as the electoral party lists. A symbolic reaffirmation of these changes prior to the 2010 election was intended by the pilgrimage all parliamentary candidates had to make to Orbán's country estate for a face to face hearing and to place an oath of loyalty. Exactly as in Coppola's film, *The Godfather*.

As a logical sequel of the foregoing, in the course of the infighting that unfolded around the 2010 municipal elections held after the parliamentary, the old Fidesz members, the local politicians who were considered cadres of other leaders within the party were replaced—or arranged to be beaten—by Fidesz candidates loyal to the top boss, and tied in to him through the chain of vassalage. So within the established patron–client relations it was no longer enough to be loyal to the party, but to the leader himself.

Fidesz cadres also learned that not only was all rebelliousness out of the question, decisions from above were not to be questioned, or even discussed openly, as a mere slip of the tongue could mean the end of a career. This eventuality befell László Mádi, Fidesz founder and MP, who inadvertently gave a public word of support to the introduction of the real estate tax prior to the 2010 parliamentary elections, not having noticed that in consequence of the populist turn his party was already against it. Only allegiance gives protection, while insubordination, sovereignty results in banishment and existential annihilation. Nor is there a limitation period, only forgiveness may help. The first in Hungary to learn that the boss is not kidding were the members of Fidesz.

The companions of the Fidesz president depicted as the godfather on the journal title page gradually disappearing, they were replaced by successive generations of *chinovniks* (Russian for subservient bureaucrats). They were no longer the heroic knights of political jousts with autonomous personalities, but instead the terminators in the "parrot-commandos" of Fidesz communications. Though they may eventually retire to some quieter political backwater with the discharge bonus received upon years of compulsory moral depreciation, they may be called back for some character-destroying auxiliary duty on occasion. What was meted out as punishment to the Fidesz founders and one-time comrades in arms of the Boss is granted as a reward to these latter.

The transmission belt party. By 2010 the encoding of the personal decision-making capacities of the president in the Fidesz constitution relativized the competencies of the party's decision-making bodies and established a culture of centralized, one-person control. At this point however the line of Fidesz's progress diverged from the autocratic model before the regime change. In the communist regime the chief overseeing body of the party did not wholly lose its importance even in parallel to the autarchy of the first secretary. For example, anyone who counted as a current confidant, or favorite of Stalin was at the same time member of the formal decision-making body, the politburo. This is why one of the favorite subjects of the literature of Kremlinology was the analysis of the composition and changes of this body, focusing on informal coalitions therein.

In the case of the "leading force" of the post-communist mafia state the actual decisions are taken away from the—nevertheless strictly controlled—bodies of the party, and through the president/godfather transferred to the decision-making pool of the inner circle of his minions, the adopted political family, lacking formal structure and legitimacy. We can no longer speak of transmission belts by which the party confers its will upon the people and oils the mechanisms of implementation—like the trade unions, women's association, etc., in the communist period—, *the party itself becomes the transmission belt of the adopted political family*. In other words, the center of power in the mafia state is in fact the adopted political family, which gains formal legitimacy to the realization of its will by means of the mediation of the party. After all it functions behind the scenes of democracy, where the party itself is the political stooge for the adopted political family.

There is then no point in the Kremlinologist-like approach, which keeps searching for the slightest sign of a crack in the party bodies, and tries to politically interpret a few winks and nods to those outside with heated optimism. Following upon a few decades of democracy, this type of thinking would be a return to the state of mind pervasive under socialism. Of course there are many in Fidesz who would feel much better if they did not have to serve by sacrificing all their moral reservations unconditionally and represent things they know are quite different from how they appear in their communication. But they also take share in the collective coercion committed by their party, they also vote for the disenfranchising laws. This is exemplified by the fate of people described as "Fidesz's human face," from Tibor Navracsics (parliamentary faction leader, the minister of public administration, later EU Commissioner) to Zoltán Pokorni (member of the Fidesz presidency, minister of education, then mayor), or János Áder (parliamentary faction leader, EU Commissioner, then President of the Republic), and Mihály Varga (minister of finance). The intelligentsia that does not like Fidesz in many ways has retained the same mindset as in the soft communist dictatorship of the Kádár era. However the situation was then the other way round: at that time it was still reassuring that János Kádár as first secretary was under all odds better than a hardline Muscovite such as Béla Biszku would be, who had directed the retributions following the revolution of 1956. Now, to the contrary, many would like to believe that there exists a better Fidesz, but without Viktor Orbán.

2.7.2. Socialist erosion, liberal vaporization and Fidesz's accomplishment of social embeddedness

After the regime change—when party membership was no longer a pre-requisite for career advancement at work—it was plainly apparent that mass parties like the communist party used to be would not come about any more. The only question was also for the MSZP how far its membership would shrink, though even after the shock its membership totaled more than all members of the rest of the parties taken together. In comparison to the earlier state of affairs therefore all the other parties inevitably became media-bound parties, though meanwhile it was clear that for the local organizations there was a minimum without which—if only due to the specificities of the electoral system—they could not exist. For a secure spread countrywide a minimum of 5–10 thousand committed activists was required. Even with the impetus of their launching, the new political parties had much fewer members than the party that had once been communist, and the numbers continued to decrease over time.

In the case of the *socialists* the remaining members were also strongly attached to either the ruins of the earlier organs of the regime, or the remaining structures of the vast care systems (public administration, healthcare, education). And though aging constantly, it retained its nostalgic, bureaucratic, apparatchik nature. The atmosphere in the party—for those who remained—showed the old intimacy in terms of custom and behavior, even if it no longer fed back into their workplaces as it had before: the representatives and the represented had similar preferences in terms of taste thanks to their background. This community of interests and taste-preferences helped to preserve the party base even in times lacking in political tasks and action, being a social form of coexistence and a safety built on reciprocal relationships. Though it was not able to enter into up-to-date spheres of life opening up in the new world, its day to day sense of security, tradition and the mass nature maintained the party as a widely, and rather evenly spread, well oiled "mutual aid" network. This network was even capable of surprises, as for example at the 2002 elections that toppled the Fidesz government. Yet even so, it was limited to such a degree in adopting new communications technologies and reaching new groups of the society that by 2010 it simply buckled under, to become the social club of those— essentially pensioners—who had lost out after being part of the one-time administrative middle class.

Among the liberals, in the *SZDSZ* everyday party activities required awkwardly obligatory attendance since the party leadership and the intellectual circles surrounding it did not really have cultural chemistry with the general majority of the membership. This also meant that they did not share social partnership and lifestyle. After the successes of the early nineties, the liberals—concerning the institutionalized social networks—could hold on only in the local government offices. With worse and worse election results the consistently decreasing number of local government positions turned the local party organizations, which were essentially arranged around these seats, against recruitment of new political figures, and the party organizations could no longer step out of this diminishing circle and get renewed.

At the time of regime change, a significant portion of the *Fidesz* organizations were formed under the wings of SZDSZ, and their membership remained far below that of its rivals. The contradiction between the popularity of the party measured in opinion polls and its organization weaknesses at the beginning of the nineties was reflected in the by-elections as well, as the young democrats (Fidesz) were never able to validate their 30–40 percent popularity in polls with an individual electoral district victory.

While the socialists had inherited the powerless middle and lower layers of the once truly powerful nomenclature, the story of Fidesz can be described as a reversed process: a chain of hierarchic vassal (patron-client) relations had replaced the communist nomenclature by 2010. The process can best be observed in the dynamically changing ties between the party and the organizations helping to embed it in society. The disciplining of the party with its small membership was complete by 1994: the power of the president could no longer be questioned. Not only the structure of the party, but the selection for local government positions were aligned in such a way as to make the emergence of autonomous positions opposed to the party president impossible. Thereby the party became capable of overwhelming other political organizations, or pressing non-political organizations into service. Fidesz completed its modernized organizational halo and network in gradual steps.

- At the 1998 national elections the Catholic and Calvinist **churches** already ensured Fidesz's otherwise lacking organizational background, since it had returned to the Christian fold. Not only did this spare Fidesz a lot on campaign expenses, but also meant nationwide outreach, and influenced the type of social groups that brought their electoral decisions not on the basis of rational considerations, but ties of faith.

- An intensive process of clientele building that began in the period of 1998–2002, stalled with the lost election of 2002. In the aftermath of the close election results Fidesz capitalized on the disappointment felt by half of the populace to establish the **Polgári Körök (Citizens' Circles) movement**, which was not integrated directly into the party, but could be mobilized effectively when occasionally needed. By these means the threat that the hierarchical discipline of the party would be eroded by a mass overflow was avoided on the one hand, and a shared identity was formed for their followers who were most ready to fight. This constituted the foundations of the database, which spread beyond party boundaries, listing potential supporters at shorter or longer range for eventual actions.

- Following the 2004 referendum on dual-citizenship and the signature campaign that preceded it, the collection and entry of contacts for voters well disposed towards Fidesz took on industrial proportions. The "social referendum" of 2008—on the annulment of higher education, healthcare and hospital checkup fees—and other campaigns collecting signatures only served to fatten and update the availability of potential supporters. Later, the database widely called the **Kubatov lists** after the director and campaign chief of the party was further extended to keep track also of those who did not sympathize with the party.

- Upon return to power in 2010—after an interval of eight years—the instruments of state and government also became tools to clientele building. In the operation termed *"national consultation"* a manipulated questionnaire—related to a range of societal issues in a populist rendering—was sent to every citizen of voting age in the form of letters to be responded post prepaid. However the real aim of collecting the often referenced but never verifiable replies—whether loyal or confronting—was to refine and update the Kubatov lists.

The above measures were essentially suited to needs when the party was in opposition. Though they survive as means to mobilize followers not included in the party or the adopted political family, after taking power in 2010 the party and state recruitment of cadres (HR) have grown virtually indistinguishable, and together with rooting out the institutions of social autonomy, the establishment of a post-communist model of patron-client relations is underway.

2.8. Pre-2010 political cold war, and the erosion of the institutional, two-thirds constraint

2.8.1. Political cold war

Though Fidesz unexpectedly lost the 2002 elections, the conclusion that it drew from this was not to return from highly confrontational politics to the culture of concord regulated by the institutions of the separation of powers in democracies built on consensus, but quite the contrary: in opposition it consequently employed the tools of political cold war. This was when questioning the cleanness of the elections (conducted by its own administrative apparatus!) and the legitimacy of the new socialist-liberal government, refusal to cooperate to the degree required by the democratic institutional system, character assassination, intensive use of verbal aggression against the personalities, measures and programs of the government, and a permanent installment of street demonstrations—turning violent at times—all these were added to the Fidesz inventory of tools. For Fidesz, the positions guaranteed by the separation of powers served *not to control government, but to put it under siege*. The slogan that gave this siege its cohesive ideological framework, "the fatherland cannot be in opposition," proclaimed by Orbán in the speech he gave after losing the 2002 elections, meant no less than an attempt to exclude the followers óf the socialist-liberal government from the nation. As a result a sort of *dual power* came into existence from 2002 onwards, but even more pronouncedly after the elections of 2006, when the MSZP–SZDSZ coalition won a mandate to continue in government. The means by which the positions intended to serve as checks on government was a *personnel policy* wholly subordinated to the goal. Just as it would have been impossible to carry out the constitutional coup-d'état after 2010 without the order of vassalage and discipline within the party, it would have been impossible to maintain the siege on consensus-based democracy, were the people delegated to the institutions meant to ensure the checks and balances not filled with obedient sword bearers of the party rather than impartial professionals.

In the Hungarian constitutional system the cornerstone of the system of checks and balances was the requirement of a qualified majority, that is, a two-thirds constraint. A parliamentary majority of this proportion was needed for amendments to the constitution and a number of so called cardinal laws (on local government, media, association, elections, etc.). This guaranteed that within the circle of political decisions concerning the fundamentals of the political establishment, the liberal democratic principle of separation of powers would be imposed through the enforced consensus between governing and opposition forces. The MDF–SZDSZ agreement following the 1990 elections decreased the number of laws bound by the two-thirds constraint in order to ensure that the responsibility of government is truly in the hands of whichever party takes power. The dilemma was real. On the one hand, the two-thirds constraint had grown into a formidable obstacle to the implementation of necessary reforms from the mid-nineties onwards, because in the hands of Fidesz—lacking the wish to reach consensus—it had become a weapon for blackmailing the government: they would only vote for something (even if they agreed with) if they received something in return, or they would not vote for anything, to preempt any success of the government. On the other hand the requirement of a qualified majority also meant a necessary protection of the institutional system of liberal democracy from an eastern-type political culture that prevailed, and because customary law was on a weak footing. The fact that instead of nurturing a culture of seeking consensus, the two-thirds constraint led to a culture of blackmail and destruction of political rivals only reflects on the wretchedness of Hungarian political life after the regime change. If one of the opposed forces is willing to go to the ultimate lengths to sabotage the search for consensus in order to acquire and keep hold of power, the system will eventually become dysfunctional. In response—sensing the ineffectuality only—society will come to desire resolute, strong-handed leadership.

Appointments to positions of leadership in institutions independent of the government was also mostly tied to a qualified parliamentary majority, or the involvement of the president of the republic. In these negotiations over posts, lasting years at times, where opposed stances faced off it was never Fidesz that would swing the steering wheel—to avoid collision course—but the socialists, weighed down by the inferiority complex of being the successor party of the communists, afraid of the excessive influ-

ence of the liberals, and incapacitated for action by their oligarchic structure. As a result Fidesz regularly came out as the winner of these tests of
strength where appointments were concerned. In government—when
necessary—Fidesz would declare overseeing bodies with positions unfilled
as operational, such as the Hungarian media and news agency, when only
half of the positions of its board of trustees were filled, those of the government. In opposition it would not refrain from completely unhinging
operations of the given bodies. The result was that while the delegates of
Fidesz in these decision-making bodies behaved as completely loyal disciplined droids—with the rarest exception—the delegates of MSZP, who
usually had not the party to thank for their positions, but a group within it,
usually rival to other factions, would often not only free themselves of the
shackles of the ethos that gave meaning to the position, but even from the
delegating party, hoping for personal political survival. According to a witty
remark by Gábor Kuncze, president of the liberal SZDSZ: "For each position the socialists have at least two unsuitable candidates." The difference
between the processes of delegation in these two parties pushed a majority
of members of these joint bodies to try and win the favors of Fidesz in their
first cycle as delegates—in hopes of being reelected.

The two most important fields Fidesz had pressed into service in the
period before 2010, in spite of the existing system of separation of powers,
was the Office of Prosecution and, partially, the Constitutional Court.

The unexpected resignation of the impeccable and generally respected
Kálmán Györgyi from the position of Chief Prosecutor in 2000, having
been elected with the support of 82 percent of parliament in 1990, resembles a Greek tragedy. The public was only presented with the conflict that
he caused by considering the truncated boards composed only of Fidesz
delegates as being illegal.[15] Rumors—that better explain his unbroken
silence since then—mentioned a personal blackmail. Fidesz's influence in
the *Prosecutor's Office* has since been constant, irrespective of changes in
governing party. Led until now with minor breaks by previous Member of
Parliament for Fidesz, Péter Polt, the organization became an active participant of the election campaigns—as a tool of *politically selective law
enforcement*—with its material chosen for campaign purposes streamed to
the public through Fidesz's media channels at the best-timed moments. If
for example someone would wish to get an overview of the matter of corruption in Hungary on the basis of actions at the Prosecutor's Office led by
Polt, it would seem that the central and local government areas controlled

by Fidesz are completely devoid of corruption, while the areas controlled by political rivals are rather contaminated by it. While "the number of complaints has fallen to half, or even one-thirds of the earlier annual averages, their dismissals have risen to three times the earlier figure. Moreover, if investigations are even initiated, since 2010 they have been cancelled twice as often."[16] A comparison of the activities of two "government commissioners for accountability" in cases of government corruption clarifies a great deal. It would seem as if the earlier socialist commissioner László Keller had tried to drag a number of innocent people before the court, but the Prosecutor's Office, as a committed human rights organization had prevented this on every occasion. In contrast, the charges filed by the Fidesz member appointed next, Gyula Budai—who began his career at the military prosecution under the communists before the regime change—generally pass through the Prosecutor's Office without the slightest hindrance, then to regularly stall at the stage when they enter the court process. The activity of the Fidesz delegated commissioners for accountability and the political expectation they are faced with do not follow the patterns of a cultured, legally justified oversight of one's own public administration that would be found in a well versed democracy, but rather that of the Spanish inquisition: regularly raised suspicions will destroy people even without court sentences, as their moral and professional capital is worn down.

Fidesz's confrontational policy on appointments did not leave the **Constitutional Court** unharmed either. In the course of selection of constitutional judges, the initial, largely renowned, respected row of judges with conservative convictions was counterbalanced through the machinations of MSZP, with individuals of neither liberal, nor often even socialist leanings, but people of humble experience representing an eclectic assortment of views. Furthermore, the fact that a prohibition of extending the nine-year mandate of a judge was canceled often meant that the socialist delegates also complied with the expectations formed by Fidesz. This is exemplified, as previously mentioned, by the approval of the referendum on the annulment of the 300 forint (app. 1 euro) clinic and days in hospital fees, and annual higher education tuition fees of 100,000 forint (app. 300 euro) in 2008. The Court made way for this initiative—legitimizing social populism—in spite of the fact that the constitution expressly forbids referenda on issues related to the state budget. This had a decisive role in the collapse of the socialist-liberal government, in the destruction of all attempts at carrying through any reforms, and in Fidesz's two-thirds election victory in 2010.

2.8.2. Economic trench truce: 70/30

At the same time, the cold war tactics did not preclude a common under-standing on the acceptance of "political realities" and "economic compul-sions," the **consensus on the practical application of illegitimate instru-ments in party financing**. The 70/30 meant that the illegitimate resources acquired (or simply acknowledged) in common, would be divided with 70 percent going to the governing party, and 30 going to the opposition. The reason was that until 2010 neither access to sources, nor means of sanc-tioning could be wholly monopolized by either political side. The parliamen-tary majority was normally surrounded by a colorful composition of parties in local government, and within the system, a number of joint, or at least multi-party committees had a say in the distribution of resources under state control. This generated the system of sharing the resources of ille-gitimately collected allowances in proportion to share of influence between government and opposition forces, colloquially called the 70/30 regime. The unmasking of corruption outside the range of shared deals provided the free hunting ground in the political struggle between the rival parties.

The parties cooperating in the 70/30 system acted with different models of operation. The single-channel order of accountability established in the political family run by Fidesz marginalized, and over time repressed, and thereby penalized the private foragers cashing in under the Fidesz banner, ensuring the unity of taxation on centrally sanctioned corruption income across all levels of the established order of patron-client relations. This made sure that businesses would never be approached simultane-ously by parallel channels from Fidesz, and that the public service that was offered in exchange for the toll would indeed be realized. This manner of illegitimate taxation established expensive, but reliable conditions in cor-ruption transactions. While in opposition, the political family represented by Orbán collaborated with the rival government forces: this cooperation on party financing evoked a friendly sense of trench-truce. The actors on the government side, however, were not driven by uniform motives. Firstly, fields that promised revenues from corruption were assailed by francs-tireurs of the party out on their own initiatives and local oligarchs, and sec-ondly, others made repeated efforts to break the established ties of corrup-tion collaboration of the two rival parties.

Following the decisive blows suffered by the socialist-liberal govern-ment in 2006, but even more so in 2008, Fidesz set out to secure a two-thirds, qualified majority in parliament already in campaign gear, and with the help of the Prosecutor's Office, which they controlled already in opposition, they succeeded in depositing the full weight of corruption cases at the doorstep of the government forces so far as public opinion was concerned. The Prosecutor's Office leapt to the service of the electoral battle fought by Fidesz with campaign-actions of criminalization. Moreover the business circles, acknowledging the unavoidability of forced illegitimate taxation, unanimously closed ranks behind Fidesz, supposing: if the payment of corrupt allowances is unavoidable, at least it should be carried out under reliable circumstances.

With the sea change in 2010, in possession of the two-thirds majority ensuring quasi absolute power, Fidesz no longer had any reason to maintain the 70/30 system. Yet the **business ethics of the mafia family** continued to hold sway: while the political partners that were "aboveboard" in the business collaboration enjoyed immunity, all weapons were allowed in settling of accounts with the individual takers of corrupt tax and those who attacked the Fidesz political family, from character assassinations in a media they ruled to politically selected and ordered processes of the Prosecutor's Office.

2.8.3. Alternating corrupt regimes

Corruption, oligarchies, state capture—these are perhaps the most often used categories in describing the relationship between politics and economy in the systems that were raised over the ruins of the Soviet Empire. An undifferentiated use of these terms in the analysis of systemic features of various type and weight obliterates the difference between the alternation of corrupt post-communist regimes and the mafia state. An essential characteristic of the first is that it cannot produce a situation in which any political force gains practically absolute monopoly of power—that is, no party secures all-round constitutive powers along with unlimited freedom to appoint people to all key positions of the state.

The post-communist states that were admitted to the EU—with the exception of Hungary—can be described in varying degrees as the alternation of corrupt regimes. In their cases an electoral system that is proportionate—or only slightly disproportionate—guarantees the most secure institutional constraint on any political force gaining exclusive power. At the same time, this situation ensures the relative autonomy of the oligarchs appearing in the given society, and thereby their bargaining position against the various political forces aspiring to government. Therefore they can make deals with a number of rival political forces simultaneously, without the danger of any one of these forces subjugating them through pure political violence. They may become the beneficiaries or sufferers of unequal distribution or withdrawals, but will not be exposed to complete subjugation. This is a sort of permanent mating dance. Naturally the extent of how widespread corruption is can differ from one case of alternating corrupt regimes to another, as well as the favorite methods, or the influence of corruption on legislation. If the latter is systematically subjugated to private interests, and if members of the political elite, or its institutions for that matter, become the systemic, and not merely occasional parts of the machinery of corruption, the phenomenon of state capture is realized. But when state capture is observed within the frame of the alternating corrupt regimes, the initiative is taken by the oligarch: the oligarch's needs dictate the orders to be fulfilled by the political sphere, the channeling of public goods and services to private interests. In this conception state capture is never total.

The mafia state however is not the qualified case of state capture produced by classical underworld conditions, but represents rather a case where the head of a political venture disciplines and domesticates the oligarchs in the capacity, as it were, of the godfather, settling them into his own chain of command. A more fitting description would be *"oligarch capture."* For in this instance it is not partial economic interests that capture the state, but a political venture that captures the economy through gaining monopoly of power. Of course this could also be interpreted as an extreme form of state capture, but this would probably explode the original meaning of the concept, as it would follow from this that any autocracy—replacing a democratic establishment—could be described as state capture.

NOTES

[1] Hungary was first officially declared a republic between 1918–1919, for the second time between 1946–1949, and third between 1989–2012. Although the country remains a republic, its official name was shortened to Hungary in the current constitution.

[2] Péter Tölgyessy, "Rajtunk múlik," *Index*, December 23, 2014, http://index.hu/belfold/2014/12/23/tolgyessy_peter_elemzes_masodik_resz/.

3 Tamás Keller, *Magyarország helye a világ értéktérképén* [Hungary on the world values map]. Budapest: Tárki, 2009. http://www.tarsadalomkutatas.hu/kkk. php?TPUBL-A-920/publikaciok/tpubl_a_920.pdf.

4 Péter Esterházy, *Búcsúszimfónia* [Farewell symphony] (Budapest: Helikon, 1994).

5 Survey by Medián Opinion and Market Research Institute. In András Gyekiczki, ed., *Hol tart a szabad gondolat?* (Budapest: Politikai Tanulmányok Intézete Alapítvány, 1991).

6 János Kis, "Az összetorlódott idő – második nekirugaszkodás," [Times arrested—A second attempt], *Beszélő* (5 May 2013).

7 Pál Teleki (1879–1941), conservative politician. The parliament ratified the first anti-Jewish law on the limitation of admission of students of Jewish origin to universities called *Numerus clausus* (Act XXV of 1920) under his first term as prime minister. His second term in office saw the ratification of the second anti-Jewish law (Act IV of 1939). In protest to Hungary's role in the German occupation of Yugoslavia, he committed suicide in 1941.

8 Albert Wass (1908–1998), right-wing, antisemitic writer. Lived as an emigré in America after World War Two.

9 "Nőtt a 'pirézekkel' szembeni elutasítás." Tárki, 8 March 2007.

10 A speech by prime minister Ferenc Gyurcsány, president of MSZP at the closed door faction meeting of the party on 26 May 2006 where he encouraged self-criticism with regard to the mistakes made by his party and government.

11 Klára Sándor, linguist and politician in an article at the Internet magazine *Galamus*, "Miért nemzeti a trafik?" *Galamus*, July 2, 2013, http://www.galamus. hu/index.php?option=com_content&view=article&id=219953_miert-nemzeti-a-trafik.

12 One of the slogans used by MSZP in its 1994 parliamentary election campaign.

13 *Fidesz* stands for *Fiatal Demokraták Szövetsége*: Alliance of Young Democrats.

14 *Heti Világgazdaság*, December 18, 1999.

15 Dávid Mesterházi, "A legfőbb ügyész lelépésének háttere," *Index*, March 7, 2000, http://index.hu/belfold/gyorgyi2/.

16 http://atlatszo.hu/2015/02/06/polt-peter-kinevezese-ota-meredeken-zuhan-a-politikai-korrupcios-ugyekben-inditott-buntetoeljarasok-szama/.

3. Approaches of interpretation: from the functional disorders of democracy to a critique of the system[1]

After the collapse of the Soviet Empire, the illusion that only a western form of liberal democracy could follow the communist dictatorship—in European countries at least—was generally accepted in Hungary. And though the path ahead did not seem free of tribulations, there was a consensus that Hungary was on track for a linear, progressive process of development in this direction. Occasional deviations from the norms of liberal democracy seemed like growth pains, rather than adult character traits. Though ideas along the line of a Third Way also emerged in the historical moment of transformation, these were overwritten by the desire to belong to Europe and the necessity of institutional adjustment. A number of the transition countries—earning EU membership—passed the entrance exam on account of geopolitical considerations on the part of the European Union, though some only did so with eased requirements and the help of a crash course. Those enlarging the European Union believed that the countries were motivated not only by the desire to belong to a community of consumers, with its restrictions on entry, but also that of belonging to a voluntarily assumed community of values. As it became increasingly difficult to overlook the disappointment in this regard, the related subject area of the literature on transitology grew richer.

3.1. Trapped in an interpretation along the democracy–dictatorship axis

Interpreting the democratic deficit and functional disorders that followed the dissolution of the communist regimes in Eastern Europe presents a scene of great variety. Attempts at a description usually tried to interpret the political processes that took place in the post-communist states *along the liberal democracy-dictatorship axis*. The post-communist countries set off in the direction of the liberal democratic world, but had not yet arrived. Alternatively: though they had progressed a great deal along this path, they stalled, perhaps turned around. Transitology appears not only as a transformation of social systems, but also as a reference to its own literal meaning: these systems are underway, and form different models according to the rate of their distance or deviation from liberal democracy.

Some analysts label the systems in transition with specific phrases, *adding a restrictive qualifier or a privative suffix to the term of democracy*: illiberal,[2] controlled, restricted, quasi, partial, etc. democracy—trying to determine the level of deviance on the basis of various institutional indicators, and they assess whether the respective system passes the democracy test in light of such aggregated scores.

Others have come to feel that a more accurate impression is offered by describing these systems as versions of *autocracies or dictatorships with the addition of softening adjectives*—semi-autocratic regime, soft dictatorship or for that matter, competitive, electoral autocracy.[3]

Terms like hybrid regimes or related labels are also indicative of *attempts to place the systems along the democracy-dictatorship scale*, but these no longer seek to define the respective establishment in correlation to one or the other ends of the scale.[4]

The foregoing define the various ruling establishments by formal and technical features rather than in a substantive sense. The intrinsic weakness of these scaling procedures along the democracy-dictatorship axis is that they reduce the institutional distortions of liberal democracies to mere quantitative indicators, moreover, they do not treat them as sovereign systems, but as sets of isolated, uncorrelated indicators. Of course scaling seems to allow for a quantitative comparison of various autocratic regimes, but at the same time excludes specific systemic differences from the analysis. So these—otherwise politically useful and orienting—procedures and aggregates of democratic deficit indicators allow for a perception of the degree of deviation from the "ideal" state of affairs, but they are no help in terms of the specific, systemic nature of the deviation. All the more so, because they are stuck in a language that tries to apply categories descriptive of liberal democracies by adding privative suffixes that mark the level of deviance to the analysis of systems that are in fact already of a fundamentally different type.

3.2. Moving on to substantive concepts of description

Other analytical approaches refer to the **subjects of the regimes** that challenge liberal democracy, such as majoritarian democracy, dominant-party system, one-party system, or authoritarian democracy.

While these definitions do not directly link issues of power concentration and wealth accumulation, the two are partly combined by labels that allude to the **illegitimate beneficiaries of the regime**, such as the clientelist regime, crony capitalism,[5] or kleptocratic authoritarianism.[6] These definitions are fertile shifts of perception in the explanation of post-communist systems, but the adjectives used as complex categories provide only a limited understanding due to their presuppositions and underlying subtext (often not conscious at all):

Clientelist, as an adjective, does not express the illegitimacy of the relationship;

The term *crony*, in the context of corrupt transactions, assumes parties, partners of equal rank (even if acting in different roles), voluntary transactions—occasional, though repeatable—that can be terminated or continued by either party at their will, and without consequences;

As to the arrangement implied by the term **kleptocratic**, it differs from the mafia state in a number of ways:

- first, the mafia state carries out an aggressive takeover of property in contrast to the kleptocratic system, which mostly hijacks current revenue only, using classical mechanisms of corruption;
- second, the kleptocratic regime does not establish a system based on permanent patron-client relations of subservience, unlike the mafia state;

- third, the kleptocratic system is not necessarily centralized or monopo- lized (could also be decentralized, or eventually anarchic);
- fourth, in contrast to the mafia state, kleptocratic regimes do not employ coercion, or criminalize at all cost, but merely exploit the opportunities offered by the circumstances.

Besides highlighting the deviation from the norms of liberal democracy or the techniques of power concentration, the conceptual framework of the post-communist mafia state also attempts to depict the underlying nature of the ruling elite.

In terms of analytical tools, Henry E. Hale's outstanding book, *Patronal Politics—Eurasian Regime Dynamics in Comparative Perspective* comes closest to the conceptual framework drawn up in this volume. He sums up the essence of his approach as follows: "Patronal politics refers to politics in societies where individuals organize their political and eco- nomic pursuits primarily around the personalized exchange of concrete rewards and punishments through chains of actual acquaintance, and not primarily around abstract, impersonal principles such as ideological belief or categorizations like economic class that include many people one has not actually met in person. In this politics of individual reward and punishment, power goes to those who can mete these out, those who can position themselves as patrons with a large and dependent base of clients. The sinews of power in post-Soviet countries, therefore, tend to be roughly hierarchical networks through which resources are distrib- uted and coercion applied. [...] The most important distinction among patronalistic polities is whether these patronal networks are arranged in a single pyramid or multiple, usually competing pyramids."[7] Post-2010 Hungary is also discussed as one of those "patronalistic post-communist countries" in which the "single-pyramid system" came to be established in the present volume. Yet "patronal politics," as key to Hale's conceptual system, also aptly describes earlier eras in the history of Eurasian soci- eties. In contrast, the conceptual order of the "post-communist mafia state" that is applied in this volume is more limited in terms of histor- ical validity. It indicates on the one hand, the form of organization taken by the conveyor of the single-pyramid arrangement, that of the adopted political family, the political clan—as befitting its cultural models of rule—and on the other, its illegitimacy, even according to the legal norms it has itself declared.

3.3. The limited validity of historical analogies

Noting that the deviations amount to defining a system in Hungary, analysts searched for historical analogies too.

Some found the phenomena of centralization and nationalization, carried through in opposition to the free-market, decentralizing ethos of liberal democracy—in which the role of the state is to establish and uphold the rules of fair competition—reminiscent of late communism under the Kádár regime.[8] The metaphor of ***neo-communism*** is however misleading on at least two levels. First, the classical communist systems are built on the monopoly of state ownership, and second, the communist ruling elite, the nomenclature was not organized upon the patterns of mafia culture.

Others interpreted the assertive reincarnation of the ideological and cultural inventory and language patterns of the Horthy regime or the Southern European corporativist regimes preceding World War Two, as phenomena in the formation of a ***fascistoid*** system.[9]

And yet, while the fascistoid, corporativist, or for that matter communist systems are essentially ideology driven, the post-communist mafia state uses ideology with value-free pragmatism. (This will later be dealt with in greater detail.) It assembles the ideological garb suitable to the anatomy of its autocratic nature from an eclectic assortment of ideological frames: in other words, it is not the ideology that shapes the system by which it rules, but the system shapes the ideology—with huge degree of freedom and variability. Attempting to explain the driving forces underlying the power machinery of the post-communist mafia state from nationalism, religious values or a commitment to state property is as futile an experiment as trying to deduce the nature and operations of the Sicilian mafia from local patriotism, family centeredness and Christian devotion.

For observers of changes in the praxis of power and the administration, attentive to the expansion of personal chains of command, the growing distance from liberal democracy sometimes suggests features of a reincarnated ***feudal system of vassalage***. This is often labeled—following Max Weber—as a ***neopatrimonial*** system.[10] Yet even as the term is suitable to spotlight the historical regression taking place in public administration and the professional apparatus, it does not describe the system as a whole. For in the case of the feudal forerunners the real nature of power and its legitimacy overlapped in a kind of natural harmony, and required no illegitimate mechanisms for alignment, as it does in the post-communist mafia state.

3.4. Proclamation of the Hungarian "illiberal state"

After 2010, when Fidesz dismantled the institutional system of the liberal democracy, rather than reaching back to one or another historical model, it established a new system that can be related not to one of those found in the past, but in the post-communist present of the former soviet republics (Russia under Putin, Azerbaijan under Aliyev, and some Central Asian republics). It is there that the basic model evolved, though Orbán's system approaches the Putin model of the mafia state by a detour, through the West, and establishes itself as *a Trojan horse of the post-communist mafia states within the ramparts of the European Union*. While Orbán's regime grew out of the corrupt state administration of liberal democracy, in Russia the post-communist mafia state a regime combining an anarchy of the oligarchs with a weak central power was replaced by a pyramid like chain of command built on the networks of patron-client relationships, a shift that could not have occurred without the monopolization of political power.

Viktor Orbán had declared even in advance of the parliamentary elections of 2010 that he was not planning on a mere change of government, but rather the creation of a *"central field of power"* that would secure him the opportunity for decades of "calm" governing undisturbed by rival political forces. He gave the new model established after the elections the name **System of National Cooperation** (*Nemzeti Együttműködés Rendszere—NER*), demarking it from the period he described as the "two troubled decades of transition." The results of the "revolution fought within the limits of the constitution" were then placed under the protection of the ideology of the "national freedom fight" and "unorthodox" economic instruments. While in his speech of 2009 (in the village of Kötcse near Lake Balaton) he only promulgated a program for regime change in euphemistic terms, in a 2014 speech he gave in Băile Tuşnad (in Hungarian Tusnádfürdő) in Transylvania, Romania, Orbán announced—as in a business report—the liquidation of liberal democracy and the establishment of the *Hungarian "illiberal state"* as accomplished facts. He also named certain autocratic regimes as examples leading the way, the "stars of international surveys": Russia, Turkey, China and Singapore.

Though all of these regimes may indeed be considered illiberal democracies, the differing natures of their various power structures is not genuinely explained by the notion illiberal. Fareed Zakaria, who coined the term, also sensed this disparity, when in relation to Orbán's regime he speaks not merely of an illiberal democracy, but as one of its subtypes: "Putinism."[11] While the label marks the similarity between the nature of rule of the two systems, is not followed up by an analysis, since the categories with which he intends to describe Putinism—nationalism, religion, social conservatism, state capitalism, and government domination of the media—are not suitable to capture the *differentia specifica* of the current reigning systems of either Orbán or Putin, or else other former Soviet republics. Stanislav Belkovsky's formulation in describing the system under Putin points more expressively to the essence of the Russian mafia state, which served as an inspiration for the Hungarian one, when he names it as the ***"authoritarian regime of total corruption."***[12] It should also be noted however that Yegor Gaidar, one-time Russian deputy prime minister, had already written as early as the mid-1990s: "A union between mafia and [bureaucratic] corruption can create a monster which has no equivalent in Russian history—an all-powerful mafia state, a real octopus."[13] Though he still speaks of the Russia of Yeltsin, in which political power is not absolute and a relative autonomy of the oligarchs still prevails. Furthermore there is a strong interwovenness with the organized underworld. It is this very horizontal, symbiotic, chaotic relationship that Putin's model later reorganizes into a more hierarchical order in accordance with a chain of command. Ben Judah's eloquent description of Putin's regime properly fits to the conceptual framework of the post-communist mafia state.[14]

For the public in the western democracies, Viktor Orbán's announcement of the illiberal model for the Hungarian state can be taken as an admission of guilt, too strong for the western political elite to ignore without comment. Though the systematic construction of the model was constantly underway during the previous term of Fidesz government, no acknowledgement of its systemic nature—apart from a few exceptions[15]—were forthcoming, censuring only individual elements as isolated cases. The proclamation of the system as the Hungarian illiberal state however, makes it unavoidable for them to discuss the conditions in Hungarian politics as a systemic challenge to liberal democracy, rather than sporadic aberrations.

The Hungarian public however, interprets the illiberal state in a different linguistic context: while the expression self-evidently bears negative connotations for a close group formed by the liberal intellectual elite, it carries a different meaning for Orbán's followers and the wider audience less receptive to the subtleties of the political use of language. For the wider public, through years of unstinting effort, Orbán has linked the concept of liberal democracy, and liberalism especially with that of the "two troubled decades" following the change of regimes, the growth of poverty, corruption, sterile political rivalry, indifference to the Magyars as a "global nation," to gypsies prone to criminality, powerlessness towards the unemployed who live parasitically of state support, while in terms of the imagery of an immediate enemy, liberalism conjured the dependence on the West, the multinationals bearing down on Hungarian businesses, bank capital preying on the citizens, the alien-hearted Jews and other deviants, homosexuals, pedophiles. Thus, when Orbán speaks about the illiberal state and illiberal democracy, he also implies that by means of his ideal of the state he wishes to liberate Hungarians of all of the above, and on the whole is about to realize the strong state that holds the interests of the nation above all else. Therefore, if within the local communications environment his political opponents get stuck in the rut of the linguistic formula of illiberal democracy, they will fail to notice that what is understood abroad as a privative suffix, already operates as a positive qualifier for the broader Hungarian public. And meanwhile the ideologists of the regime have already begun to reinterpret "illiberal democracy" in the—faux-naïve, fake compartmentalized—terms of "community-focused and national democracy"[16]—akin to Putin's "sovereign democracy."

Meanwhile—between 2010 and 2014—Hungarian opposition critics of the new system, rather than assuming a stance critical of the system as a whole, lay down their arms by remaining stuck in the paradigm of criticizing government. More recently however, attuned to discussing illiberalism, their arguments only fall on deaf ears at best, and at worst inadvertently serve the communications goals of the ruling regime. And even now—when Orbán spoon-feeds them the fact that he is systematically demolishing the institutional system of liberal democracy—they are torn between considering his reign in terms of "bad government" or as an illegitimate system. For a long while critics were not even clear about what system they were the domesticated subjects of. Their criticism was frozen at the stage of moaning while coming nowhere close to a diagnosis, not to mention a cure. For in order to arrive at a system-critical paradigm, a conceptual framework fitting the phenomenon has to be built, in which this novel type of political predator can find interpretation. Without a conceptual framework gained from descriptive criticism they are helplessly exposed to the verbal aggression of the new regime's self-definition: they are only victims not an opposition.

NOTES

[1] For more on this see the study by Balázs Trencsényi, "How shall I Call you?," in: *Twenty-Four Sides of a Post-Communist Mafia State*, edited by Bálint Magyar and Júlia Vásárhelyi, CEU Press – Noran Libro, forthcoming in 2016.

[2] Fareed Zakaria, "The Rise of Illiberal Democracy," *Foreign Affairs* 76/6 (November/December 1997), https://www.foreignaffairs.com/articles/1997-11-01/rise-illiberal-democracy ; Fareed Zakaria, "The Rise of Putinism," *Washington Post*, July 31, 2014. http://www.washingtonpost.com/opinions/fareed-zakaria-the-rise-of-putinism/2014/07/31/2c9711d6-18e7-11e4-9e3b-7f2f110c6265_story.html.

[3] Andreas Schedler, *Electoral Authoritarianism: The Dynamics of Unfree Competition* (Boulder and London: Lynne Rienner Publishers, 2006); Steven Levitsky and Lucan A. Way, *Competitive Authoritarism. Hybrid Regimes after the Cold War* (Cambridge: Cambridge University Press, 2010).

[4] Among Hungarian analysts thinking in terms of hybrid systems the clearest comparative model was elaborated by János Kornai, who delineates three types of the post-communist state: post-communist democracies, post-communist autocracies, and post-communist dictatorships. Hungary—in his interpretation—is on its way from the first to the second. (János Kornai, "Fenyegető veszélyek" [Menacing threats], *Élet és Irodalom*, May 23, 2014; as well as János Kornai, "Hungary's U-Turn," Prepublication working paper (January 2015), http://www.kornai-janos.hu/Kornai2015-Hungarys_U-turn.pdf.

[5] Helen Hughes, "Crony Capitalism and the East Asian Currency and Financial 'Crises,'" http://www.cis.org.au/images/stories/policy-magazine/1999-spring/1999-15-3-helen-hughes.pdf.

[6] Karen Dawisha, *Putin's Kleptocracy—Who Owns Russia?* (New York: Simon and Schuster, 2014).

[7] Henry E. Hale, *Patronal Politics—Eurasian Regime Dynamics in Comparative Perspective* (Cambridge, MA: Cambridge University Press, 2015), 9–10.

[8] Lajos Bokros's speech in front of the University of Technology on 23 October 2013 (https://www.youtube.com/watch?v=ADFX3wM4Qpk). But later he himself used the expressions "Hungarian polyp" and the "mafia state created by Orbán," in Lajos Bokros, "Képzelt varázsló és törpe bohóc" [Imagined magician and dwarf joker], *Élet és Irodalom*, March 6, 2015.

[9] Rudolf Ungváry, *A láthatatlan valóság – A fasisztoid mutáció a mai Magyarországon* [The invisible reality—Fascistoid mutation in present-day Hungary] (Bratislava: Kalligram, 2014).

[10] Iván Szelényi and Katarzyna Wilk, "From socialist workfare to capitalist welfare state: Competing strategies and outcomes of transformation of social institutions in European neo-patrimonial and neo-liberal post-communist regimes during the second phase of reforms," Paper presented at the "1989: Twenty Years After" conference at UC-/Irvine, November 6–8, 2009; Tamás Csillag and Iván Szelényi, Drifting from liberal democracy, Neo-conservative ideology of managed illiberal democratic capitalism in post-communist Europe, 2014. http://intersections.tk.mta.hu/index.php/intersections/article/view/28/2.

[11] Fareed Zakaria, "The Rise of Putinism," *Washington Post*, July 31, 2014. http://www.washingtonpost.com/opinions/fareed-zakaria-the-rise-of-putinism/2014/07/31/2c9711d6-18e7-11e4-9e3b-7f2f110c6265_story.html.

[12] Stanislav Belkovsky, *Putin. The man who wasn't there* – Az ember, aki nem létezett (Budapest: Athenaeum, 2014), 177–178.

[13] http://www.economist.com/news/books-and-arts/21633785-academic-investigation-networks-control-russia-band-brothers.

[14] Ben Judah, *Fragile Empire* (New Haven and London: Yale University Press, 2013).

[15] Kim Lane Scheppele, "Legal but not Fair: Viktor Orbán's New Supermajority," 13 April 2014, http://krugman.blogs.nytimes.com/?s=Scheppele.
"The European Union imagines itself as a club of democracies, but now must face the reality of a Potemkin democracy in its midst. The EU is now going into its own parliamentary elections, after which it will have to decide whether Hungary still qualifies to be a member of the club."

[16] Tamás Fricz, "Illiberális helyett inkább: közösségelvű és nemzeti demokrácia" [Replace illiberal with: community-based and national democracy], *MNO.hu*, August 11, 2014, http://mno.hu/fricztamasblogja/illiberalis-helyett-inkabb-kozossegelvu-es-nemzeti-demokracia-1241777.

4. Definition of the post-communist mafia state

All that has occurred since 2010 was prefigured quite clearly for anyone who had followed Fidesz's course up till then, especially in its first term at the reins of government from 1998–2002. Neither intent, nor objectives have changed, only circumstances: with a two-thirds parliamentary majority, most institutional constraints on the exercise of power were removed. After everything and everyone in the party had become dependent on Orbán a long while back, after 2010 the state also came under his control, so he could now apply the same methods that he had used to enforce obedience within Fidesz to the whole of society. In the first years in power the citizens of Hungary were only meted out what members of Fidesz had suffered before. *"I learned when you have a chance to kill a rival you don't think, just do it,"* Viktor Orbán said to ambassadors on 26 June 2007, as quoted in a dispatch found in WikiLeaks. A few years later the time had come.

The regime that has been established in Hungary since 2010 is a stand-alone form among authoritarian, autocratic systems, with particular traits to be discovered only in post-Soviet states outside of the EU until now, which cannot be placed in any of the existing categories. Though one or other feature does suggest relation to certain other forms of autocracy, it defines a sui generis type through the eclectic configuration of unique traits, **a subtype of the autocratic regime**. The conceptual framework describing it discusses not only the methods of achieving a concentration of power, but also how that is related to the relationships, which in turn determine the distribution of wealth and revenues, as well as the nature of the ruling elite. At the same time, beyond its capacity as a conceptual framework, to provide grounds for a scientifically consistent analysis of the current form of the autocratic regime, it adequately determines a basic political stance for a critique of the system and furthermore, has the potential of providing a linguistic frame onto which the citizens can string their own everyday critical observations with regard to the regime.

4.1. Post-communist

The use of *post-communist* in the designation does not refer merely to a historical sequence, but rather to the fact that the conditions preceding the democratic big bang have a decisive role in the formation of the system. Namely that *it came about on the foundations of a communist dictatorship, as a product of the debris left by its decay.*

The political system of communist dictatorship dissolved more consistently in east and central Europe, and less consistently—with the exception of the Baltic states—in the former Soviet republics. While the institutional system of the western political system, liberal democracy, never even developed fully in the former Soviet republics, and historical precedents were also lacking, in the east and central European states the western institutional system was more-or-less established, even if the struggle with an eastern mentality and political culture wears on incessantly.

Usually in post-communist transitions outside the European Union the ruling-economic elite is recruited in significant measure from the former party and secret service elite, or their circles. Yet this is not their most important aspect, rather the inner structure, links and operational mode of the system, into which those recruited from elsewhere can also fit in. The last two decades do not show a linear progress shifting from dictatorship towards an increasingly clean democracy in most of the Soviet successor states. While Russia represents a softer version of the post-communist mafia state, a few Central Asian former Soviet republics present more extreme cases. But even among the European—non EU-member—communist successor states other than former Soviet republics, Macedonia or Montenegro can also be quite certainly ranked among autocratic regimes in the category of mafia states. That which seems like the stalling, or stagnation of the process of democratization in these countries, is in fact the consolidation of the post-communist mafia state. It is no coincidence that the OCCRP (Organized Crime and Corruption Reporting Project) awarded Vladimir Putin (Russia), Viktor Orbán (Hungary), and Milo Đukanović (Montenegro) the titles of man of the year in 2014, with earlier awardees including Ilham Aliyev (Azerbaijan).[1] Of course, in their case the misleading implications of the regularized terminology (corruption and links to organized crime, the organized underworld) no longer apply, the fact is that they themselves operate the mafia state, the organized upperworld—as the heads of their own adopted political families. Hungary, in all events, approaches the Putin model from the angle of liberal democracy. Meanwhile, quite a few other European post-communist countries are uncertain, adrift in the bi-polar gravitational space, torn between the uncertainty of the divergent attraction of east and west, still not having become one of the mafia states. In their cases that monopoly on power—tied to one political actor—which is an indispensable condition of the formation of a mafia state is missing. For this reason, one of the earlier winners of the OCCRP corruption award, the Romanian parliament—however widespread and mass-scale the practice of corruption could be—only serves as an example of the alternation of corrupt regimes, and not the mafia state.

The other meaningful reference of **post-communist** is that the collapsed systems of these countries were built on the **monopoly of state ownership**. In the case of other autocratic systems, either the sequence is reversed, that is, private property is converted to property quasi belonging to the state/community, or the formal disposition of property is left more-or-less untouched, perhaps redistributed in smaller measure. However, no historical example can be found of an instance where state property is transformed en-masse into private property, on the basis of dubious norms—at least so far as their social acceptance is concerned. When the intention is to create a layer of private owners, it seems as if they were intent on producing a fish out of the fish soup.

The two implications of the adjective of post-communist described above are of decisive force in the formation of the new system.

4.2. Mafia state

The use of mafia state is neither impulsive, nor sensationalist, it is not an indictment or cheap insult. The term refers to the **nature of organization and the order of the new ruling elite**. The characteristics of the relatively small new ruling elite are largely unlike the ruling elites of the variously analogous regimes earlier mentioned. Primarily in that it is built on a network of contacts grounded essentially in family relationships—as is the case in the mafia—or the *adopted family* sealed by businesses in common. New, and then further families link up to the organization along ties of kinship and loyalty, fitting into the highly hierarchic, pyramid-like order of subordination that has the head of the *adopted political family* at its summit.

4.3. The expansion of the entitlements of the patriarchal head of the family: mafia, mafia state

The *classical mafia*—as the *organized underworld*—is no more than a violent, illegitimate attempt at giving sanction to the pre-modern powers vested in the patriarchal head of the family in a society established along the lines of modern equality of rights. This attempt is at the same time being thwarted, as far as possible, by the state organs of public authority. The mafia is an adopted family, "the form of artificial kinship, which implied the greatest and most solemn obligations of mutual help on the contracting parties."[2] **The mafia is an illegitimate neo-archaism.**

Though two types of mafia have developed historically, this is not relevant in terms of the line of argument advanced here, concerning the illegitimate extension of the authority of the patriarchal head of the family. Nevertheless it is worth noting[3] that though the Sicilian mafia had aspired to the handling of quasi state functions in the face of Italian ambitions of unification, the American mafia was merely the unorthodox tool of advancement and social mobility for recently arrived Italian emigrants. A number of new groups of immigrants invested efforts in "making it" by means of organized crime, among others.

The **mafia state** on the other hand—as the **organized upperworld**[4]—is a project to sanction the authority of the patriarchal head of the family on the level of a country, among the scenes of the democratic institutional system, with an invasion of the powers of state and its set of tools. All that was achieved by the classical mafia by means of threats, blackmail, and—if necessary—violent bloodshed, in the mafia state is ensured through the bloodless, illegitimate coercion of the state ruled by the adopted political family. **The mafia state is the privatized form of the parasitic state, the**

business venture of the adopted political family managed through the instruments of public authority. In terms of the patterns of leadership the exercise of sovereign power by the godfather, the prime minister, the patriarchal family, the household, the estate, and the country are isomorphous concepts. On all these levels the same cultural patterns of applying power are followed. In the same manner as the patriarchal head of the family is decisive in instances disposing of personal and property matters, also defining status (the status that regulates all aspects of the personal roles and competencies among the "people of his household"), so the head of the adopted political family is leader of the country, where the reinterpreted nation signifies his "household." He does not appropriate, only disposes. He has a share, he dispenses justice, and imparts some of this share and justice on the "people of his household," his nation, to all according to their status and merit.

In the same way that the classical mafia eliminates "the private thief,"[5] the mafia state also sets out to end partisan, anarchic corruption, which is replaced by a centralized, largely legalized enforcement of tribute organized from the top.

NOTES

[1] *"Putin has been a finalist every year so you might consider this a lifetime achievement award," said Drew Sullivan, editor of OCCRP. "He has been a real innovator in working with organized crime. He has created a military-industrial-political-criminal complex that furthers Russia's and Putin's personal interests. I think Putin sees those interests as one and the same."* OCCRP (Organized Crime and Corruption Reporting Project).

[2] Hobsbawm, *Primitive Rebels*, 35.

[3] Based on observation by Ákos Róna-Tas.

[4] Bálint Magyar, "Magyar polip – a szervezett felvilág" [Hungarian octopus—The organized upperworld], *Magyar Hírlap*, February 21, 2001.

[5] Hobsbawm, *Primitive Rebels*, 40.

5. Specific features of the mafia state: a subtype of autocratic regimes

The post-communist mafia state is not a mere deviation from liberal democracy, nor a transitional formation, but an independent subtype of autocracy. An analytical review of the system-specific characteristics of the post-communist mafia state will substantiate the statement.

5.1. Concentration of power and accumulation of wealth

The concentration of political power and an accumulation of wealth by the adopted political family are carried through concomitantly, as they mutually presuppose each other: they are one another's tools and objectives at the same time. Public interest is permanently, and not incidentally subordinated to private goals, determining political decisions fundamentally, in a systematic way. Public policy objectives as reasons for political decisions are relegated to the background. Par excellence public policies are eliminated: decisions have no professional motives only consequences. ***Decisions regard both power and wealth accumulation at once.*** In the course of private wealth accumulation derived from political power, public, or state property and the possessions of the adopted political family inevitably reach across into one another.[1]

Inexplicably, even analysts who are critical of the system show great modesty and separate their descriptions of political power concentration on the one hand and phenomena of corruption on the other, and thus their explanations as well. As if they were two separate stories. Seen through the prism of this approach, all that happens in the political sphere is a self-serving, devilish lust for power, while the outrageous "thefts" appear as mere problems about party financing. The narrative of the first is, "they are at it again, destroying democracy," while the second simply states, "there, that is their scam." Yet these descriptions do not explain the essence of the system. For the concentration of power is no mere obsession, even if a certain kind of mentality and moral defect are required for it. And the corruption of the organized upperworld is not just incidental, sporadic "scam," a decision of the moment or a deviance, but a robbery directed centrally and carried out rationally, a quintessential part of the system. It has to be acknowledged that in the organized upperworld the *adopted political family cannot operate a concentration of power and the accumulation of wealth as separate systems*. But while the traditional mafia achieves its aims through blackmail, intimidation and open violence—in lieu of public authority—, in the case of the mafia state the quasi-legal tools of enforcement can manipulate spheres of influence. This means that the organized upperworld legalizes its own business, as it were. It no longer hoards wealth clandestinely, in the hidden sphere, but has elevated their operations to the rank of state politics.

5.2. Key players of the mafia state: the ruling elite and its accessories

5.2.1. The poligarch

The poligarch[2] acquires illegitimate economic wealth by means of legitimate political power, running a political business venture. While his political power is public, the economic power, his wealth itself is hidden. His previously inexistent personal wealth is secured from his political position and decisions. He manages his family business in the form of a political venture. His illegitimate financial advantages overstep the limits of privileged allowances that could be related to his position, and revenues from classical corruption. He also establishes land leases, real estate possessions and a network of companies through stooges (frontmen, who legally stand for his illegally acquired property and authority). At times he piles up private fortunes in the frame of pseudo-civil organizations or foundations sourced from billions in public funds—where he has informal decision-making competencies over the money. (An example of this would be the football stadium and academy on the private estate of the prime minister's family in his home town of Felcsút, built and maintained from tax benefits and public funds redirected as a form of "protection money.")

The top-most poligarch, head of the political family—and controller of all legitimate executive powers at the same time—is Viktor Orbán, also the prime minister in the case of Hungary. The poligarchs are key figures in the machine of public authority, which is operated as a political-family business. The two most decisive poligarchs are: János Lázár, minister of the Prime Minister's Office, and Antal Rogán, leader of the parliamentary Fidesz faction. The pattern shown by the bloating circle of duties and apparatus at the Prime Minister's Office give a revealing imprint of the nature of rule and economic strategy of the mafia state. Its growing competencies are not standards of some sort of "good governance," but merely follow the needs for power and wealth-accumulation within the political family. At the same time, the parliamentary faction with the majority required for constitutional changes plays a docile role in the removal of normative conditions through legislative means.

5.2.2. The oligarch

Sometimes the oligarch uses his legitimate fortune to also build political power: the economic power is public, but the political power is kept hidden.

A distinction has to be made between the ideal types of the major entrepreneur, the organized underworld's entrepreneur, and the oligarch. The **major entrepreneur** undertakes **legitimate economic activity, and his access to this activity is also legitimate**, meaning it is conducted according to the accepted social norms: he secures both market and state contracts through transparent competition. The political powers do not infringe on his autonomous position guaranteed by law. In contrast, **the entrepreneur of the organized underworld** mainly carries on **illegal economic activities** (drug trade, prostitution, oil bleaching, extortion, protection racket, etc.) **under illegal conditions**. He stands in conflict with representatives of public authority and seeks to draw them under his influence by illegitimate means (bribery, threats, blackmail, occasionally physical violence). After the regime-change in Hungary, the 1990s brought the rise of the organized underworld, as well as its regression later. The **oligarch of the post-communist systems** however, seeks to secure **illegal support for legal economic** *activity* by means of corruption. Until a single political force wholly takes over political power, he is assured relative autonomy, a bargaining position and a competitive edge. Such are the current conditions typical in varying degrees of the former communist states that are now EU members—all of them, that is, but Hungary.

However, the post-communist mafia state reduces the autonomy of the major entrepreneur, while restricts, domesticates, or eliminates the organized underworld. Drawing upon its monopoly of power it destroys the relative autonomy of the oligarchs, and aims to integrate them into its own chain of command. The patron-client relationship also turns around in the mafia state: basically it is no longer the economic players approach the political sphere with their claims, but it is the political regime that milks the economic actors as well as the taxpayers, by way of contracts and privileges ensured to its subjugated oligarchs. A network of subcontractors and suppliers then extends this patron-client relationship to the lower reaches of the economy.

5.2.2.1. Major entrepreneurs versus oligarchs

The oligarch is not only distinguished from the ideal type of the major entrepreneur by the advantages a regime ensures, but also by the measure of vulnerability to power; the degree in which the oligarch's particular economic activity and existential conditions make it possible to force him into a patron-client type of relationship.

*Model differences in the positions of the ideal typical
major entrepreneurs and oligarchs*

	Major entrepreneur	Oligarch
Relationship to the adopted political family	not embedded	embedded
Economic activity	legitimate	legitimate
Economic activity ordered on basis of	competition, market terms, legitimate	personal contacts, illegitimate or legalized illegitimate practices
Business performance	dependent primarily on performance in the market	dependent primarily on political relationships

	Major entrepreneur	Oligarch
Target group for products and services	largely not domestic consumers	largely local, domestic consumers
Mobility of activity	geographically mobile	place-bound, immobile
Nature of activity	difficult, or impossible to monopolize by the state	easily monopolized by the state
Conditions for the business venture	not directly under the influence, or hardly influenced by state arbitrariness, thus not easy to blackmail, less vulnerable to political decisions	established by state arbitrariness and therefore wholly prone to state influence, even to the extent of liquidation, and therefore open to blackmail
Source of wealth accumulation	mainly market, though also possibly competitive privatization	mainly directed privatization, state concessions, state procurement, guided bid for tenders
Nature of risk	independent of the state, market dependent	under influence of the state, based on patron-client relationship
Utilization of profit	utilized in transparent fashion, largely reinvested	drawn out of the venture, utilized in other (less transparent) fashion
Status of business	autonomous	dependent, tribute-bound
Type of venture	profit oriented by market, innovative	tribute exacting through non-market tools, non-innovative

5.2.2.2. A typology of the oligarchs

In the full-fledged mafia state one can identify different **types of oligarchs**:

The **inner circle oligarchs** did not have significant wealth to begin with, and actually managed to secure their startup capital from positions weaving through politics—building on what would be called greenfield investments. These may have been party business ventures at the earliest stages (e.g., some of the earliest Fidesz ventures), which later either folded, or continued as personal businesses, throwing off their party limitations. Their wealth can be compared to that of those who made it as a result of the chaotic, spontaneous privatizations of the regime-change. Forming the inner circle of oligarchs with ties to political ventures, most of them belong to the **top spheres of the adopted political family, and also play active roles in shaping politics without legitimate position in public office.**

In Hungary Lajos Simicska[3] could be considered as the par excellence case, also Zsolt Nyerges, who made it into this circle at a later stage. Yet it was also possible to drop out of the starting lineup, as in the case of Tamás Varga, who endangered the businesses of the political family through large-scale, criminal tax evasion, or Gyula Gansperger, who got caught up in business deals separate from the political family.

The *adopted oligarchs* accumulated their wealth in the period of the alternation of corrupt regimes, and their admission into the political family only stabilizes their position and protects them in the world of politically motivated, violent redistributions of wealth. They can access opportunities offered by the adopted political family, and provide benefits in return: their contributions are exacted as the economic or political demands of the political family would have it at any given time. Their account balance nevertheless remains in the positive by a wide margin.

Among representatives of this type of oligarch are Gábor Széles,[4] who made his riches in the course of the spontaneous privatizations and operates the pro-government TV channel, or the owners of the CBA chain store for groceries, László Baldauf[5] and the Lázár brothers,[6] for whom acceptance in to the club is a heart-felt, reverential experience. They never have a say in determining the political family's strategy, only serve its purposes: they organize loyalty campaigns and demonstration and partly finance them (see for example the mass demonstrations involving hundreds of thousands of participants in support of government, the so called Peace Marches).

The *surrendered oligarchs* earlier enjoyed relative autonomy or had "played in the rival team." Reasons for their surrender may have been contracts petering out under the mafia state, or non-market tools of state coercion—tax authorities, prosecutor's office, police—enforcing the change indirectly. Since they are struggling to survive economically, with a lot to lose but no protected bargaining position with the regime, they are compelled to find their place in the chain of command under the political family. They enjoy privileges, but pay their corruption taxes to the political family as required, meeting all expectations.

A typical figure among this type of oligarchs is Tamás Leisztinger, who originally had left-wing ties. In the first cycle of the Fidesz government he had been stripped of a part of his wealth (BÁV Rt, the privatized national pawnshop network) through the non-market coercive instruments of the state, from tax authorities to law enforcement. During the second term of Fidesz government after 2010 he changed sides, and as a surrendered oligarch he was given the task of financing the godfather's hobby: to be the owner of one of the football teams, that of Diósgyőr in northern Hungary.

The surrender to the political family must at the same time also result in a demonstrative break with rival political forces and figures. Being loyal is not enough, seeming loyal is also a must for surrendered oligarchs. In 1998, when Fidesz first formed government, an important western automobile manufacturer made the outgoing socialist minister of industry head of its Hungarian branch, following a western tradition. A mistake: the new government gave them to understand that they should not dream of the state purchase of a single car of theirs until the ex-minister has been removed. They complied within half a year. It was under the second Fidesz government after 2010 that the former finance minister under the socialists was unceremoniously fired from the position of the president of the supervisory board of an internationally active Hungarian transport company. This was the price to pay for a strategic agreement concluded between the company and the government which ensured tax benefits. But in another example of similar tactics, immediately prior to the 2010 elections a company managing a large real estate development showed the door to its president of the board who had been minister of the interior—not for Fidesz of course—in anticipation of the election results. These few examples are only meant to illustrate the nature of state blackmail practiced widely and on massive scale as well as the eventual preventive accommodation to it.

Escort oligarchs are basically not beholden for their wealth to the political business venture of the mafia state, but rather, their network reaches back to the period before regime-change. They are the greatest oligarchs of the "two troubled decades of transition," whose favors were courted by both political sides for support. They were further reinforced by this mutual dependence. However, the position of "equal accommodation and equal distance" towards the rival political forces was undermined by the disruption of political balance following 2006, and it became apparent that the disintegrating socialist-liberal government forces would most likely be replaced by a long-term reign of Fidesz in government. The encroaching advance of the adopted political family tipped the earlier autonomous oligarchs out of their balancing act between various political forces, and in the first round, forced them into the roles of committed adjuncts in the venture. Though as allied oligarchs they have not been included in the political family's chain of command, they had to close any given ties of support to rival political forces, or at least restrict them to a minimum.

The emblematic figures of this group include Sándor Csányi,[7] who usually leads the list of richest Hungarians, and had been the chairman and chief executive-officer of OTP Bank, the largest retail—once state-owned—bank in Hungary, and Sándor Demján,[8] chairman of the TriGránit real estate company, and the National Federation of Savings Cooperatives.

After Fidesz had overrun the political institutional system in 2010, it felt the time had come to begin forcing the allied oligarchs to surrender. In the case of Sándor Demján, the plunder of the savings cooperatives by the legislative means of nationalization meant the launch of the assault, while Sándor Csányi received a message through the media from János Lázár,[9] the politician leading the Prime Minister's Office that in lieu of his surrender, he may well be demoted from the position of respected chairman of the largest Hungarian bank to the "no. 1 usurer of the country."[10] The size, influence, and type of wealth is largely decisive in regards to the outcome of these efforts. While the composition of Sándor Demján's businesses made it possible for his social standing to be shaken, in the case of Sándor Csányi this could not be achieved. Launching "total war" on the chief executive officer of the largest bank of the country, and the oligarch recognized as the richest Hungarian would have meant a significant risk to both the political family and the economic stability of the country. Therefore Orbán—having suspended the attempt at making him surrender—has been satisfied for the moment to keep Csányi in the role of a loyal, escort oligarch.

Yet the first term of Fidesz in government showed that even an almost fraternal relationship was no guarantee for holding back the plundering instincts. This was the fate of Gábor Princz,[11] the CEO of Postabank, which had gone bankrupt. Following Fidesz's taking power in 1998 the assets of the bank were doubly over-consolidated, and in exchange for a free withdrawal, avoiding to be jailed, Princz kept silent about the bank's relationship to, and financing of parties and politicians. Then in a situation where he had been removed and put under trial he could not take steps against an organized heist on a heretofore unprecedented scale of size, masked as consolidation of the bank.

The **autonomous oligarchs** do not commit themselves permanently to any political force. While attempting to establish corrupt business relations with actors in the political sphere, they try to keep their integrity. This, however, is only possible if no political party manages to monopolize all the political power. Their freedom of manoeuvre becomes sharply limited by conditions under the mafia state: they are either forced to surrender, and if they balk at this solution—considered rival oligarchs—they become the targets of efforts at economic annihilation. Their relationships with any political force rivalrous with the adopted political family are criminalized and used as a pretext for their destruction—by means of selective law enforcement.

The adopted political family of the mafia state considers those **rival oligarchs** the most dangerous, who have their own political ambitions. They are meted out direct state coercion (as in the Khodorkovsky model). Those who don't have personal political ambitions and only support alternative political forces, can count on more peaceful forms of expulsion (Berezovsky model). In addition, those who try to resist the efforts of the adopted political family to make them surrender will also find themselves in the status of a rival oligarch.

Under the alternation of corrupt regimes, the questions would still be relevant as to who of those with partial political power on the one hand and economic power on the other is leader, who depends on the other, who gives orders and who executes them. In the post-communist mafia state however it becomes an obvious fact that the boss is the one who can outlaw his rival by means of the legislature, the tax authorities, the prosecutor's office or the police. The one who can eject the other from the game using state powers is the winner who takes all. Therefore, those who think that in the post-communist mafia state **oligarchs** have captured the state are down the wrong track, because the relationship is the reverse. In the mafia state a tight political venture, the political family appoints its own oligarchs, and gives them power. The oligarch cannot blackmail the godfather here, since the classical mafia technique assumes publicity and the institutions of democracy, which can be activated when wrongdoing is unveiled. The indebted politician is not blackmailed with the threat of physical violence, but that of disclosure. As the tax authorities, the prosecutor's office, the parliament, and so on, belong to the godfather in the mafia state of the organized upperworld, the chances of an oligarch blackmailing him is rather thin.

The relationship of the head of the political family and an oligarch is more like—as an old anecdote from Moscow would have it—the time Stalin threatened Krupskaya: unless she behaved appropriately, he would appoint someone else as Lenin's widow. Such is the process of being broken, being readied for submission. Independent oligarchs only exist temporarily, in the mafia state *everyone works to fill the same family purse, from which everyone receives their share according to the rules of the political family.* There is no invisible free-enterprise corruption—as in the "two troubled decades" prior to 2010—but rather the family estate is run by the permission of the godfather, within the frame clarified for each field in which concessions are granted. While the mafia state derails the bureaucratic administration, it organizes, monopolizes the channels of corruption and keeps them in order. Yet to use the word corruption—as an expression—to describe the foregoing seems altogether below the mark, after all, this is family-building, under the guise of "nation-building," where private interest is recast as public good.

In the mafia state a number of instruments of state enforcement applied with the precepts of a mafia culture can be accounted for. It is of course not irrelevant where on the scale between "peaceful" coercion and bloody violence the tools of exclusion, discipline, and enforced subservience are to be located. Though the classical mafia often applies physical violence—lacking the bloodless instruments of enforcement through public authority—they still must not be mixed up with wanton murderers, as they use physical violence as a means to an end, and not and end in itself. The mafia state naturally "needs" to turn to physical violence less often, but "when necessary" it does not shrink from using it. In fact the *coercion thresholds* of the post-communist mafia states are different, depending on their geopolitical position. The threshold constraining the use of violence in the case of the EU-member Hungary is higher than in Russia, which is not a member, and even in Russia it is higher than in the case of a post-communist mafia state in Central Asia.

5.2.2.3. *The Orbán–Simicska conflict: the first mafia war within the organized upperworld*

Nonetheless, even the "top oligarch" within the inner circle of oligarchs can lose his privileged position. In spite of Viktor Orbán declaring still in April 1989 that "Lajos Simicska[12] was the brightest among us." In spite of the fact that it is known to have been Simicska's initiative, his creative input to base party financing on business ventures, so the oiling of the party machine would not be dependent solely on occasional bribes. In spite of the fact that he poured the illegitimate funds acquired with the help of the party into the party treasury and private family purse from the beginning. In spite of the fact that during the eight (not the biblical seven) lean years of Fidesz in opposition that followed their defeat after their first term in government in 2002, he ensured the financial resources needed for the party's existence, and the survival of a Fidesz-serving, hard-hitting anti-government media. His exceptional position was assured by his role as the college roommate, the mentor, the knower of family and party secrets, the number one confidant and economic strategist. But this was not all: it was also assured by the fact that he could operatively manage the centralized collection of illegitimate revenues and place them at the disposal of the discretional decisions they made together with the godfather-party president. This made sure that the flock would not disperse in the lean years, and that everyone in the political family was absolutely clear about whom obedience was owed to.

While in opposition—in lieu of the offices and apparatus of public authority—it was a matter of survival whether oversight of financial resources could be centralized, yet following the change of governments in 2010, Simicska's exceptional position remained, even if the situation no longer demanded it. By way of the mega-corporations he owned (the construction enterprise Közgép, the advertising company Mahír, etc.) the state and EU contracts and resources poured in throughout the first term in government. Beyond this, however, to tighten the process, the government itself relayed these contracts through Simicska's stooges. "Lajos built up a network which had permeated almost every field of the state apparatus. Since his people were placed everywhere, no political decision could be carried through without his consent. This curtailed the prime minister's freedom of choice far more than Brussels or the multinationals. Viktor's real freedom fight is actually only now in the offing."[13] This is how an influential businessman summed up the Simicska-Orbán conflict.

Orbán wanted to avoid becoming "honorary godfather" and let his economic decisions, and thereby even some of his political ones be filtered by the top oligarch, pending his approval or even refusal. For this reason, after the 2014 election victory—ensuring two-thirds of the seats in parliament, that is absolute power for another four years—Orbán began to restrict further encroachments of Lajos Simicska within the apparatus of public authority, when they were difficult to control and verged on derailing, or even overriding his decisions. "Our insider sources report: Orbán proposes a novel system for clientelism, and in this system there are no Lajos Simicskas, and there are especially no separate realms for power nodes that tend towards independence. There are only individual actors dependent on the prime minister, with individual interests. Under this regime only the prime minister can give a key to the safe overseen by János Lázár for the next four years."[14]

Only oligarchs, or stooges with much smaller personal authority can win access to those areas that Simicska was ejected from. To take the example of the Ministry of National Development, which had been ruled by the Simicska–Nyerges oligarch duo via their stooge, Mrs. Lászlóné Németh,[15] who headed the ministry. In 2014 she was replaced by Miklós Seszták,[16] who had as a lawyer previously administered the registration of hundreds of dubious Russian and Ukrainian companies to a single address in a remote small town, later liquidated with significant public debt. He is not an independent personality in any way, but someone who can be handled, blackmailed by the poligarch. Indeed he immediately forbade any state companies reporting to the ministry from signing contracts without his—in fact, the godfather's—permission. Furthermore, "he promised a complete screening, a review of all the old contracts, and a settling of accounts with certain interest groups. It was clear that this message was directed at Lajos Simicska: 'You are no longer the one pulling strings here.'"[17] After the conflict became open in February 2015, Simicska's stooge in charge of the Hungarian National Asset Management Inc. was also removed. The weight of the situation is reflected in the fact that this corporation, and through it the state, had a majority stake in 255 companies, and less than a majority stake in 160 firms. "What really gets Lajos upset, much more than losing even a contract worth a billion forint, is that they are trying to take his people away from him. He built up a network, every corner belonged to him. They have not struck these people off now. They have just been told that from now on they are working for someone else. His will really goes under when he has lost his network. He won't build that up again."[18] These are the words of a participant in the battle who tried to give a sense of the stakes through this comparison with drug dealing.

A stooge for Lajos Simicska, Minister of National Development László Németh "had to go" in spite of the fact that, as quoted by the US Ambassador from one of their conversation, "she met Orbán every week, looked over the list of public projects, and decided which ones to prioritize and which bids to accept."[19]

This is a struggle for the real chips within the mafia state—and not a single, one-off business opportunity. After the reshuffling of government following the 2014 elections the godfather first excluded the stooges tied to Simicska from the state apparatus, and drew under his own oversight not only the advantages that could be acquired by other oligarchs and favorites, but also the benefits that until then could only be secured by the top oligarch himself. A further signal was sent by the lack of compensation from other state resources for the Fidesz-affiliated media—largely owned by Simicska—when a starkly progressive advertisement tax was imposed mainly with the intent of blackmailing the German-owned market-leading television station RTL Klub. In fact, in the beginning of 2015 the godfather informed the media organs tied to the political family, which had till then been pumped with state adverts, that they would have to find their own footing from there onwards, as state resources were to be concentrated on a state media that had been converted to become the mouthpiece of the ruling party. At a later stage it was announced that the discriminative progressiveness of the advertisement tax would be repealed, a measure taken under the combined pressure of RTL Klub sharpening the critical edge in its news programs, a visit by Angela Merkel, and the measure's foreseeable defeat at the European Court. This move on the other hand threatened to take a serious financial toll on Simicska's media empire, too. However the event that was most undeniably befitting the mafia culture was when managers of Simicska's media companies collectively resigned and signed over to the state media overseen by the godfather.

What unfolded after this can be termed a *mafia war within the organized upperworld*, because it openly crosses the line on the rules of loyalty and obedience within the family. For in the beginning of the *"Orbán-Simicska war"* the "semi-contact" economic strikes dealt by the prime-minister-poligarch were returned in the form of "semi-contact" political strikes back: the publication of pieces critical of the government in the media empire belonging to Simicska. In reality he must have been aware of the fact that his demotion was final, even if its extent could still have been a subject of bargain. He must also have known that if, as the conflict escalated, the contending parties had brought forward their full war arsenal, both sides would have suffered major losses. Yet Simicska—the oligarch facing the poligarch—could have lost everything. He could even only

permit himself even his offended resistance rather than an obedient acquiescence to the new situation on account of his having once been the college
roommate, "first among the brothers in arms."

The godfather made the inner-most leading cadres of Simicska's media
empire an offer that could not be refused: to switch to the media loyal
to Orbán. It was a message of no compromise, complete surrender was
expected. A dramatic situation, reminiscent of gangster movies: as the
boss faces betrayal and shot in the back by his own closest body guards.
Simicska's brutally uncouth expletives—public, moral denunciation of the
godfather[20] were made under this shock, at the same time it was a symbolic announcement of the fact that he was not willing to change from his
equal role to that of the role of subject. From this point onwards, within
the mafia state, in a war that now unfolded not only behind the scenes,
the strikes against each other could be "full contact." An end to the conflict could no longer be reached by agreement. Simicska had dropped out
of the political family. This is why a heightened sense of despair can be felt
among his subordinates who had rightfully felt, until then, that in serving
him they were also serving the godfather, but now they had to face the fact
that they would inevitably become the targets of liquidation by either one
party or the other.

Another sign of the irrevocable desertion and expulsion from the
family is that in the first three months of 2015 Simicska's company, Közgép
lost seven tenders to the tune of 11 billion forint (approximately 37 million
euro).[21] Paradoxically, this proves by reverse effect the closely directed
hijacking of tenders: for if Simicska's companies had not won the series of
state and EU tenders due to his position within the political family, this line
of wins should not have come to an abrupt halt at this moment. Yet "it has
now become Simicska's favorite habit to make offers for tenders—usually
being realized from EU sources—at a consistently lower price than that of
the newly favored oligarchs of the godfather. He creates increasingly difficult situations by this means, as his bid has to be disqualified from the
competition through the strangest of false claims, such as the construction of the development work being priced too low in the bid. Looking for
a more stable solution by the summer of 2015 the political family excluded
him from a road construction tender worth 7 billion forint on the ground
that he had 'filed false data.'"[22] The Arbitration Committee of Public
Procurements (Közbeszerzési Döntőbizottság—KDB) has already excluded
Simicska's mammoth company, Közgép from all Hungarian public procure-

ments for a period of three years on the basis of this accusation. Simicska has turned to the court for legal redress, which has suspended the ban issued by the KDB until the case is closed. The outcome of the court proceedings will show how much is left of juridical independence in Hungary.[23]

But the new government is not only an obstacle to Simicska securing any new procurements, it also seeks to undo his present contracts, currently in force: claiming EU criticism as the reason, the commission of Közgép to build the M4 highway has been annulled, and the leadership of Budapest has suddenly realized it made an unfavorable contract with Simicska's company Mahír in 2006, for the establishment of advertising columns in the streets of Budapest, annulling the contract and requiring the company to destroy the columns.[24]

In another new development the agricultural state-owned lands rented without tenders to companies affiliated with Simicska until now under contracts that were automatically extended every year, will now be offered for "tenders" by the National Land Trust, and his companies are expected to lose an annual 100 million forint (335 thousand euro) in EU agricultural support as a result.[25] Finally his exclusion from the leasing of land is to be completed by the sale of the, till now rented thousands of hectares of state-owned land by a bid for offers that has already been issued.

The conflict does not leave the media empire unscathed either. Not only are the companies belonging to the one-time ally stripped of the funds from state advertising, but the production of TV programs for the state channels, which had functioned as directed cash funnels out of the system, are also either being cancelled, or handed over to other producers where possible. This amounts to losses on the scale of billions.[26] In response the companies Simicska owns have ceased to support the Ferenc Puskás Football Academy in Felcsút.[27] A resignation from the list of sponsors of the godfather's favorite hobby is a demonstrative sign of quitting the adopted political family. The symbols with which family belonging are expressed and its iconographic imprint—in this case the list of supporters on the website of the Academy—is an expression of the marks that differentiate the mafia state from other autocracies.

The war therefore continues, waging on thousands of battlefields, all earlier points of contact. Thereby a map of retributions retrospectively outlines the circle of illegitimate benefits. This could be considered a particular form of self-denunciation in a situation where there was an independent judiciary.

Needless to point out that the war within the political family, between Orbán and Simicska shows stark differences from settling of scores between members of the ruling elite in dictatorships and autocracies such as the Night of the Long Knives under Hitler, or Stalin's terror.

5.2.3. The stooge

The stooge has no real power: his formal position, legal standing—whether in the field of politics or that of economy—serves only to bridge the gap between the legitimate and illegitimate spheres. The reason why the regime in question can be considered a mafia state, a sort of neo-archaism and not a reincarnation of historical prefigurations is that in their case—whether it was a feudal system or one or another version of dictatorship—the sociological nature of power and its legitimacy coincide, and the position of a stooge—as it is not needed—never appears in any way. The members of society are all positioned in various orders organized along lines of chains of command, and no one has the role of mediating between the actual keepers of either political or economic authority and the formal actors of these spheres. In other words, no extra players are required to hide the difference between the actual, and the legally declared social positions of those who fill these roles.

With the formation of unbridled power over the shaping of the constitution and the appointments of personnel, the institutional system of liberal democracy becomes the domain of stooges. It is not just a matter of a political force in possession of all power placing its followers into offices in the executive arms of state and government, but that the same treatment is given the key positions in the institutions that are supposed to check and control them (Constitutional Court, President of the Republic, State Audit Office, ombudsman, National Office for the Judiciary, Media Council, Prosecutor's Office, tax authorities, National Bank, etc.), which would be fine if adherents to a party's values would nevertheless act in an autonomous fashion and in keeping with the ethos of their positions. But this is not the case here. It is in fact misleading to describe the people filling the positions captured at the latter mentioned institutions as people who tow the party line, because in fact they are not loyal to the party, but directly, or indirectly to the head of the adopted political family: they have come by their appointments through him, and report to him alone. *The political stooges are governors, while the stooges of the business ventures are stewards, so far as their sociological function is concerned.*

Those who can be considered *political stooges* do not use the authority vested in them on the basis of their public office autonomously, in other words their formal authorizations contradict their actual scope of action. To begin with, the political stooges are shaped from the first-generation of leading Fidesz comrades in arms (faction leader, President of the Republic, Speaker of the House), and then the placing of external experts and family members into these positions begins (Chief Prosecutor's, head of the National Office for the Judiciary), to finally include, in the last round, the adopted political family's businessmen, accountants, managers, and even the lawyers of these businesses in the key economic positions of executive authority (Ministry of National Development, Ministry of the Interior, National Development Agency). In their case the omertà, the code of silence applies even to their rare public appearances, and neither public opinion, nor the politicians of the opposition consider them political actors of authority, who could be held accountable. The people filling most of the functions of public authority in the mafia state can practically be considered the godfather's political stooges positioned at various levels.

Changes of political stooges can have various reasons. The change of one Fidesz cadre for another appears senseless at first sight. The real motivation behind these changes in the period of establishment of the mafia state is that the Fidesz cadres, or clients of other leaders within Fidesz are replaced by the personal clients of the head of the political family. Following the repeated Fidesz victory in 2014, the replacement of the "top stooges" of the Simicska-Nyerges axis, László Baranyai from the helm of the Hungarian Development Bank and the already mentioned replacement of Lászlóné Németh, minister of national development for Miklós Seszták, the lawyer without any party or professional record. His appointment was followed by a change of over two hundred personnel across the whole chain of the administration dealing with development resources. Purges of such depth are unprecedented even in case where governments change hands between political forces. We were witnesses to a bloodless liquidation, a gang war within the mafia state, played out using the powers of public authority.[28] One of the tools of this move was the diversification of appointees to positions of state control and oversight of the economy, and moreover placing a person in charge of a significant segment of these positions, who reports directly to the head of the political family, can be blackmailed with the means offered by public authority, and is a new oligarch, not an old one of the inner circle. Another tool was to place "disciplinary" economic sanctions in prospect (e.g., retrospective tax on revenues from freeway construction), then imposition of penalties (e.g., advertisement tax), or the failing at public procurement tenders intended as a warning. While disciplining his unruly family members discretely, the godfather persecutes his rivals from outside the family with the instruments of public authority (tax authorities, Prosecutor's Office, secret services, police). He will expel, or isolate his own familiars when necessary, but not outlaw them, whilst his rivals can expect criminalization.

The *economic stooges* represent poligarchs in the economic sphere, and especially in the fields dependent on the state. But oligarchs might also have economic stooges, when they do not wish to reveal the full gamut of their economic activities resulting from their political contacts. The economic sector they have covered is the most dynamically expanding segment in the Hungarian world of business, since its success is determined not by fair competition, but the monopolized political environment. The economic stooges could not be mistaken for oligarchs even if someone were to try: their servile body language, visible at a glance, declares that they are not the actual owners of what formally belongs to them.

The economic stooges of the poligarchs can be either insignificant businessmen, or oligarchs of the adopted family of the inner circle.

An example of the first kind—among the people close to the head of the political family—would be Lőrinc Mészáros, the quickly risen gas repairman from the home village of the prime minister. "The Felcsút resident, known as a confidant of Viktor Orbán has risen to the foremost ranks of rich Hungarians in four years, as the winner of state procurements for water supply systems, roads, agricultural land leases and (monopolized) tobacco shop concessions."[29] The estimated value of his assets has grown to a hundred times what it was at the change of governments in 2010, making him the 85th richest Hungarian with 7.7 billion forint (24 million euro). Symptomatically of a stooge's ambiguity about the separation of his and his patron's possession he "forgot" to add a 1 billion forint (3 million euro) dividend from his yearly asset declaration. "God's will, good luck, and the person of Viktor Orbán have a role in his having achieved such wealth," he says.[30] But *Forbes Magazine* already listed him as the 30th richest Hungarians in 2015, with an estimated fortune of 24 billion forints (78 million euro).[31] His business ventures virtually cover the gammut of economic activities: from agriculture to construction, mineral water production to canning, tram, air conditioning and car repair workshops, hotels to golf clubs.[32] He is at the same time "mayor of Felcsút and the president of the Ferenc Puskás Football Academy [...] in recent years he has established a real mini empire in the Felcsút, Alcsútdoboz and Bicske region."[33] His lands lease holds, won at the state tender for bids on agricultural land distributed among those in the political family—which they can later purchase at discount rates—are in excess of a thousand hectares. This was how, among others, he acquired the rental of state lands that had been leased until then to a shepherd of Felcsút, András Váradi.[34] Váradi, who took a virulent stand against the land racket, and registered as a contender to him for the post of mayor in the municipal elections in the autumn of 2014, died in an accident a few days before polls—under circumstances that have still not been cleared. Mészáros is mayor of Felcsút, landowner, the president of the Foundation for Felcsút Youth Football Development that operates the Football Academy, businessman. Political and economic stooge, governor and steward—all rolled in one. This is not the case of an oligarch who has made a lot of money under whatever circumstances establishing a close relationship with a poligarch, but rather that of the poligarch delegating him the management of a part of the illegitimately acquired wealth.

Interestingly, not only an individual, but an institution may also act as a "stooge." As founder of the Foundation for Felcsút Youth Football Development, Viktor Orbán appoints the Board of Trustees. In actual fact, he controls decisions of the foundation. In the meanwhile, public funds can be freely channeled into the foundation, which rather than serving the common good, actually serves to finance the hobby of the head of the political family. One of the prime examples of the above: an amendment to tax laws made it possible for businesses to direct a part of their corporate taxes to support spectator sports, among them football. The football team of the village of Felcsút, with a population of 1,800 received 6.8 billion forint (app. 22 million euro) from 2010–2013 out of this source, a sum that is 4.5 times the amount received by the recipient of the next largest amount. These were the funds used in part to build the stadium seating 3,500 viewers.[35]

Felcsút and its neighborhood are also a symbolic place for the godfather: signifying the household, the estate, the village. These are the origins of his patterns of rule: the patriarchal family in a broader sense, which he rules over as head of family. However he does not have legitimacy to rule the country this way. Not even in Felcsút. Though this is his world, it can only be partly on his name. This is what Lőrinc Mészáros, and other local businessmen are required to bridge. And though formally Mészáros is the mayor, landowner and major entrepreneur, everyone is aware—including himself—that he is only a servant. *It is this institution of the stooge, among others, that separates the classical mafia and, by the same token, the mafia state from those systems where the nature of power and its legitimation coincide.*

To repress the top oligarch, Lajos Simicska, a company was needed that had grown up by the side of, or rather in opposition to his Közgép: the new company was Duna Aszfalt Zrt., whose "first major pitch in 2012, was to snatch the construction contract for the M43 highway from Makó to the Romanian border, actually right from Közgép. The company figures have only become prettier since. By 2013 it filed revenues of 54.3 billion, which is like a dream compared with the 18.2 billion forint of 2010. The growth of its balance accounts are even more impressive, having risen from 424 million in 2010, to 2.3 billion in 2013. And the dividends paid out have virtually catapulted: rounding out from 40 million to 2 billion."[36] Thereafter the company, as the Orbán-Simicska war became open, used a dormant company with no revenues called Kőrösaszfalt Zrt. to buy itself into a building concern that had at one time been one of the largest in Hungary, but had since 2010 gone a sharp decline of state contracts since, the Magyar Építő Zrt. The transaction is a fine demonstration of the methods used by the political family for economic expansion. Firstly the owners of the company with experience, expertise and capacities, had to be given to understand that with the current owners they would not be able to gain state contracts, and secondly the company would have to be drawn into the hold of the political family at the lowered price these unfavorable future prospects had cut them down to. The CEO of the purchasing company, Kőrösaszfalt Zrt. is no other than Lőrinc Mészáros's future son-in-law. Meanwhile the ousted earlier owner of the bought company, Magyar Építő Zrt. felt it necessary to issue a statement saying that he is satisfied with the price, and "nothing forced him to resign," adding nonetheless that "in concluding the sale of his company his first consideration was that his 108 employees would have a job under the direction of the new leadership as well."[37] Of course this is quite revealing with regard to the fact that a company's market performance is irrelevant when success at state contracts requires an ownership suiting the political family. Besides, the price of the company must have been lowered by circumstance that cannot be ignored, the political family's complete domination of the field of state contracts. Therefore the value of the company, excluded from potential deals, would plummet further with time.

As the observer moves further away from the location of the estate (whether Felcsút, or the wine yard of the Orbán family at Tokaj, etc.), the circle of stooges for the head of the political family becomes less conspicuous. Nevertheless, the sudden rise of new oligarchs suggests that they are, in part at least, also the latest circle of new stooges for the godfather. István Garancsi[38] stands out among them, who in addition to being the owner of the Videoton FC, the football team of the city of Székesfehérvár—the closest major city to Felcsút—is the owner of the only savings cooperative not to have been forcibly nationalized, namely the Duna Savings Cooperative, as well as having been "given the opportunity" to buy the majority shares of the company Market Építő Zrt., which has won huge tenders from the state, also co-owning the offshore company that earned 55 billion forint on the gas deal concluded with the Hungarian Electricity Ltd.,[39] all of this while "subletting" a flat in Buda to Orbán's son.[40] Another example of the emerging oligarch-stooge, two-in-one model with direct ties to the godfather is Andy Vajna,[41] American film producer of Hungarian origin who was granted a vast majority of the casino concessions in Hungary.[42]

The existence of the stooges—while they fill an indispensable role in the mafia state—raises a problem in terms of the legalization, the laundering of the revenues they make for poligarchs. This is a rather bothersome task with high "additional costs." For though revenues from outstanding profits of business ventures under stooges and deputized oligarchs can be redirected to the illegal end-user through "payment" to an offshore company, the utilization of these funds by the poligarch still meets with some difficulty. The organized upperworld provided a solution to the problem, making the tool of tax amnesty that can be applied occasionally and for a limited period of time, the ***permanent instrument of money laundering***. "The Stability Savings Account is the latest tax amnesty, which began at the end of 2013, the idea being that at least 5 million forint must be placed on an account at an authorized bank in Hungarian sovereign bonds, and the tax authorities will not ask the owner of the account where the money has come from, or whether tax has even been paid after the amount. The amount ***becomes legal immediately*** upon the account being opened. (Law qualifies the sum that had been transferred abroad under unclear circumstances—or simply disappeared from the sight of the tax authorities—as domestic income, essentially legalizing it.) According to the regulations in place in the first half of 2015 it is better to keep the money parked on the account for a few years, because at first a rather hefty tax has to be paid on the sum transferred to the account and its yields, if the 'deposits' are broken prematurely: twice the personal income tax for the first 3 years, which is 32 percent; 16 percent in the fourth year; and 8 percent in the fifth year; after which the amount can be taken off the account free of tax. Amounts can only be placed on the account when it is opened, however there is no upper limit, and any number of accounts may also be opened. While this in itself was no mean deal, what came next was paradise itself, so long as you have a bit of dirty money: upon the proposal of Mihály Varga[43] (minister of finance) only 20 per cent tax has to be paid on amounts placed in the Stability Savings Accounts after July 2015, if the 'laundered' amount is taken off the account within an year, but if it is left on the account for over an year, the rate is decreased to 10 percent. A pretty attractive offer at first glance, but what a brilliant offer once you calculate what would be left if you had paid the fair rate of tax into the public account."[44] And moreover, the funds do not even have to take the roundabout way abroad: they can be delivered straight to the account in cash. Some experts believe sate supported money laundering might strengthen a reversal in the direction of cash flow, serving effectively not to bring the dubious revenues parked abroad back to Hungary, but the transfer of money cleaned and freed of any tax liabilities in Hungary to safe havens abroad.[45]

5.2.3.1. The head of the political family and the family VIP box

The family VIP box by the football pitch paints the clearest picture of real power relations in Hungarian society, as the head of the political family cheers in the awkward intimacy of his circle, **poligarchs, oligarchs, stooges, governors, executives, stewards, and security guards** (in their civil roles under a rule of law: minister, mayor, chief prosecutor, president of the State Audit Office, bank chairman, leaders of NGOs, businessmen, and so on)—in a word, the people of his household. No liberal principles like the separation of powers or conflict of interests can be allowed to disturb the national-fraternal unity, the harmony of the VIP box.

The cultural models of the head of the political family, the features of his rule differ vastly from the models of other—e.g., Fascist or communist—autocrats and dictators. He does not show his power in parades, party congresses. The manifestations of his rule bear the characteristics of relations within the patriarchal family. If we were to place it in historical-logical order we would find that the role of the head of the mafia state's adopted political family begins with the archaic patriarchal head, followed by the Roman pater familias, and the godfather of the mafia. What is common in the concept of the roles can best be described through the role of the pater familias. The Roman family unit, as a household community subject to the initially unbridled power of the pater familias enjoyed a rather high degree of autonomy from the state. The scope of public law, the *ius publicum*, that is, the power of the magistrates in a sense came to a stop (in principle and in general) at the border of the private estates, on the doorstep of the private houses, from where the rules of private law, *ius privatum* were instated, ensuring absolute power to the head of the family."[46] This power extended to all matters of life, individuals, property and activity. The "existence of the family is the sum of those who stand beneath the power of the head of the family,"[47] from the head of the family down, through the wife, as well as the children by blood and adopted children, and other relatives living in the household, down to the servants and menials of various statuses. "Our Hungarian expression for family, 'család' goes back to the word 'cseléd' (meaning servant)—of old Slavic roots—so the word family originally meant the people of the house, or rather the servants. A faint, but living trace of these roots in our language is the occasional use of the word 'család' for the children."[48] Historically we have the opportunity to bear witness to the process by which the people belonging to the household of the patriarchal head of the family, subjected to him under various statuses, are gradually becoming emancipated, and finding ways out of all-round personal and material dependence. Along the centuries the process is taking we have only now reached, for example, prohibition of domestic violence. In the classical mafia tradition however the patriarchal head of the family extends his entitlements over persons, property and activities by illegitimate and violent means to citizens and families who are legally in all ways independent from him. Belonging to the adopted family of the mafia is at once both a grace and a compulsion. As to the mafia state, the head of the political family seeks to establish this model of rule on a national level, by the means of a monopoly on the enforcement of state power.

In the same way as the family, the household, the estate and the country belong to the same pattern for the head of the political family, so do those who act within them. The child is finicky or unbridled, women "sniffle" at weddings, the opposition throws a tantrum about everything—none of them are manly, a tough hand is needed. For the head of the political family, leading the country is essentially the same as leading the patriarchal family. Rather than rights, its members have rules of conduct prescribed by the head of the family. The alienated, formalized, impersonal institutional relations of liberal democracy are replaced by the personal, jovial forms of rule and leadership that however, brook no contradiction. In a country where leadership is characterized by the division of labor typical of the patriarchal family, differently legitimized people may fill roles of similar function in the adopted political family. This reveals the true guiding principles and scope of each role, to which the mere formalities of the rule of law are then assigned as required by occasion.

The head of the political family commands the cultural patterns belonging to the patriarchal head of family with natural ease: a clear hierarchy reigns between the people of his household without the need for formalized roles; the informal codes of speech are also dressed up in respectful forms mirroring the higher and lower positions: "Would you please prime minister—Come on now Lőrinc..." (using the informal address, but keeping to formal modes of address in Hungarian). The bonds across class boundaries are reflected in tax free home distilling of *pálinka* (Hungarian fruit brandy), the filling of sausages at home and at gastronomy festivals, the manly singing of vulgar songs in wine cellars, and the SUV driven by the godfather himself in the snow blizzard—"Let me take the reins a bit, Józsi!" he says. The same culture finds expression not least, in the eating of sunflower seeds and spitting the shells around in shirts and short vests at the football games in the family stadiums, without social distinction. But let the jovial atmosphere fool no one, the goodwill of the godfather cannot be abused, for the disobedient will get clapped on the ear that is coming to them, and if still not understood, the next steps are exclusion, or expropriation of property.

As the *estate*—with the house, country mansion, stadium, lands, even a narrow-gauge railway—belongs to the familiarly symbolic representation of the regime, so do the people of the household and the *close family*. And though it cannot fully unfold, the dynastic principle also comes into play. If the eldest daughter of the godfather gets married, she deserves a royal wedding in Felcsút, with the full protocol of guests, local roads with freshly lain asphalt, security from the Counter Terrorism Center. If the girl is interested in catering, let her study at the most expensive private school in Switzerland, and as a place to practice, why not find her a coffee shop or restaurant "of her own": "A little research has revealed who owns the fine dining restaurant at the center of the city, on Erzsébet tér, a spot simply overrun by tourists. All clues woven through a complex network of companies led to István Tiborcz, the son-in-law of the head of government" writes *HVG*, the leading Hungarian financial weekly.[49] However the son-in-law, in order to make him worthy of the daughter, has to be enriched through a drove of state and EU projects won in dubious public procurement procedures (from the LED external light fixtures for Fidesz-led local governments, to yacht harbors on the Balaton), and his acquisitions are further expanded through the tools of state threats and blackmail. "Even if public lighting projects costing over 150 million HUF were open tenders, a single company, Elios [owned by Orbán's son-in-law] alone submitted bids for all but one of the tenders. Thus, lacking competition, they won the contracts with an offer barely a few thousand forints short of the cost calculated in advance by the municipality." The reason for this was built into the custom-tailored public lighting tenders issued, which even fixed details of the following magnitude: "the color code of the spray paint to be used on the frame for the lamps and in some cases even the type of glass—curved—to be used for the lamp covers."[50]

This is the dowry that comes with the godfather's daughter. Though the new law on public procurement in effect since 1 November 2015 accidentally came to include a passage saying that the highest state functionaries and their families cannot make bids for public procurements, the parliament rushed to correct this "mistake" a month later: making it possible for family of state leaders to take part in bids so long as they do not live in the same household.[51] Meanwhile his other daughter's young partner has the opportunity for a schooling in ways to gather and use a network of contacts at the cabinet of a Hungarian EU commissioner in Brussels, a scene reminiscent of young aristocrats in the past attending the imperial court in Vienna.

Every despot has his own hobby. In Hungary the prime minister likes football, so the punishment all vassals are given, is that to prove their loyalty they must each adopt and sponsor a football team, and watch the weakest of weak matches with the godfather, devotedly wrecking their nerves through the match with him. And their humiliating, pathetic efforts are even broadcast on television...

The new standard of the mafia state is also proven by comparison of the history of the construction of ***two new Hungarian football stadiums***. The only great wish of the self-made billionaire, József Stadler,[52] was a stadium of his own in the *puszta* (the Hungarian plains, or steppes). But since he was a simple tax evader with an economic background and no political power, a sort of "oligarch of the plains," he was caught, jailed, and the stadium has stood empty ever since, falling into ruin. In contrast, in the world of the organized upperworld the public land is handed over to a stooge through a state tender, and the narrow-gauge railway (padded with a special state development investment) transferred from the state to the Football Academy, which—as previously mentioned—the parliament had ensured tax-exempt private donations. Time for miracles, a wave of altruistic enthusiasm can be seen all around: two-thirds of the financial offerings made by companies flow into the village team of the godfather that, as a result, rises up the divisions. Those who newly belong to the court purveyors know well that if they wish to receive state procurement contracts and EU funds, such charity will mean an advantage. The godfather of the organized upperworld builds a stadium next to his home by adding a tax-benefit to sweeten the pill to the "protection money" collected for his hobby.

Though football is the great favorite, with the closest poligarchs and oligarchs as owners or leaders of a football club each, the members of the adopted political family have nevertheless taken control of a majority of the rest of the sports as well, along with disposition over the state funds accorded to these sports: "an annual fifty billion forint (app. 170 million euro) of public funds from corporate tax is directed to the spectator sports (football, handball, water polo, basketball, ice hockey), and in addition 16 further branches of sport will get 135 billion forint (app. 450 million euro) in total for development until 2020." (See Annex 1.)

5.2.3.2. The business ventures of the poligarchs, the inner circle oligarchs, and their stooges

As if these business ventures were not subject to the basic laws of economics. In distinguishing them from the businesses that do not receive the benefits of political favor, the following peculiarities can be outlined:

They have an incredibly fast ramp-up phase and become "national champions" in spite of the fact that they were established immediately prior to their first state procurement order being announced, or even after that. They are able to win huge state contracts without appropriate references or base capital, and secure loans if necessary—under rather favorable terms—without any capital cover.

The expansion or downsizing of their activities follows political cycles, rather than economic ones. In most of the tenders they won, businesses offering more favorable terms were excluded by administrative means, or they were the only ones to submit a bid. According to the EU's anti-corruption report "a very high proportion of public procurement procedures involved a single bidder: 54.3% in 2010 and 49.1% in 2011. This figure was even higher when a negotiated procedure was used (on average 61%)."[53] This is because ventures not propped up politically learn pretty fast: they do not even apply for tenders that require significant material and intellectual input, which they do not have hope of winning.

As winners of state contracts and procurements they are essentially administrative, rent seeking coordinators, and not technology coordinators. They usually function as gateways of accessing to state contracts, and partner with such large subcontractors or associates in a consortium, who under proper rules of competition would be able to carry out the tasks specified by the procurement contract on their own. The rent seeking coordinator normally establishes a system with more tiers of subcontractors than what the technology coordination of the given task would require. The vulnerability of those at the base of the pyramid of subcontractors is borne out by the fact that they work as pariah outsource companies, with virtually no profit margin. Moreover nonpayment to subcontractors does not entail a ban from further public procurements.

The scale of taxed profits within the total revenue significantly outrides those at businesses in the same field, but not enjoying political support. This disproportion in scale indicates the venture's nature as tapper of public funds and rent seeking.

The scale of dividends paid out of the taxed profits of the venture far outdo that of dividends taken out of politically unsupported ones that are exposed to the market. In the case of companies participating in fair market competition—especially the startups and developing ones—a decisive majority, if not all the profits are reinvested in the company, as would be only natural in the case both of an expanding field of activities needing investment and the likelihood of market fluctuation. However in the case of the companies of the oligarchs or stooges, the burden of necessary investments in equipment is transferred to the partner in the forced consortium, or the subcontractor. And any risks meant by possible market fluctuations are annulled by stable, politically directed contracts. These two factors in themselves indirectly indicate that these winning companies are largely merely there for rent seeking, and can be liquidated without further losses if the political situation changes.

If by some chance the economic stooge also becomes a political stooge at the same time, on account of this office he must prepare a public asset declaration, and the gap between the dividends taken out of his company profits and the financial situation reflected by the asset declaration becomes apparent. This contradiction is surmounted if the stooge's property is only actually a premium, a transaction cost, and the missing amount lands somewhere in the proximity of his patron.

While a not insignificant segment of successful businesses without ties to the adopted political family are exposed to attempts at expropriation by coercive means often employing the instruments of public authority, the companies owned by the inner circle of oligarchs and stooges are never. And though this would be understandable in the case of oligarchs within the inner circle or adopted oligarchs, it would still need to be explained why business proprietors in seemingly week political positions also enjoy protection. The most prominent identifier of companies belonging to the poligarchs and oligarchs of the inner circle that are directed by stooges is the apparent disparity between the weak political-legal standing and untouchability of their legal owners.

5.2.4. The corruption broker

The corruption broker[54] connects participants of a corrupt transaction as a mediator, or legitimizes the illegitimate business deal as a judicial expert. His activities and position have changed a great deal during the two decades following the regime-change. Under the conditions of the socialist shortage economy the "business client" and the "corrupt service provider" would connect directly in almost all walks of life. The end of the shortage economy after the regime change eliminated the market foundations of these corrupt relations in such dimensions. At the same time, forms of more robust corrupt transactions demanding greater expertise came into being. This created the situation in which the mediator's position came to be established, in which the main fields of activity, apart from the expected reliance on a network of contacts, were organized around the **writing of bids for tenders, legal advocacy, and the preparation of draft laws.**

In the fluid conditions following upon regime change, the corruption brokers could simultaneously be at the service of clients with different political ties. Later, with the stabilization of the party structure, the more constant bonds of corruption brokers in a mercenary role under one or another political figure was established, and the party's own financial network was built and operated with these corruption brokers. Personnel did not normally mix or match between different networks during the period of the alternation of corrupt regimes. But this did not exclude their being in contact for negotiations naturally, as required by the deals between various political actors. With a monopoly on political power, the mafia state assembled its own corruption brokers under the adopted political family in strict order, and also employs a number of them in the roles of political stooges.

In parallel to this, naturally, while seeking to liquidate the financial background of rival political and economic forces, it also eliminates their network of corruption brokers. On the new grounds of the mafia state's monopoly on power the proportions of fields of activity among its own corruption brokers also changes internally: with the systemic legalization of the adopted political family's channels of corruption, the field of planning draft laws makes it into the foreground of their activities, and the services provided by the writers of bids is also largely taken over by the now essentially unchecked state. In the same way that legislation and preparation of draft laws are in the mafia state no longer the tools of creating normative regulation applicable to everyone, and the normative status of equality before the law is undermined by laws arbitrarily tailored to individuals and businesses, so the transparent and legitimate agencies for the preparation of laws (competent ministries, administrative organs and legitimate supporting institutions) also shrink into the background, with the field of activity relegated to private law firms and other, often newly established "professional" background institutions belonging to the adopted political family that cannot be monitored by instruments at the disposal of the public authorities. In the meanwhile "the parliament has repealed the compulsory requirement for law firms to make their financial reports publicly available, even though the regulation had been so recently introduced that the revenues should have been published for the first time on 1 June 2015. According to Fidesz politicians the repeal is to be attributed to successful lobbying by legal bars. The national and Budapest bars however have stated that they have not been involved in anything of the sort, and would have been moreover: pleased if it became public, who was receiving the major state contracts."[55]

Under the conditions created by the mafia state, there are two types of lower-level, day-to-day corruption broker[56] that gain vast importance, and simultaneously go through a strange metamorphosis.

One of these is the **gatekeeper**, who ensures the bureaucratic background and protection of the illegitimate deal within the public administration. In the earlier stage he is the official of the bureaucracy as posited by Max Weber, who is led astray by an occasional commission. With the establishment of the mafia state however, not only the appointment of the official in charge, but orders for continued activity as a corruption broker also come from above. The entry of the political stooge indicates that the transformation of public good to private benefit has turned from an occasional deviance into a systemic operation.

The other type is the **representative broker**, who under the mafia state, in a role as deputy for poligarchs may even give his name to the ownership of major corporations. In terms of the size of his wealth, his business, he may even be considered an oligarch, and yet is not, only an **economic stooge**. Of course it is also frequent that an oligarch and stooge are embodied in one and the same person.

5.2.5. The family security guard and the secret services

The **family security guard** is composed of a wide spectrum of elements: from the Counter Terrorism Center, newly established following the Fidesz victory in 2010, through the security services guarding the family estates (which are allowed to close public roads as private ways), down to the infamous radical football fans of the most popular Hungarian football team, Ferencváros, the so called, Fradi B-közép (B-box, designating their sector in the stadium). The latter were ready when needed to siege state television and set fire to it (2006), or defend the Fidesz headquarter from students at a protest (2013). But they can also be mobilized to disrupt student rallies critical of the government. Certain lower levels of this multi-tiered "security service" that can be mobilized to fill various functions, permanently remains under private disposition. The personal interweaving is quite bewildering: the Fidesz party director who handles the databank on supporters who can be mobilized for elections, Gábor Kubatov, is at the same time—in his role as the president of the Ferencváros Sports Club—mentor to its football ultras who riot to take up the causes favored by the political family. While opposition politicians are constantly exposed to offences committed against them by the pro-government rabble as a result of a police that "can't control" the situation, the security services offer the head of the political family tight protection.

The leader of the **Counter Terrorism Center**—Viktor Orbán's former personal bodyguard, who advanced in one step from major to brigadier general, János Hajdú[57]—has practically unlimited powers for "prevention" in both arms of state apparatus, the police and secret services. Though formally under the oversight of the minister of the interior—who, while a political stooge, owned a vast security services company while Fidesz was in opposition—he is without doubt tied in directly to the godfather. Not only is there no opposition control over the state enforcement apparatus, but even institutional control on the government side is replaced by personal dependence, the patron-client relationship. Thus in the event of a change of government the functions of personal bodyguard and security services can be withdrawn into their earlier position in the private sector.

The personal protection of the President of the Republic, the prime minister and the Speaker of the house had previously been the province of the Republican Regiment. This was taken over by the Counter Terrorism Center. However, of the two concerned "Fidesz-founding" public dignitaries, first László Kövér[58] freed himself of the "personal security," which informed Viktor Orbán of every step he took, by establishing the Parliamentary Guard that he also entrusted with his protection. Then the President of the Republic, János Áder[59] attempted to free himself of the yoke of the godfather's all-seeing eyes by establishing an independent presidential security guard. While this attempt was put down, he nevertheless succeeded in having his personal protection to the Operational Police, thus giving the slip to surveillance from the Counter Terrorism Center.

Similarly to how the **private security guard** of the head of the political family gained a new state organizational form through the Counter Terrorism Center, there is also an intermixture between the private and official secret services. However, as a particular of the mafia state these are no longer party cadres, but the personal confidants of the head of the political family.

A part of the old communist and the new political elite had been in touch with each other before the regime-change of 1989–1990 as recruiters and informers of the **secret services**. Others, among them Fidesz, recognized opportunities in rescuing and exploiting the informers, apparatus, and networks from before. These explain the partial survival of the secret services, whereby the culture of blackmail, and susceptibility to blackmail has remained virtually unscathed. Among the former socialist countries entering the European Union, Hungary had the strongest alliance of those with a vested interest in obstructing the full disclosure of one-time secret service documents. Only the leadership of the liberal Alliance of Free Democrats (SZDSZ)—having largely emerged from the anti-communist dissident movement of those times—were an exception to this rule, that is, immune to the infiltration of the secret services. The political clout borne by the SZDSZ however, was not enough to crash through the wall of opposing interests aligned on this matter, composed of the Hungarian Socialist Party (MSZP), the right-wing Hungarian Democratic Forum (MDF), and Fidesz. The "predictably erratic" behavior of blackmailed people, whether in parliament, or other walks of political life signalled the continued vitality of this culture. The distinction drawn by a popular explanation between former informers in rival parties, "my informer is a patriot, but your informer is a traitor," sounded especially dissonant on the part of those political forces, whose ideology was typified by demonstrative hackling of "commies." And these "patriots" continue to be kept firmly in various positions and roles of political power by the current government forces. Beyond the blackmail and employment of the one-time informers, one of the least clarified questions regarding the secret services (which had integrated some of the former political police force as well), is its—obviously opaque—influence on post–regime-change politics in Hungary.

Securing control over the **secret services** was a key issue for Fidesz, right from the beginning: already in 1990, in exchange for supporting the election of the liberal Gábor Demszky as lord mayor of Budapest they bargained, and secured his previous position in parliament as chairman of the Committee on National Security for themselves. Until the middle of the first decade of the 2000s, even in opposition, Fidesz used this position to ensure its influence over the national security apparatus. But in 2006, the governing socialists ended the services' practice of "reporting both ways"—i.e., to the socialists and Fidesz—which had been established till then, resulting in serious conflicts between the two political parties. This development lent importance to private companies undertaking shady secret service activities, such as the UD Zrt., described by the leading Hungarian economic weekly as "a private intelligence agency that organizes party coups."[60] The pensioned secret service agents working there were reactivated by Fidesz in the official security organizations, after their return to power in 2010. However, since 2010, as minister of the interior, Sándor Pintér oversees not only the police, but also the secret services, which meant reversing the decision on the separation of the two bodies, which was a symbolic act during the regime-change.

Though after 2010—empowered by the two-thirds majority in parliament—Fidesz could have ensured the opening of the communist regime's political police documents to the public on its own, the steps they have taken, such as the dismissal of the archival research committee headed by the once outstanding activist of the anti-communist dissident movement, János Kenedi,[61] or an absurd statement by the secretary of state for public administration and justice (to the effect that "all the people under surveillance in the previous regime can claim the originals of all written material, and documents pertaining to them,"[62] i.e., take them home) rather suggest that the way is being paved for the destruction of the information not yet selected on the basis of political interests. In Eastern Europe, this is the unique case of **the survival of this system of political blackmail**. What's more, the possibilities for the collection of data on various groups of citizens are extended on every pretext. All such measures increase the surveillance and blackmailing potential of the government.

The Counter Terrorism Center is furthermore legally authorized to secretly collect information on citizens without judicial authorization. A licence, that not even the national secret services have. This does raise the scepter of third-world models where the autocratic political leader has his very own elite commando, tied only to his person, and invested with such intelligence authorizations. Though a human rights organization, the Eötvös Károly Institute turned to the Constitutional Court, taking issue with the fact that "the probing of the most sensitive, most intimate parts of our lives depends not on the independent, impartial court, which is in the final run called upon to enforce the primacy of our basic human rights, but the decision of the minister who merely serves the interests of the government, and oversees justice,"[63] the Court did not give place to the complaint. The case now stands before the European Court of Human Rights in Brussels. There is no institutional oversight of the Counter Terrorism Center, neither real governmental, nor parliamentary, nor from the ruling party. A stark difference in model from the case, for example, of the communist regimes, where the secret services were tied into the highest organ of the party, and the first secretary could not "keep control of it" after losing the position.

5.3. The political family's expropriation of databases ensuring democratic control

The following databases—including software necessary to handle the data—were appropriated in order to ensure, by illegitimate means, the power of Fidesz and the adopted political family, as well as to oil the operation of the system of patron-client relationships:

Secret service data: Fidesz is obstructing the all-round public accessibility of the list of informers, their recruiters, and the document material on the one hand, while on the other, it is able to use the information available in them to protect its surrendered followers, or when necessary, to blackmail and stigmatize its political rivals.

Tax authority documents: upon taking government in 1998, one of the first measures taken by Fidesz was to appoint Lajos Simicska, the—then still—closest confidant of the prime minister, the most reliable oligarch of the inner circle to the helm of the tax authorities. In a—widely reported, but never officially proven—operation lasting three days, with the staff sent on vacation, and called the "night of the long bytes," he succeeded in securing for Fidesz the "maintenance" of the compromising database.[64] Of key importance in the instance of a possible change of government, "clearing" the database minimizes the chances of penalization. The lack of confidence in the tax authorities under Fidesz—in its function as a tool to apply political pressure or selectively enforce laws—is indicated by the way in which the media evaluated the maintenance operation on the eve of the last parliamentary elections in 2014 along the same lines.[65]

The Hungarian National Bank (MNB) has bought up *GIRO Zrt., which handles all of the retail and corporate transfers*. The company was founded before the regime change by 12 financial institutions, among them the MNB. Approximately 300 million orders for payment went through it annually. It covers almost all of the retail and real economic company transactions. As a possible explanation for state acquisition, reflected in "the only interpretation independently formulated by a number of experts, was... that 'practically every retail and corporate transaction is visible in this system, our bank transfers, credit payments, and payments to public utility companies.'"[66]

The *software and digital database that handles tenders for EU resources* could be one of the foremost tools in an investigation of abuses committed in the course of distributing EU fund and procurement contracts. But since the software formed the property of a private company (Welt 2000 Kft.), the acquisition of the company through forced nationalization was of paramount importance to Fidesz. The fact that the circumstances of the acquisition were not fair was signaled by the long drawn out series of negotiations between the owner and the state, and that the government, in order to indicate the seriousness of its intentions to buy, "sent the armed investigators of the Hungarian tax authorities to search the offices of Welt 2000, and the homes of its owners, [... where] early in the morning, they seized documents and computers. Unofficial sources say they were investigating VAT fraud."[67] On the day after the contract of sale was signed the earlier owner of the company suddenly died—though his close friends were not aware of his being ill.

The software used for the parliamentary and municipal elections was owned and operated by a private company composed of former experts who had worked at the Ministry of the Interior, and no doubts as to the proper functioning of the system had ever been raised. In this case, curiously, private ownership was the guarantee of the digital collection of the votes not becoming a tool to the falsification of the election results. Fidesz however used both government pressure and overpayment from the budget to gain possession of the software through nationalization. The motivations for nationalization are plainly revealed by the fact that while the experts of the parties that form national lists were earlier allowed to delegate IT specialists to inspect the operation of the database and the software, this practice was abolished by Fidesz upon nationalization.

The *so-called Kubatov lists* are an umbrella term used to describe the databases established and updated by the Fidesz party director in the course of various *elections, referenda and signature campaigns*, as well as the *so-called national consultations* conducted by Fidesz after taking government. Within the continuously updated and expanded database containing entries in the millions, the individual target groups can be filtered according to categories defined in terms of level of activity, commitment, availability, regional distribution, among others. From mobilization of those listed to the building of a clientele, they serve the needs of the adopted political family. For many years now they include not only the data of committed sympathizers, but also those of people critical about Fidesz—in as much as this could be established in the course of data collection.

5.4. Polipburo, in place of the former communist politburo[68]

Effectively, political and economic decision-making is transferred from the organs of formalized, legitimate public authority, and even from the "politburo" of the party, to the "poli*p*buro" of the adopted political family. (The "politburo" was the top level body of the Bolshevik-type communist parties. Fidesz has no politburo, its highest organ is the Presidium. The actual top power center is however an informal close network the virtual feelers of which are like arms of the *octopus*, called *polip* in Hungarian, which was also the Hungarian title of the film series about the Sicilian mafia screened to wide acclaim in Hungary during the 1980s, titled in Italian *La piovra*.) Of course the polipburo—as it is not a formalized body with legally determined membership—does not have any legitimacy deriving from its nature of power. The difficulty for conventional analytic approach does not mainly lie in the fact that people who do not bear any real power are also to be found in profuse numbers among those on the top bodies of formalized public authority or party organization, but rather the fact that individuals without membership in any formalized organization or body apparently have considerable influence and power. The conventional approach of political science, accustomed to its regular Kremlinology, attempting to identify informal nodes of authority with actual influence within the formalized organs of leadership cannot resolve this contradiction. With regards to Soviet type societies, it was still admissible to assume that the communist party defined as the "leading force of society" took charge of the formal competencies of government, and the rivalry between the political figures with various measures of influence was contained within the leading organs of the party. In such a case, anyone with real power needed automatically to be member of the formalized, legitimate ruling body. In the case of Fidesz however, no one could seriously presume that for example, out of the four deputy presidents of the party, Ildikó Pelczné Gáll, who leads the women's section and is a European Parliament representative, or Zoltán Pokorni, who has withdrawn into voluntary exile as mayor of one of the districts of Budapest, can have any significant influence on any decision. Yet it is also evident that the oligarchs of the inner circle without any legitimate position, as well as the confidant of the prime minister, the communications and campaign guru Árpád Habony, who holds no position, office in formal public authority, and receives no remunerations, do have real power and play a determining role in the decisions of the adopted political family.

This makes it more accurate to speak of **polipburo, rather than polit-buro**, with the topmost close circle of the adopted political family forming the real center of power—though not operating as a formalized, legitimate body. In contrast to the communist—or a number of other—dictatorships, it is not the party, Fidesz that has organizations that function as a transmission belt for the implementation of its will, but the party itself has become the main transmission belt for the adopted political family. Not only can the central power not be described as a legitimate, formalized organization, but practically there are no decisions taken by formal bodies. No conceptual work for political objectives is carried on in the organs of the party Fidesz, the party only mediates between the illegitimate and politically determinative decisions of the adopted political family and their legitimized implementation by Parliament, government, or municipality.

5.4.1. Delineation of the mafia state's ruling elite from other historical analogies

It is only possible to make a very limited, metaphoric comparison between the adopted political family of the mafia state and the ruling elites of other systems, the clans and dynastic houses of premodern society, the feudal orders, Christian middle class of the period of Austro-Hungarian Monarchy, or Hungary between the two world wars, the nomenclature of the communist regimes in the more recent past, or even the rule of the oligarchs in the transition period.

- **The clans and dynastic houses of premodern society** were on the one hand, organized on the basis of bloodlines, but they also took in outsiders as they expanded on a personal, family basis. When the network outgrows the hierarchy based on bloodlines, the system becomes more complex—this is a characteristic to be witnessed in a more definitive form also at the traditional mafia-like organization. In the elite of the mafia state, the family organized along bloodlines is continuously complemented by families not connected to them on the basis of bloodlines, that is, they become members of the adopted political family. On the other hand, the entitlements and competencies of the leaders of the clans formed a part of the natural law in the premodern state.

In contrast, the mafia ekes out unlawful entitlements for the clan-like adopted family by the means of corruption, threats, and violence. If all of this is carried out from the position of monopolized public authority, then it is a mafia state.

- Though certain sheikhdoms by the Persian Gulf—as forms of **post-modern monarchy**—are built on the family, or adopted family network with ties to the ruling dynasty, they are nonetheless legitimate. This is a type of monarchy, in which the head of the clan, by reason of that role, is also the ruler: his situation in the family and his broader legitimacy as ruler coincide. Unlike the mafia state, where this position is set as a desire, as the status of the godfather is not legitimate. The head of the political family in the mafia state might only wish for the position of the sheikh, which is determined by the following: the dynastic inheritance of power, the appointed and at most partially elected parliament, which nevertheless has authority to give advice only. While the citizens of the state are members of the quasi-adopted family, enjoying its state allowances, those at the bottom of the pyramid—multiply outnumbering the citizens—the guest workers do not have citizenship, and therefore do not enjoy the benefit of the allowances ensured by membership in the adopted family either. The treasury has no welfare obligations towards the children and elders they have left in their countries outside of the sheikhdom. At the same time they can even host a Football World Cup with the oil revenues they have (like Qatar). What the sheikh is given by natural course—as the head of a family venture would have it on his own "estate," the head of the adopted political family in the mafia state is forced to achieve through blackmail, made to look legitimate at that. The sheikh's power is legitimate by its nature, while he owes "social solidarity" only to his dynasty and adopted family—in possession of a citizenship.
- **The feudal orders** still stood in some sort of legitimate contractual relationship with the monarch, with rights even in his regard that they were entitled to on the basis of their status. While the vassal owns his property by rights, so the lord could also take that property from him rightfully. The system is legitimately built on this, and so the legal status and social position of the vassal coincide. The essence of the mafia state is to use coercion—in this case that of the state—to expropriate the property of certain people, and to give it to others by illegitimate ways and means, while formally upholding the formal equality of rights. In the

mafia state the vassal does not have the legal status of a vassal but only the vassal's social position, and while equal rights are not de jure eliminated, the social position of vassals is created en masse.

- Members of **the Christian middle class of the Horthy regime, that held power between the two world wars**, though they were existentially shaken, and with their gentry status became increasingly dependent on the opportunities offered by the state bureaucracy or the army, still disposed of certain privileges in their own right on account of their status in the social order. They were accorded differential care, though social recognition was shown basically through the state bureaucracy, the military, and other state dependent organizations. An entry into the Christian middle class by accumulation of wealth through the market was legitimized through inclusion by the genteel classes. The crony relationships of the socially declining, genteel middle class are in general of a personal nature, but are not organized into the mono-centered hierarchy with its chain of command, that typifies the adopted political family of the mafia state. They rather form the privileged network of contacts composed of fraternities that base their status on social order, and guilds, on grounds of solidarity among people of the genteel middle class.
- In spite of the inequality of opportunities due to differences in wealth and culture, **the middle class in capitalist societies** nevertheless come by their social status through competition, and are not typified by ties of social order or vassalage.
- **The ruling elite of the Southern European fascist dictatorships** was grounded in the fascist parties, and only constrained, disciplined the economic elite and propertied classes, but did not expropriate them. In its Nazi versions—as they unfolded during World War Two—it looted the "Jewish capital," and passed it on to Aryan owners or melted it into the state budget through sale.
- **The ruling elite of the communist regimes** fitted into the hierarchy of the communist parties, while the positions in the state or public authority were filled according to a strict order imposed by the nomenclature. But individuals, rather than families belonged to the nomenclature—on ideological grounds. In their cases dynastic characteristics rarely and only exceptionally appeared, in fact loyalty would have to be demonstrated by turning traitor to family ties—in the classical Stalinist formations. The propertied class was liquidated—by means of nationalization or collectivization.

The communist nomenclature
> - did not organizationally follow the logic of the adopted political family in the way it organizes itself in the mafia state; was not built on patriarchal patterns of chains of command;
> - its personal privileges manifested themselves in limited consumer advantages and that only bore significance in a shortage economy, there was no significant accumulation of wealth in the family;
> - its power was purely of a political—and not mixed, political and economic—source and nature, so political power was limited to the period in office, unlike the power of the adopted political family in the mafia state, which does of course take a shock after a political defeat, but in its economic sphere of influence it continues to possess significant reserves to paralyze or influence politics;
> - the nationalization the communists carried out was the final station of the appropriation of private property belonging to businesses, and not a transit station for the redistribution of property.

- The *oligarchs* comprising the economic elite of the *alternating corrupt regimes* make up a group of rivals who can only partially influence or oversee public authority, but not rule over it in its totality, and do not fit into a single order forming a chain of command.
- *In the mafia state*—since the family is sacred, just as in the traditional mafia—the trial by fire is not the sacrifice of family ties as in the Stalinist regimes, but quite the opposite, *to gain inclusion into the adopted political family means the acknowledgement and sanctification of loyalty*. As it happens in the case of today's Hungary, demonstrated by the measures taken even in favor of the lower layers of the adopted political family based not on merely ideological or party ties, such as the concessions for tobacconists, or the granting of state land leases, or the protectionist distribution of state and EU tenders. The community of interests brought about by Fidesz is a community which has stronger (party) affiliations than normally encountered in liberal democracies. In the adopted political family members participate through their income and wealth privileges not only as individuals, but often in tow with all their family relations. Thereby the tight, hierarchic group originally composed of the team that was small, but already disciplined in the course of the 1990s, then expanded in concentric circles, stringing along other circles from loyal social groups onto the

system, but thereon with different statuses, with different entitlements and privileges.

5.5. "Law of rule" in place of the "rule of law"

After conquest of the party itself—and with Fidesz's victory in the 2010 elections resulting in two-thirds of parliamentary seats—the path opened to a demolition of the liberal democratic system and an institutionalization of Orbán's autocratic political position. The winner takes all: in the manner of some gaseous political substance, he filled out all the political spaces that could be filled. Any form of self-restraint would have only been a sign of weakness. The system was not drifting along, but deliberately progressed towards an autocratic arrangement. This was the central guiding principle of political action. The hypothesis of the objective, of what sort of arrangement the government envisioned, was clear: it should be of a kind in which by ideologically representing itself as the subject of the *"central field of power"* and the creator of the *"national middle-class"* and captain of the *"national freedom fight"* it could force through its interests and will without any further obstacles.

Since the decisions that determine the future of society are brought outside of the formalized bodies, and are pragmatically customized to the needs of the adopted political family where both economy and power are concerned, materialistic and autocratic action take the place of formal and legal processes in the established political institutional system without checks and balances. The prime minister does not govern, but disposes of the country as if it were his own property. In the institutions of public authority—from the parliament, through the government, to the tax authorities and the prosecutor's office—the autocratically brought decisions are merely registered and implemented. A materialistic dispensation of justice takes the place of formal judicial services. *The "rule of law" is replaced by the "law of rule."*

5.5.1. Constitutional coup d'état—the institutionalization of autocracy

Under the banner of a politics based on symbols, Fidesz believed a *new constitution* would be fitting for the new system, as a demonstration of drawing the line after the troubled decades in politics. It is not coincidental that autocrats unable to legitimate their power by a line of succession usually portray the beginning of their reign, planned to last a long while, as the *start of a new historical era*. The new *Fundamental Law* while even rejecting the word constitution steeped in ideological elements with the first line of the Hungarian national anthem, "God bless the Hungarians," and reference to the Christian heritage and Holy Crown of Hungary. Furthermore, the date on which parliament passed it on the day of Easter Sunday (18 April 2011) also seems to indicate some confusion of roles and lack of a sense of proportion: suggesting that a parallel could be drawn between the resurrection of Jesus and the resurrection of—in good faith—Hungary.

The two-thirds parliamentary majority won by Fidesz in 2010, with the votes of much less than half the eligible voters, and the support of only 53 percent of valid votes made it possible for Fidesz to systematically dismantle the system of checks and balances that characterize a liberal democracy, and the development in turn of a new state of balance for the autocratic regime, a consolidation by means of restriction of individual liberties based on illegitimate coercion. The conditions were established for the absolute position of the head of the political family within his circle, till then limited where the world beyond Fidesz was concerned, to grow into the position of the autocrat.

The concept of the "constitutional coup" used by the literature on the subject is only acceptable—according to former constitutional judge, Imre Vörös—in as much as this is intended to mean *"an overthrow of the state using the instruments of constitutional law, under the cover of the constitution, through constitutional legislation, and a series of constitutional amendments: an unconstitutional coup d'état."*[69] "Overall, the balance of the assessments of the new constitution in the legal literature has been extremely disapproving. Critics suggest that instead of effecting amendments necessary for a consolidation, the new constitution, building on a romantic construction of the past, is ill-adapted to set limits to the state's power—a crucial function of any constitution. In reality, the Fundamental Law's real purpose was to cement the power of the Fidesz."[70]

The two-thirds majority in parliament provided the opportunity to "eliminate while seemingly keeping" the separation of powers. The creation of the constitution became the monopoly of one political actor, along with its five amendments in the following two years, the legislation of all the laws and subsidiary regulations, as well as the appointment of the key figures supposed to guarantee the system of checks and balances. So the executive powers controlled by the political family forced all of the other branches of power into its command. The new Fundamental Law:

- limited the possibility of turning to the **Constitutional Court** (actio popularis). The jurisdiction of the Constitutional Court over budget and tax laws ceased. Whenever the Constitutional Court, with its powers curtailed, would qualify a law as anti-constitutional, it would simply be added to the constitution;
- terminated the **Supreme Court**, and removed its president from office. Though the judgment given by the European Court of Human Rights in Strasbourg decided that the former president, András Baka—who had turned to the court with the case of his removal—was right, the ruling only resulted in payment of financial damages, but no reinstatement of the framework required by the rule of law. The courts' system of self-regulation was disposed with and the National Office for the Judiciary installed, with its president Tünde Handó authorized to move cases between courts in spite of the terms dictated by law, without required justification or means of legal remedy, thereby violating the independence of courts and the constitutional right of citizens to decent and impartial court decisions. Incidentally, she is the wife of József Szájer, Member of the European Parliament, who boasted about drafting the Fundamental Law on his laptop while commuting between Budapest and Strasbourg;
- gave the **Fiscal Council** the right to veto the annual budget accepted by parliament at its discretion; meanwhile the President of the Republic now has the right to dissolve the parliament even shortly after the elections, if the budget is pending;
- abolished the independence of **municipal governments** from the row of fundamental rights, and following from this of course, their right to property: which de facto ends municipal autonomy and prepares any and all of its segments for nationalization;
- also eliminated citizens' right to **social security**, which enabled the systematic dismantling of the established structure of normative social entitlements and support.

After tackling the constitution came the laws guaranteeing the rule of law, which also required a two-thirds majority to change, from the media law to the election act, and from the act of association to the act on strikes, without looking for any form of consensus.

5.5.2. Hostile takeover of the institutions of public authority

The steps taken by the new regime are subject to the aims and logic of power and wealth accumulation. The seemingly improvised measures reflect merely the variety of solutions when this purpose comes up against a wall to be demolished, or obstacle to be bypassed. This is the *demise of public policies*.

The institutions of public authority cease to be the sites where real decisions are taken, those having been removed from the institutions into the realm of the adopted political family. The institutions of public authority are only required to quasi keep the books on decisions taken elsewhere, since they must operate within the settings of a democratic institutional system. Like the party, the institutions of public authority are no longer decision-making bodies either, but mere institutions of implementation carrying out the will of the political family. All that the classical mafia ensures through the coercive power of illegitimate violence within the environs of rule of law, the adopted political family of the post-communist mafia state achieves without bloodshed, by means of the legitimate instruments in the hands of public authority.

This puts an end to equality before the law. Though not in general, nor in legal terms, since it does not establish a feudal order of social groups permanently differentiated in legal standing, or a dictatorship. But it is systemic, because it *suspends equality before the law both individually and en masse*. It is not consistent in a doctrinarian fashion, but rather takes steps only when necessary.

5.5.3. Government: not there to take decisions, but to manage decisions taken by the political family

The composition of *the government* shows an unprecedented growth in the powers of the prime minister. The people occupying top government positions after 2010 have been recruited largely from three categories: either they are former members of the ruling party of the communist regime and/ or tied to the secret services of the times; or friends, business partners and stooges; or thirdly, political light-weights, who can easily be expelled from their positions. The first category can be blackmailed, the second is already part of the organized upperworld, while the third can be replaced at pleasure. Hardly any exceptions can be found. Though the prime minister showed an inclination for bringing back earlier ministers into his cabinet, he only took back those who had no political weight or backing within Fidesz. It is beyond debate that the prime minister can impose his will within government and the parliamentary faction unhindered. Internal wrangling lasts until he has his say, and stops at his word. Even in the first period of Fidesz governance—from 1998–2002—cabinet members would stand up for the entrance of the prime minister at the start of the cabinet meetings.

Disposing with the constraints meant by the separation of powers is simply the institutionalization of autocracy. The godfather-prime minister can have any law accepted by the set of MPs selected at his Felcsút estate. There are practically no cases of desertion, their infrequency has even surprised his own expectations. When he speaks about certain decisions not as his own, but as sovereign decisions of his party or the parliament, he can scarce avoid an ironic smile. His will can assume the form of constitutional legislation, law, or decree without any resistance or external consideration.

5.5.4. The lexes—custom tailored legislation

Legislation is no longer a field of legal and normative rules that are applicable to all and can be called to account, but the adopted political family's "tailor shop for fitted garments," where laws are tailored to fit the needs of the family. The parliament only serves to give the stamp of approval for the autocratic decisions. ***Equality before the law has been replaced by inequality after the law.*** Travel back in time has become possible with retroactive laws, and legislation tailored to individuals, groups, political friends and foes is carried on with the precision of a surgeon using laser technology based on the case-by-case authorizations given by the head of the political family: offering reward or punishment, privilege or discrimination.[71] This is the era of occasional arbitrary laws (commonly named "lex ..."), when the legal environment is adjusted to the continuously changing whims of the political family, with mass ad hoc procedures that shame legislative principles. They form incidental exceptions rather than general rules.

The no longer normative, but autocratic procedure of ***legislation in the mafia state*** can be sorted into five times two specific types based on the beneficiaries/harmed or the privileges/damages engendered by the law:[72]

- ***I/A*** To ensure that the stooges of the adopted political family can be ***appointed to public positions*** even in cases where conflicts of interest would not permit it: *lex Baranyay* (President-Chief Executive Officer of the Hungarian Development Bank), *lex Vida* (President of the tax authorities), *lex Szapáry* (ambassador in spite of his being 72 years old), *lex Domokos* (member of the Fiscal Council), *lex Polt* (exemption from the requirement to retire from position of Chief Prosecutor), *lex Borkai* (allowing him to run for position of mayor, though he had retired from the military 4, rather than 5 years before), *lex Töröcskei* (not being required to renounce his property, which had till then been in conflict of interest with his leadership of the State Motorway Management), *lex L. Simon* (so there is no conflict of interest between the position of state secretary and leading the National Cultural Fund), *lex Mocsai* and *lex Schmitt 3.0* (in the case of certain functions the earlier prescribed doctoral degree should not be required), etc.

I/B The arbitrary removal of persons from public offices enabled by legislation: *lex Nagy* (President of the Competition Authority), *lex Baka* (President of the Supreme Court, the chief justice had to be removed from his position, because he frequently criticized government), or *lex Jóri* (Ombudsman for information protection), etc.

- *II/A Growing remunerations or support for political stooges of the adopted political family, or the civil and political organization, municipal governments dominated by them*: *lex Szász* (President of the Hungarian Financial Supervisory Authority—PSZÁF), *lex Járai* (to allow earnings of 1.2 million forint as Chairman of the Board of Trustees of the Hungarian National Bank—MNB), *lex Schmitt* (to ensure him benefits due to past presidents of the republic, while not having filled the position for a full term), *lex Kovács* (the remuneration of the chairman of the Fiscal Council was raised to nine times the amount it had been before, 2 million forint), *lex Hódmezővásárhely* (1.7 billion forint support prior to municipal elections to this city), *lex Dalma Mádl* (ensures widows of former presidents of the republic a residence, the use of a car, two secretaries and free health care), *lex Anita Hercegh* (tax payers fund the insurance of the spouse of the current president of the republic as well), *Lex Szász 3.0* (ensures that the "severance pay" of Károly Szász and fellow leaders will be available to the leaders of PSZÁF even if MNB and PSZÁF are merged, and not fall under the effect of the otherwise due 98% special tax), etc.

II/B Decrease in the remunerations or support of political opponents of the regime in public positions and critical civil or political organizations, municipal governments: lex Simor (the lowering of the National Bank president's remunerations to a monthly 2 million forint), *lex defiant members of parliament* (fines can be drawn from the remunerations of the MPs, but the European Court of Human Rights in Strasbourg found this contradictory to the freedom of expression, and stipulated the payment of compensation for penalties given on this basis), *lex communist pensions* (withdrawal of outstanding pensions established by the former communist regime), *lex debt settlement of Esztergom* (the opposition mayor was stripped of one of her options), *lex Esztergom* (nationalization of certain health care services of the city that was withdrawn after the Fidesz candidate won), *lex retired judges* (the retirement age is reduced from 65 to 62 years, in the case of judges and prosecutors), *lex Fapál* (state appointed professional military personal should not be able to claim service home from the defense department), *lex Margaret Island* (the Municipality of Budapest expropriates the island from the 13th district municipality), *lex Demokratikus Koalíció* (the party of the former socialist prime minister should not be able to form an independent parliamentary faction), etc.

- **III/A Extension of the competencies of the institutions under political stooges, after they are appointed**: lex Szalai (authorizing the president of the media authorities to pass decrees), *lex Handó* (authorizing the president of the National Office for the Judiciary to move judges and cases between courts at her discretion), *lex Tarlós* (after reelection as lord mayor of Budapest he receives veto rights against decisions of the Municipal Assembly in important matters), *lex old constitutional judges* (judges after their 70th year should be able to keep their positions if they were elected for twelve-year terms) *lex Polt* (the Chief Prosecutor could not be interpellated in the parliament any more, his term in office grew to nine years, and the selection of his successor requires the approval of a two-thirds parliamentary majority), etc.

III/B Narrowing competencies of institutions, or municipal and professional bodies monitoring government: lex Constitutional Court (a drastic reduction of the sphere of issues on which it can pass judgment, and an annulment of the referential status of their earlier decisions), *lex (higher education) Accreditation Committee* (its autonomy taken away, followed by the suspension of its membership of the international body ENQA), *lex Mészáros*, mayor of Felcsút, Orbán's "steward" (leaves the decision of whether to reply to "abuses of requests of information" from journalists/citizens up to the state institutions), *lex Papcsák*, accountability *commissioner of the* Fidesz government (changes procedure for civil suites in court, so it becomes more difficult to enter as an intervener), *lex átlátszó.hu*, government-critical investigative website (significantly decreases access to information of public interest), *lex kuruc.info*, extreme-right website hosted in the United States of America (the Hungarian state can block websites hosted abroad, which the Hungarian court has decided is illegal), *lex NGOs* (charging high fees for obtaining information of public interest), etc.

• *IV/A Ensuring positions of advantage to loyal business ventures*: *lex MOL*, *lex OTP I.* and *II.* (I.: certain tax liabilities should be favorable to OTP Bank, II.: banks losses from their "related ventures located in Ukraine" can thereon be written off their special taxes), *lex CBA* (relieves the Fidesz associated shopping chain of some of its tax liabilities), *lex Mahir* (ensures benefits to the business interests of Lajos Simicska), *lex Duna Takarék* (the savings cooperative owned by István Garancsi, Viktor Orbán's new favorite oligarch and stooge was one of the few to escape the "full nationalization" of over a hundred savings cooperatives), *lex Andy Vajna I.* and *II.* (casino concessions can be won without even entering a bid; while sports betting sites can only be operated by the state owned Szerencsejáték Zrt., online card games and casinos can only be operated by those who possess a Hungarian concession for casino businesses, with only two persons or businesses meeting that condition: Andy Vajna and Gábor Szima), *lex TV2* (a condition for decreasing the current year tax base is that the tax subject had a zero, or negative result for revenues for 2013, which meant that the television RTL Klub, that resisted the government's intentions to buy up the channel lost out on this opportunity), *lex FHB* (the "allied" banks gain, so called, easier capital adequacy requirements, as well as access to a 136 billion HUF in public funds along with their yields), *lex Continental* (a central distribution agency is installed between the tobacco factories/wholesalers and the retailers), etc.

IV/B Removal of businesses not integrated into the adopted political family from the market, or their expropriation, or ensuring the conditions for doing so by legislative means: *lex MAL* (even on situations only threatening environmental disasters the management of privately owned companies can be taken over by the state), *lex ESMA* (the named business, which is critical of government, should not be able to place certain types of billboards on the sites they had even till then possessed by concession), *lex Klubrádió* (allowing the Media Council to demand tens of millions from this radio for the frequency they were awarded), the other lexes belonging in this category—such as the *lex shops shut down on Sunday, lex branch specific special taxes, lex plaza stop, lex inspection fee for food store chains, lex RTL Klub I* and *II*—have already been addressed in the book, or will be.

- *V/A Achieving political benefits through legitimate objectives*: *lex Biszku* (making it possible to hold the former minister of the interior responsible for his role in the repression of the 1956 revolution), *lex Brad Pitt* (weapons used for film productions should also be subject to the law on firearms), *lex Szaniszló* (frees the minister from having to hand a government award over to an extreme right-wing journalist), *lex Varga* (the tougher penalization of domestic violence made necessary by embarrassing incidents involving Fidesz politicians), *lex Hajdú-Bét* (compensates the suppliers who had suffered damages because of an agricultural company that had gone bankrupt), *lex Laborc* (forces those concerned to appear before the parliamentary investigation committees), *lex election video from Baja County* (anyone preparing a sound or video recording that is fake or has falsified contents in order to malign people's dignity can be sentenced to a year in prison), *lex Rezesová* (discretional switch between release for house arrest), *lex KGBéla* (on account of the suspicious Russian connections of the extreme-right Jobbik party's member of the European Parliament, a new provision entered into the criminal code under "spying on the institutions of the European Union"), *lex Balettintézet* (the possibility of the state buying back buildings part of the national heritage, that are kept in dilapidated conditions by their private owners), etc.

V/B Achieving political benefits through illegitimate objectives: *lex informer-caretakers of apartment buildings* (a new, quasi political

requirement to supply information applying to caretakers of apartment complexes), *lex gang of Árokt*ő (extends permanently the period
of pre-trial detention in the case of certain, serious criminal offences),
lex National Consultation (creates the appropriate legal background for
the direct mail campaigns of the government on which it builds its
electoral databases), *lex Normafa* (re-qualifies an environmentally protected area as a historical sports area, so less stringent environmental
regulations apply to it), *lex election-year budget* (the government gets
time to hand in the budget for the following year after the municipal
elections), *lex Turul* (the illegally raised sculpture of the Turul—a
mythical bird used as a symbol by the Hungarian extreme right—could
remain in place in Budapest), etc.

The arbitrariness of legislation on lower levels, specifically for *local governments*, was guaranteed by the Constitutional Court in a decree of 2015, by
the allowing them to regulate the compulsory norms of local coexistence
and sanctions to be imposed upon those overstepping them by decree,
without any form of judicial guarantee. It did so even though the Supreme
Court of Justice expressly indicated that "without the area of legislation
being circumscribed the regulation gives way to arbitrariness and in terms
of its scope, lack of substantive control."[73]

5.5.5. Suppressing the control functions of other institutions of public authority

After parliament passes legislation the ***President of the Republic*** is the first
who is in a position to stop the law, since he can either send it back to parliament, or forward it to the Constitutional Court. Orbán struck down the
effort for the reelection of László Sólyom, President of the Republic (2005–
2010) who, though loyal to Fidesz, was still somewhat too independent. He
needed a rubber stamp, a figure he found in the person of Pál Schmitt, a
favorite of the communist party in its day, vice-president of the National
Physical Education and Sports Office, who in that position had a rank of
deputy minister. After having Schmitt resign following a plagiarism scandal
concerning his university doctorate, he ordered the return to Hungary of
János Áder, who had been exiled to the European Parliament after having
been earlier caught, as faction leader, "plotting" in the ranks of Fidesz.
Áder had rehabilitated himself with the drafting of the manipulative elec-

tion law after 2010, and also proved as President of the Republic that he is worthy of the godfather's confidence: carefully choreographed sovereignty of the President of the Republic is completely exhausted in legal needling in insignificant matters, rather than taking steps against the winding up of constitutionalism. He returns some laws to the parliament for further consideration in full knowledge of the fact that he is participating in a humiliating theatre piece: the parliament regularly approves the laws he returns without any further meaningful debate, instead adding more of what had been objected to, for good measure. After this he can no longer turn to the Constitutional Court. The symbolic demotion of the highest dignitary of state is indicated by his falling behind the prime minister in the ceremonial protocols. The President of the Republic is in fact *not an expression of the unity of the nation, but the unity of the political family*, not a guardian of liberal democracy, but of the order of the mafia state.

The next obstacle in the way of a law could be the **Constitutional Court**. However the process of straightening out this body has also been completed. The number of members has been raised by the parliament, while it eliminated the requirement of political parity for the parliamentary committees proposing the new constitutional judges, so that the government majority could delegate its loyal cadres to the body without any hindrance. But since in the case of some members of the Court their immovability proved a double-edged sword, and gave them the courage to test their sovereignty, after 2010 either their authorities were limited by legislative means, or the constitution was altered in order to circumvent the Court's ability to take steps against laws that they had judged as anti-constitutional before. But on occasion Orbán would send a message already in advance of the decision of the Constitutional Court, for example in the case of the plundering of the private pensions funds: "It would be a pity to even try and create the illusion, as if [...] this situation could be changed by a Constitutional Court decision. It cannot. This is a finalized system. A two-pillared Hungarian pension system."[74] In these words the death certificate of the Court had been issued. Indeed, they took the words seriously: e.g., the text of the decision about the unconstitutionality of the termination of government officials without reasoning was taken by the Court in such a way that Fidesz could eat its cake, but the Court could have it too. In place of defending those who lost out on the unconstitutional practice of termination the Constitutional Court even extended the period in which the unconstitutional procedure could be continued by three months, just in case Fidesz had not yet finished the comprehensive political cleansing of the public sector.

At the same time the Constitutional Court was stripped of its weight, political influence was secured over the **National Office for the Judiciary**, which had been established within the framework of the *"reform of the judicial services."* In place of the independent professional body, a family friend of the prime minister, the wife of a Fidesz Member of the European Parliament (see *"lex Handó"* above) now takes all decisions, at her full discretion, about the appointment, assignments, career steps of judges, and the courts to which individual cases are assigned. A minimum two-thirds parliamentary majority elects the leader of the Office for 9 years, so if the absolute majority is not forthcoming in the future, according to the new regulation the head of the office could stay in that position for life. Following criticism from the European Union this possibility was later extended to the position going to a deputy she herself appointed. A significant number of leading judges were removed through enforced retirement, while retirement age—contrary to this practice—was raised for the general public. The judges were brought into an existentially dependent situation. And meanwhile suspects and accused can be intimidated through the exclusion of their advocates.

Under the wings of the **blitzkrieg of power concentration** the rest of the independent institutions had also been overrun by the spring of 2011, including the **State Audit Office of Hungary**, the **Fiscal Council**, the **Hungarian Competition Authority**, and the **national public media channels**. In spite of the character assassination campaigns launched at the president of the **National Bank**—appointed by the previous government in 2007—and due to an international uproar, the Bank's president could stay in his position until his term ended in 2013. At the same time with one of the autocratic twists of the *lex* laws concerning the **Monetary Council**, and extending both membership and powers of the deputy presidents of the National Bank— filling these positions with the cadres of the political family of course—the disliked bank president's room for maneuver was also confined.

The recruitment of new cadres for the institutions of public authority also does not follow the patterns of the classical one-party dictatorship. For while in those the channels of mobility are regulated, partly within the party itself, and partly by the nomenclature, these delegates of the mafia state are **governors and stooges**, who are usually connected to the political family through personal ties of loyalty and/or business. They could either be the oligarchs of the political family, or its accountants, as in the cases of the minister of the interior or the minister of national economy.

5.6. Administration through confidants and personal governors of the adopted political family instead of a professional bureaucratic administration

5.6.1. Array of devices employed to intimidate the professional administration

The twenty years that followed the regime change were not even enough to draw a clear and consensual line between the political and the professional positions within the government and municipal apparatuses. As a result the changes of personnel in the course of alternation of government increasingly affected the professional staff as well. This escalating process contributed in great measure to the coming about of a situation in which the governments were no longer able to govern—as previously mentioned—in a professional administrative-bureaucratic sense. The distribution of the lower and lower administrative positions as political rewards practically demolished the Max Weberian ethos of party-neutral public administration before it had even taken root.

The change of government in 2010 also brought changes in regard to this process. The subjects of the political cleansing not only lost their jobs at the "parent institution," but came under a quasi employment ban in the whole state administration, or affiliated spheres. Fidesz made every effort to systematically rend apart the networks of solidarity and to forestall any members of the public services elite not sympathetic to them from keeping afloat. According to many reports the data available on Facebook was also used to map the networks of those whose party credentials have to be checked. The fact that public servants are so underrepresented in these virtual, yet transparent communities is no coincidence. But concerns with regard to the delivery of data regarding those "recalcitrants" who stayed with the private pension funds after the plundering their assets by the government, to places of employment were also worthy of consideration. If public officials wish to keep their positions, they are compelled to voluntarily accept to be taken under secret service surveillance—without judicial approval. The campaign-like, mass changes of personnel were eased by the administrative possibility of dismissal without justification and the spread of blacklists that made it impossible for those fired to find employment in the field. For example, at the time of the wholesale divestment of the Fiscal Council of its complete professional staff, a ministerial order made certain that the experts sent away would not be hired by any other institution under the ministry. Such messages made sure that in the situation established all doors in professional administration would be closed to those who had been stigmatized by the regime. Paradoxically, the public revelation of the methods of power used by autocracy reinforced fear, adjustment, and surrender.

5.6.2. Max Weber on the historical path to modern professional bureaucratic administration

To understand the demolition of the professional bureaucratic system it is worthwhile to return to Max Weber's writings, in which he models the phases of historical evolution for the independent professional administration that is typical of modern democracies.[75]

"The master rules with or without an administrative staff. [...] The typical administrative staff is recruited from one or more of the following sources: (I) From persons who are already related to the chief by traditional ties of loyalty. This will be called patrimonial recruitment. Such persons may be a) kinsmen, b) slaves, c) dependents who are officers of the household, especially ministerial, d) clients, [etc.], and (II) Recruitment may be extra-patrimonial, including a) persons in a relation of purely personal loyalty such as all sorts of "favorites," b) persons standing in a relation of fealty to their lord (vassals), and, finally c) free men who voluntarily enter into a relation of personal loyalty as officials."[76] When the administrative tasks are dominated by vassals, that is already the feudal form of the patrimonial rule, where the "administrative staff appropriates particular powers and the corresponding economic assets," either by an organization or by individuals.[77]

Max Weber summarizes the *characteristics of professional bureaucratic administration* performed—usually in modern societies—by free officials as follows:[78]

- a continuous rule-bound conduct of official business
- a specified sphere of competence (jurisdiction)

- the organization of offices follows the principle of hierarchy
- the rules which regulate the conduct of an office may be technical rules or norms. In both cases, if their application is to be fully rational, specialized training is necessary
- it is a matter of principle that the members of the administrative staff should be completely separated from ownership of the means of production or administration
- there is also a complete absence of appropriation of his official position by the incumbent
- the principle of administration on the basis of documents is adhered to. The combination of written documents and a continuous operation by officials constitutes the "office"
- the administrative group that operates along the lines of the principles above is called the army of officials, bureaucracy.

5.6.3. Dismantling the modern professional bureaucratic administration under the conditions created by the mafia state

The process of evolution described above seems to unfold in reverse with the story that leads from the alternation of corrupt regimes into the mafia state. A sort of regression takes place, with a turn from modern professional bureaucratic administration back to archaic models of administration: "Patriarchalism and patrimonialism have an inherent tendency to regulate economic activity in terms of utilitarian, welfare or absolute values. This tendency stems from the character of the claim to legitimacy and the interest in the contentment of the subjects. It breaks down the type of formal rationality which is oriented to a technical legal order."[79]

Ever since the professional bureaucratic administration has been subject to elected bodies (parliament, government, municipality, etc.) in modern democracies, rather than lords, there has been a persistent question of where to draw the line between the competencies and positions belonging to the political administration tied to power on the one hand, and professional administration on the other. Without appropriate— socially and culturally grounded—self-constraint, there is a constant urge to treat not only the par excellence political position, but the increasingly deep levels of professional administration as part of the political plunder. *In the beginning we can only speak of the replacement of experts*, where experts loyal to the incoming party take the positions over. In the next stage the emphasis within the qualified phrase, loyal expert begins to fall on the word loyal. *Finally, expertise is completely subordinated to party commitment.* This is the world of *loyal party cadres*, when not only the segment in direct contact with the world of politics, but the whole of the administration is permeated by the hordes of officials whose basic expertise is their loyalty to the ruling party.

The top-down demolition of the bureaucratic administration in the mafia state does not however only consist of loyal party cadres taking over the leading posts of administrative control. In the sense that the *appointees of the adopted political family are its affiliates and not that of the party— they are personal governors. Service gentry*, who do not have feudal rights, but do have feudal allowances however. They are not loyal to the party, but to the lord, the head of the political family, to whom they are tied in through direct of personal chains of dependence.

Within the administrative system of the mafia state the patterns of traditional autocratic rule increasingly emerge, with the patriarchal head of the family governing in circumstances that do not adhere to the law, but giving commands himself, or through his confidants, thereby diluting and adjusting the traits of the bureaucratic administration typical in the modern state to his own demands. (On the same note, the 2016 Budget Act frees ministries from the requirement of having to post their Organizational and Operational Rules to their website.)[80]

What follows for Weber's professional bureaucratic administration from this is:[81]

- the *"clearly defined sphere of competence subject to impersonal rules,"* are loosened; the political appointees handle a great variety of roles in the adopted political family, within the legitimate sphere of administration: stooge, governor, commissar, steward, treasurer, etc., expressions that describe the real functions of their roles more accurately in sociological terms, than would the official definitions of the administrative positions;
- the *"rationally established hierarchy"* is disrupted; the affiliates of the adopted political family traverse the lower and higher regions of public administration freely;
- the normative system of *"a regular system of appointment on the basis of free contract, and orderly promotion"* is disassembled; the introduction of the life-time career models is an excuse for total political cleansing, the realignment of the whole professional apparatus at the starting line,

as well as the centralization of decisions pertaining to promotions so that by benefit of the subjective mechanisms of evaluation the normative system of promotion is replaced by discretional decision-making mechanisms driven by political interests; and if the elastic laws are still too tight for the implementation of the preferences of the adopted political family with regard to personnel, the "normative" environment is shaped to fit demands through regulations tailored to fit;

- *"technical training as a regular requirement"* is relativized; when necessary, peculiar exemptions pave the way for the positions that previously had strict prerequisites in terms of professional training;
- allowances and property entitlements added on to *"fixed salaries"* as we rise through the hierarchy are increasingly in domains well past legal sources of income, as demonstrated by a few inappropriately filled out assets declarations; these are not individual cases of corruption, but the allowances approved by the adopted political family; the individuals who rise to the status of poligarchs within the sphere of public authority, or governors who are arraigned with the right to independent income generating opportunities—that would be typical of the liege's position in "feudal patrimonialism"—in their own field, though sometimes even in fields that do not formally belong under their area of competency (to name some of them, Lajos Kósa and János Lázár, former mayors of Debrecen and Hódmezővásárhely respectively, or for that matter Andy Vajna, government commissioner for film matters, at the same time winner of the national concession for casinos).

5.6.4. Why the mafia state cannot be considered a patrimonial system

"Where domination is primarily traditional, even though it is exercised by virtue of the ruler's personal autonomy, it will be called *patrimonial authority*," writes Max Weber.[82] He continues, "where it indeed operates primarily on the basis of discretion, it will be called *sultanism*. The transition is definitely continuous. Both forms of domination are distinguished from *elementary* patriarchalism by the presence of a personal *staff*."

Still, if this description fits the administrative practices of the mafia state, why can't the system thus formed be considered patrimonial?

First, it cannot, because—as previously alluded to—the patrimonial system inherently carries its own legitimation: the lord does not require reaffirmation from his underlings, he is not chosen. To the contrary, the sociological nature of rule in the mafia state (based on discretional, rather than normative decisions, and generally on patron-client relations) and the legitimacy of the system are not in harmony with one another, do not coincide.

Second, the mafia state does not permeate the entire administration, but only those of its parts and levels that are important from the point of view of ideology, power, and wealth accumulation. In other areas—that are indifferent in terms of the above considerations—it is satisfied to ensure the option of intervention as it pleases and the loyalty of the apparatus, as well as—if it deems it worthwhile—the rewarding of its clients through the distribution of employment positions. The complete disruption of the complex system of professional administration required by modern society would not even stand in its interest: the possibilities of intervention are all-inclusive, but it only applies them when necessary. The mafia state also differs from the Hungarian autocratic regimes of the 20th century in this. The right-wing, autocratic Horthy regime, having settled on the peaks of the bureaucratic administration put forward its political expectations by legal means, without endangering the professionalism, Prussian precision, and ethos of the way the apparatus beneath it operated. The communist Rákosi or Kádár regimes regulated where each individual could end up in the nationalized society through the order of promotion dictated by the party and the nomenclature, that is, an order external to the professional apparatus on the one hand, and on the other, ensuring the supervision of the regime over the politically unreliable professionals openly through the system of political commissars and delegated party secretaries who doubled the professional administration in both economic and political arenas.

Third—though for different reason—neither democracies, nor dictatorships necessitate the institution of "stooges": in their case, everyone is simply who they are, whether on the grounds of the rule of law, or of compulsion.

5.7. Liquidation of societal autonomies

The establishment of the patron-client relationships is naturally not only valid directly for the sphere of public authority, but also for the *autonomous institutions of society that are not controlled by some public authority*: it is not only a matter of their subordination, but the *political breaking in* of all formations and institutions stretching from municipal governments through the civil sector to the world of media. A wide range of instruments are applied to achieve this: *nationalization, acquisition, forced surrender, domestication, ghettoization, exclusion, and liquidation*.

5.7.1. Liquidation of local autonomies: "caretakers" in place of local governments

The autonomy of the municipal governments was restricted through the extension of the scopes and institutions of organizations of general competencies belonging under the ministry of public administration and justice. Through the establishment of the government county offices, with historical resonances, the administrative authorities and competencies of municipal governments were significantly shortened, followed by a similar affect upon the establishment of the *district government offices* on a lower administrative level, also appropriating municipal competencies. In the follow-up, the institutional systems of education and health care, which had until then overwhelmingly been in the possession and operative control of the municipalities, were simply expropriated and centralized. *The municipalities became de facto caretakers*. Reminiscent of the communist era council system ("Soviets"), the world of "council executive secretaries" subordinated to the government and the party center has returned: the authority to appoint the staff and elite of local public administrations is once again held at levels of central government. Through the *one window administration* that has been established, *a vassal of the head of the political family looks back at the civilian from every window.*

The centralization of a significant portion of the local government institutions, and the cuts they served as a pretext for—which far exceeded the amount needed to manage these services centrally—resulted in a situation where 2,900 out of 3,200 municipalities do not have any resources that are not predetermined, that can be spent freely—e.g., on developments. This is how they turn from municipalities into caretakers of limited authority. "The target figures for municipal expenditures of the budget for 2014 were 30 percent below the actual costs in 2010. Of the local revenues of municipalities, the income from personal income tax was cut, which decreased interest in the revenues from local economies and increased dependence from central support. [...] All of this can only *operate on the condition of political loyalty and bureaucratic adjustment*. The wish to satisfy the expectations of local voters will be less important, as the results will depend on success with securing external resources and influencing individual decisions concerning the settlement. This is already a more opaque process for NGOs or the electorate to follow, and therefore raises the dangers of corruption. [...] It is a question whether it is even possible for a Weberian bureaucracy to operate efficiently in a centralized state sector, when the system of political-social calling to account is wholly missing. The asymmetry of information where decisions are brought in a centralized fashion will grow incrementally, producing new forms of corruption within the new decision-making mechanism."[83]

5.7.2. Liquidation of the autonomous positions of the intelligentsia in culture and education

5.7.2.1. Culture

In the period of the first Fidesz government, from 1998–2002, the politically multicolored elected municipal bodies stood in the way of a complete elite *change in cultural positions*. While the struggle in those days concerned positions of leadership at individual cultural institutions, or for that matter a larger state commission for a cultural product, political purposes after 2010 plainly took a quite different direction: the systematic acquisition of the positions from which various segments of cultural life are resourced became the new objective.

Under this *kulturkampf* the question raised was no longer why spend the taxpayer's money on "such stuff"—demagogically pitting artists against the tastes of the "folks"—but creative artists who are critical of the regime, or considered as such are branded as common-law criminals, as frauds, through criminalizing campaigns. On the orders of Fidesz's Government Commissioner for Accountability, judicial experts examined the "cost efficiency" of the input required for the completion of given philosophical works or pieces of fine art. The bottom-up pressure of people frustrated for various reasons caught up in the culture-destroying political passions of "what's all this empty chatter" and "why this scrawling" seconded the suspicions of the Fidesz leadership felt towards the Hungarian cultural elite, which represented western values. Fidesz does not understand this language, and fears it simultaneously, which is why it uses the tool of populism against it, molded from a mixture of common taste and jealousy. It shares in the sense of not being acknowledged, the resentment felt by the "local carvers of '*kopjafa*'" (traditional Transylvanian wooden grave markers) in their opposition with the "global non-figuratives."

But the problem is somewhat more complicated than to be explained transparently with the traditional interpretation offered by the *kulturkampf*.

The symbolic spaces of culture can by no means be left in the hands of forces alien to the nation—says Fidesz. Liberals cannot build a National Theatre for the nation, and cannot appoint its director.[84] The director appointed by the new political course even had the National Theatre consecrated, as if marking the borders of his arts censorship. This is not only a matter of positions, or divvying up state support those positions can entail: Fidesz *is sanctifying culture*, and its symbolic components cannot be the subject of bargain. *It does not consume culture, but ritualizes it and presents it as sacrament*. If for no other reason, it must do so, simply because the traditional consumers of culture do not have the stomach to take on any of this. It does not mean a problem though, because Fidesz *appeals to the audience that stays outside of culture* with its sanctified cultural symbols. Those who are followers of the new political regime no longer have to attend the National Theatre—it will do to consume culture in the form of political statements or protests. This will serve to produce enough impressions and emotional ties. Those who make and consume culture in the traditional sense can no longer even think of this process as a *kulturkampf*, a *culture war, but experience it as a war on culture*. Culture has turned from a question of taste, into a question of belief, and from appreciation of art to giving testimony and as such, into the direct taking of a political stance.

The favorites of the head of the political family oversee their given fields of culture in the name of the family as *governors*, representing both *priest and paymaster of each genre of art* simultaneously—from theatre to film, architecture to the fine arts, classical music to the Hungarian Academy of Arts and the National Cultural Fund. To distribute funds they barely trouble themselves with formally assembling juries and evaluating committees even where it is still required by law, though the operation of these bodies only make for another ritual of enforced submission. The paternalist system of vassalage is most successful, where the given genre is dependent on state support, institutional sustenance. Artists in these fields are also the most vulnerable.

The role of the governor can be played by either a prime minister's commissioner (such as Imre Kerényi, responsible "for the grounding of conscious national thought"), or a government commissioner (such as Andy Vajna, responsible for state funding or film production, or András Batta, responsible for the "development of a unified concept for classical music and its implementation"), or the president of the Hungarian Academy of Arts (György Fekete, in charge for the fine arts), or the director of theatre (Attila Vidnyánszky, responsible for theatres and also chief director of the National Theatre). In their case there are no longer any efforts expended on ensuring dominance over certain territories through pitiful majorities in various professional and organizational boards: they simply appoint the governors of the given field, and that's that. The leaders of culture then order the necessary amendments, decrees, servile juries, and character assassinating media campaigns to accompany their decisions as required. Their legitimacy is not provided by a role within the rule of law, but from the mandate they have received from the head of the political family. And even the participants of the supervised field relate to them as the anointed, omnipotent lords of the given sphere.

The cultural policy of the regime is at the same time however, not doctrinarian: its adherence to principles is calculating, its anger is rational. In certain regards however it will not budge:

- it occupies the sanctified fields, institutions;
- it will not hand over public media that can reach a wider audience;
- it does not liquidate, it only slowly wastes, starves, in other words, is not willing to support the artist, group, etc. inappropriate to its political taste from public funds;
- it does not ban, merely confines to the subculture or counterculture.

At times, when it so wishes, the artist, rather than the art he or she produced is canonized, as seen in the case of those *artists who have been brought into their protection*, but whose art is otherwise antithetical in its every element to all that the Fidesz regime culturally represents. This seeming contradiction is resolved by the artist's loyalty to the regime, or even a mere neutral silence. In fact, the oligarchs of the political family may even invest their money in alternative art ventures, workshops if they so wish, if their taste differs from the mainstream preferred by the powers that be. Such singular cases may even result in financial support (as in the case of the A38 Jazz Club on the Danube considered one of the best in Europe, and converted from a former Soviet barge) or the handover of a temporarily withheld operational permit (as in the case of the Sziget Festival, known as one of the largest summer music festivals in Europe).

The most important public institution for the support of cultural projects and institutions is the **National Cultural Fund**—established in the beginning of the 1990s—which distributed its revenues from tax contribution on media products carrying culture—from television sets, through printers to computers—and later the profits generated by the state lottery, Szerencsejáték Zrt. Professional councils decided autonomously about where the dynamically growing revenues were to go by means of rounds of applications. A decisive majority of their members were delegated by professional organizations; only 10 percent of the total revenues of the Fund comprised the so-called cultural minister's allowance. Fidesz raised the latter to 50 percent in its first term already, also raising the number of government delegated members in the juries. In 2002, the socialist leadership decreased the minister's allowance, but only to 25 percent. From 2012 however, the Fidesz government appointed the minister himself as the president of the Fund, and also granted him the right to veto any decision taken by the juries, thereby subordinating an at least partially autonomous institution for the financing of culture to wholly politically motivated interests in building and feeding its clientele.

In the beginning of the 2000s, businesses were already allowed to support the production of films from a part of their taxes. This system was extended in 2009 to the support of organizations for performing artists (*corporate tax allowance for donations to culture*), which generated a significant resource that could be distributed through decentralized channels. The principal, important system of cultural funding has however become heavily distorted over the last few years. First, spectator sports have been added to the supportable activities, among them the hobby sport of the godfather, football, which draws a great portion of the amounts that can be donated away, as "protection money." Secondly, the cultural institutions belonging to the state and the municipalities that receive funds from this source have had their budget support cut—on the grounds of this extra income. Thirdly, the large public utility providers who were important contributors have dropped out, as they have begun to make losses due to the government's populist campaign of utility price cuts, i.e., mandatory reductions in retail energy prices. Fourthly, political fears form an obstacle to support for cultural workshops that are critical of government. Finally, a whole corrupt branch of economy has developed in "competition" with the earlier cultural management companies, for the mediator's fees also on the rise as a result of the field becoming dependent on political contacts.

Art criticism has also been forced back into a ghetto. It was replaced by communication of the artist's commitment to the government. The government controlled media far outreaches the primary audience of the artist and can thus raise or doom any artist. The matter of open resistance needs serious consideration on the part of artists, as the struggle with the mafia state is usually one-sided, and results in withdrawal of existential means. Of course there are genres that can secure more of the market or an international audience, so they do not depend on public funding to such a degree.

5.7.2.2. Education and sciences

All those concerned in the world of schools—parents, students, teachers and the earlier municipal operators—have been stripped of their rights with the **total centralization of public education**. Officially redefining education from **public service to civil duty,** evoking the atmosphere of "military service," they have made barracks out of schools and drill sergeants out of teachers. In consequence:

- the minister personally appoints the principals of the over five thousand schools, while it is no longer the principal, but district government officials who decide about the employment of teachers at the schools;
- teachers in all Hungarian public schools now have only one employer, the Klebelsberg National Schools Operations Center, so their dismissal is practically equivalent to exclusion from the profession; they were compulsorily registered as members of the National Teachers' Chamber—which operates as a transmission belt of the government—while the unions' rights were curtailed; school principals and teachers can only reply to the queries of the press with the permission of the district government official for education;
- schools have been stripped of their rights to employ personnel or manage their budgets, the autonomy of the teaching faculty has been taken away, their freedom to shape the curriculum has been constrained, their right to choose school books has been limited to books recommended by the ministry;

- the ideological indoctrination of the educational system is served by the liquidation of the schoolbook market, and the state monopolization of the distribution of schoolbooks, the replacement of the professional schoolbook accreditation mechanism with the ministerial schoolbook "tenders," the legalized exclusion of private schoolbook publishers, in some cases their acquisition, in others their administrative destruction, the reform of the national curriculum in line with the ideology of the current establishment, the compulsory classes in divinity or secular ethics, and entry of this choice made by students in their reports and registers;
- the channels of mobility are drawn under political control, and preference given to church schools at the decisive high school stage;
- in order to establish a school system in the semblance of the prevalent cast-system-like social ideal, the lowering of the age of compulsory schooling from 18 to "only" 16—though planned to 15, and only reversed on account of broad protests;
- at the end of class 7, it is planned to filter out those not suitable for a high school education with a career-orienting test, and force them to choose careers early;
- the number of those receiving high school degrees are lowered, and the teaching of general knowledge subjects has been curtailed in vocational schools, especially in those which do not give high school degrees (baccalaureate), as little as 6 hours per week;
- the means of dispensing with state resources for education are centralized, so it is no longer the previous operators who decide about procurements, but the state itself (the Klebelsberg Center) who chooses the court purveyors to the system.

Universities were perhaps—in addition to the sphere of culture—the most important protected institutions of the critical intelligentsia's positions. Institutional autonomy, the professorial status, and a relatively late retirement age all served as institutional guarantees for freedom of opinion among the teaching and research based intellectuals who maintained their own feudalistic defense lines, while the freedom of the students was provided by their status as adults, though unburdened by existential dependences, and so less vulnerable.

The calling of a higher-education leadership to order—though it had never been too brave—was prepared with three threatening government actions: a campaign of criminalization and trumped procedure—officiated by the Government Control Office—against a group of liberal philosophers; the announcement of a comprehensive financial and economic investigation of universities; as well as drastic cuts in state funding. These actions ensured that the overwhelming majority of university leaders and the teaching staff acknowledged the taking away of their rights with "calm resignation":

- the new regulations for higher education ensured the minister a substantive—i.e., autocratic—say in the appointment of rectors (paradoxically this was what ended the student unions' potential position for blackmail within the institutions of higher education);
- the right to appoint the financial heads of the universities was transferred to the minister of finance—who functions as governor to the political family, and the position of chancellors introduced in 2014 gave almost unlimited powers in all financial matters to the person filling this position as delegate of the prime minister even overriding the rector; the introduction of the institution of the board (under the name of consistory) does not serve what would be the noble aim of ensuring that people with the appropriate knowledge for the professional management of large institutions are in position, but rather the complete exclusion of institutional autonomy: three members of the five-member consistory would be appointed by the minister, the fourth, the chancellor is already a government appointee, and the fifth is the rector, who can only be delegated with the approval of the minister;
- the financial autonomy of the institutions was wound up, its reserves tapped, or withdrawn;
- in place of a per capita financing of higher education, a funding system that basically followed the choices of students in a fair competition, in 2010, a system of deals between the ministry and the higher education institutions stepped in, that can be used by government to blackmail the universities;
- the government however decides not only about education financed by the state, but also tries to administratively ban fee-paid courses approved by the Hungarian Accreditation Committee at certain universities; it uses these administrative means to ensure an interest in the privileged higher education institutions;

- the universities in a financial quandary then, in order to maximize the savings possible through each laid off teacher, themselves removed a significant segment of the teaching staff in their fifties and sixties—with liberal-critical intellectuals overrepresented among them.

Furthermore, the Hungarian National Bank's establishing five foundations in 2014, with the express educational aim of propagating the government's unorthodox economic teachings to counter the liberal principles conveyed by the economics taught at universities amounts to absurdity. The foundations were financially stacked up in steps that brought them altogether to a value of 250 billion forint (800 million euro), a resource equaling one and a half times the annual budget contribution to the entire Hungarian higher education.[85]

5.7.3. Domestication of Non-Government Organizations

The mafia state aims to discipline, domesticate, and subordinate autonomous institutions in areas offering counterweights to public authority, as well as the municipalities, the fields of culture and sciences, and it follows, that this would be the case also with the world of NGOs.

In the era of liberal democracy following the regime change, quoting Ádám C. Nagy, former president of the Council of the National Civil Fund at some length, the state's approach to civil society, while replete with contradictions and gaps, was fundamentally *laissez faire* in expanding the opportunities for creating associations, the manner of acquiring the official title of "public usefulness," and modes of sponsoring. This system undoubtedly had its defects due to not being fully formed: first, the courts were arbitrary in interpreting the prerequisites of registering organizations. Second, sponsoring was anything but impartial, but this flaw remained at the lower levels of professional policy decisions rather than becoming a systemic feature of the operations.

In contrast, autocratic systems, variable as they are, work quite differently, governed by a fundamentally restrictive logic. The Horthy regime of the interwar era [1919–1944] had a mechanism that controlled the establishment and operation of associations, tending to favor local and outlaw nation-wide organizations. This entire system was eradicated in the communist era. Even civil cooperation itself was stymied via secret service or coercive measures, whereas non-profit groups were not even permitted to form. The few existing pseudo-civil organizations certainly did not meet the criteria of voluntariness and self-organization. Not even did the limited leeway granted to associations in the thawing social environment of the 1980s allow to handle social problems; these were mainly designed to convey the communist party's will to society at large.

The mafia state employs a multi-step domestication methodology. Its first step is the centralization of funding and its control by a governor. This move is "successful" with the majority of civil groups since they are primarily invested in realizing a given organizational goal rather than taking a political stand. Therefore in putting up with the governor's response—funding or the promise of it in case of waiting lists—they would not voice their discontent with this operational system. If the constrained funding does not suffice to reach its goal, the state deploys the media by, for instance, subjecting the oppositionally oriented civils to communicational pressure. On this level all but those organizations would persist which, of the three-fold task of civil society (participation, service, and control) would advocate the ethos of curbing the state's dominance. Should the communicational pressure prove ineffective, the state will employ coercive means in order to enforce the government's will. Whereas the first-step method has been used more than a few times in the context of Hungary's incompletely realized democratic model [after the regime change], the second method's application has been almost unprecedented. The deployment of central authority reveals how an unequivocally non-democratic system works.[86]

The mafia state has accomplished the atomization of the civil institutions of resistance by 2014. On the one hand the autocratic regime has built a new "national middle class" with easily outlined privileges, discipline, and a national self-consciousness—reinforced with frustration and distorted pride—while on the other hand continuously dismantling the organized, institutionally protected positions of civic autonomy and resistance. As a culmination of the process, the Governmental Control Office, arm in arm with the Prosecutor's Office and the Counter Terrorism Center occupied the Ökotárs Foundation, which handles the funding applications of the

Norwegian Civil Fund, and the minister of the Prime Minister's Office would have had the civil organizations account for their budgets, while plans were made for the legal stigmatization of the civil organizations that won foreign funding—as done in Russia. But the controlling functions of NGOs and the independent media are also under attack through the amendment of the Act on Freedom of Information, which changes the rules for requests for data of public interest on three essential points, restricting people's rights:

- There is no longer a possibility to make requests anonymously.
- The request must be accompanied by a payment of all costs, not only technical, but work related as well, and moreover, to cover it in advance.
- In the case of data protected by copyright, no copies will be made, only perusal would be possible.[87]

What can still be heard in public protests is the **voice of those pushed to the margins**. Institutionally embedded organizations either in the field of rights protection, or professional representations, chambers, public bodies or associations that have extensive networks cannot take determined steps in the face of the above cited attacks on general rights and interests. Competencies and resources are drawn away from them with the government-instituted, compulsory membership in professional chambers. And NGOs must remain on speaking terms with governments not only because of the support they may receive, but also for the sake of the people they represent. This limits their ability in committing themselves to opposition political forces. The betrayed, orphaned members of these organizations that have been uncertainly pottering their way through the last two decades have tried to establish parallel organizations, because of the passivity of the extant organizations that had either been bought out, blackmailed, or simply discredited: the NGO *Szolidaritás* (Solidarity) was established in parallel to the workers' unions, the *Hallgatói Hálózat* (Students Network) was established next to the National Union of Students, the *Oktatói Hálózat* (Teachers Network) paralleled the Workers' Union of Higher Education, etc. In lieu of institutional protection and resources these organizations were not able to gain strength and replace their compromised predecessors even though they had been paralyzed by government. The people openly giving vent to their dissatisfaction and criticism, and participants of the protests are largely those who have nothing to lose:

people who do not depend on the expanding state or people of uncertain existences, who had been fired from their jobs, pensioners or students, in other words, *people who are already, or are still outsiders.*

5.8. Patron-client relations in place of class relations

5.8.1. The changing patterns of existential vulnerability

The obedience of the citizens or at least their enforced silence is required to maintain the concentration of power. Threats based on existential vulnerability are the tool to throttle critical attitudes.

The nature of vulnerability is fundamentally different two decades after the regime-change, than the one seen under the soft-communist dictatorship. If someone had a flat in those days, since the public rent, utility and transportation costs were so low, they could manage with a relatively small income. Moreover, because of the egalitarian wage conditions, no differences in income and wealth comparable to present days existed then. Discounting sporadic cases of incitement "against community," in the late Kádár period, people did not go to prison for political reasons, and only a few score intellectuals lost their jobs for a significant length of time, mainly those who belonged to the anti-communist dissident movement. Political retributions were present mostly in the obstructions of career, or professional advancement, a ban on publications, refusal of passports, or through bureaucratic or secret service harassment.

Following the regime change, the substance of existential uncertainty also changed. *The earlier "little but guaranteed" was replaced by the "perhaps more, but no guarantees."* It is only a contradiction in appearance that in spite of the growth, the sense of existential uncertainty has risen significantly. In vain has the number of private telephones including mobiles grown from a few hundred thousand to more than that of the population of the country itself or the number of automobiles from a similar level to three million. And it does not matter if a much higher number of young people could move into their own homes, or attend university than before, or that half a million Hungarians were able to take their holidays on the Croatian seaside alone, if a massive unemployment of many hundreds of thousands (often for hopelessly long times arching across generation) has also put in an appearance in parallel to the earlier advances, and broad swaths of whole strata of the population have fallen into debt (without

reprieve as a result of the economic crisis), with a multitude of bankrupt-
cies among the small and mid-level businesses. *By now there is more to
lose,* and vast numbers can fall from one day to the next into an existentially completely hopeless situation. The loss of a job or for that matter a
contract from the state or municipality can deal a sudden, mortal blow to
what had been a stable or prosperous business. And within a society where
the number of positions and contracts related to the state (including the
municipalities) are abnormally high, this opens virtually boundless opportunities for the government to pursue its ambitions of power.

The citizen today can lose not only the expected, slow growth and
advancement of the late Kádár period. A conflict with the powers that be
may entail the loss of jobs, wealth, capital, professional and moral credibility, and sometimes even personal freedom. The bottom line is not only
a zero, but—through debt—in the minus figures. A drop in social class
does not have to be gradual, but could be precipitous. For such a person—
without an existence that can be made independent from political ret-
ribution and blackmail—confrontation seems hopeless, and dangerous.
Especially in the face of a political force that *systematically tries to force
existential circumstances into dependence from a chain of command*, meanwhile undermining the foundations of individual autonomy.

5.8.2. The variety of the patron-client relations

The basic aim of the mafia state is not merely to eliminate positions of
autonomy on an institutional level, but to do the same directly with personal positions of autonomy in the spheres of political, economic and social
life, and to transform them into a specific type of subordination, that of
the patron-client relationship. This is symptomatically reflected in the *list
of "most influential Hungarians."*[88] The lists of influential people prepared
in pluralistic societies grounded in the separation of powers will not include
people in hierarchical relationship of superiority and inferiority with each
other, but autonomous individuals in no relationship of dependence (from
politicians to businessmen, media personality to university professors). By
contrast, a decisive majority of those who made it to the list in Hungary
could thank Viktor Orbán's beneficence for their influential positions, and
if his favor were withdrawn, these people would be of no interest at their
own value. However subjective the assembly of such a list may be, it reflects
on the actual chain of command. It will depict the same form of patron-

client networks at the peak of society, as those that are typical of the lower levels of social hierarchy.

In place of social configurations that reflect class structure—with autonomous legal standings and advances through market mechanisms—, vassal relationships of the patron-client type ordered into chains of command take over the complete vertical plane of society. The adopted political family is a formation for domination that is organized around the head of the family in a monocentric, hierarchic fashion, through personal and family ties. There is no free entry to the patron-client regime of the adopted political family, only adoption, being given access, or forced surrender; and no free exit either, only to be cast out. The world of democracy that operates on the basis of multitudes of weak personal ties in the sanctuary of institutional guarantees is replaced—as the institutional guarantees fall through—by a world that is based on a few, but strong ties: the impersonal, normative and legal relationships are replaced by personal, discretional and autocratic relationships. In a dictatorship the subordination is open, total and in the final run, based on direct physical force, while the subordination takes place in a legally more-or-less homogeneous class setup. In the mafia state however, the existential patron-client relationships of dependence have to be realized with great variety of form within the props of the institutional system that formally show the characteristics of the rule of law. After all, the direct liquidation of democracy, or the open suspension of individual freedom rights would have no ideological legitimacy, not to mention other factors of constraint. Therefore the process of subordination is carried out in different social groups with the application of different techniques, meaning no sterile, institutional subordination, rather in essence a structured integration into chains of personal dependence and loyalty.

- *In the case of those working in the state administration, the distribution systems* (education, health, etc.) the political cleansing reaching down to the lowest levels was carried out with the introduction of lay-offs (without justification) and reorganizations. The unions were restricted in their scopes of activity, and a significant portion of their licenses were transferred to professional chambers managed by the government. The state administration imposes loyalty upon public servants through elastic-rules of professional conduct that can be interpreted discretionally, in any way whatsoever, as well as the centralization of decisions about advancement, prohibition on public statements, and bans that will accompany those removed throughout their careers and come in the way of their future employment.

- The centralization of a major segment of *municipal institutions* (such as the complete hierarchy of education and health care) serves to ensure that local autonomies are not be able to offer refuge to those who took a stance in opposition to the central political will. Not only has education been centralized to such a degree that every one of the principals of the country is appointed by the minister, but—as mentioned earlier—the principals appointed in such a manner can still not decide about the teachers they would employ, because the authority of employment has been transferred to the commissars of the district office of public administration.
- There are *professions* whose activities are fundamentally market oriented, some of them represented by self-governing professional guilds, which the government wishes to constrain through state monopolies. An example would be if as the government plans, *architects* would only be able to participate in projects funded by the European Union through a central state architectural firm, rather than on the basis of free competition. The work of *companies writing bids for tenders* would be mostly made redundant by the state, when their tasks are taken over by the ministries. And when the centralization or monopolization of the activity of the representatives of a profession meets with a difficulty, the regime attempts to *take over their chamber*, their professional organization with all its official functions. This is what they tried to do—unsuccessfully for the moment—in the case of the legal bar, where the stakes of the battle would have been to fill up the disciplinary committee of the bar with people loyal to the adopted political family, making it possible for them to exclude any lawyer from the bar with elastic rules on ethics, and thereby rob them of their legal practice. In the spring of 2015, the president of the Legal Bar of Budapest made a public statement disclosing that "a member of the Bar had indicated, on the basis of informal but reliable sources that state actors had 'bugged all parts' of a few law firms. There is no exact information about who are intercepting these office communications, it may be the police, the Constitution Protection Office (formerly the National Security Office), or even the Counter Terrorism Center. The case caused an outcry at the Bar, as those who bugged the offices were

violating attorney-client privilege, and so committing an illegal act. Furthermore surveillance can only be conducted in line with a specific objective, but not in general."[89]

- *In the world of academia* the constraints on the autonomy of the universities, the creation of the appointment and financial mechanisms of political blackmail—ensuring the silence and loyalty of the sector— has already been discussed. The government has only partially tempered with the institutional autonomy of the *Hungarian Academy of Sciences*, when it decreed through a parliamentary decision that the *Hungarian Academy of Arts*, an NGO ideologically loyal to the government should become on a par with the Hungarian Academy of Sciences, and has remunerated its members exceptionally—as it does with the members of the Academy of Sciences. At the same time it withdrew all financial support for the Széchenyi Arts Academy, already functioning as part of the Academy of Sciences, and thus made it inconsequential. *Research institutes* in Hungary were of two types prior to 2010: the research centers at the Academy, and the background institutions to the ministries, which supported the work of the administration. The mafia state brought about a new type appeared in the form of the *political-ideological backup institutions*—duplicating the institutes of the Academy—under the direct supervision of the prime minister or a minister: the 21st Century Institute, the Hungarian Language Strategy Institute, the Veritas Historical Research Institute, the Research Institute and Archives for the History of the Hungarian Regime Change, the National Strategy Research Institute. In their case the regime did not bother about occupying and radically transforming the existing institutions, it simply diverted significant budgetary sums to the newly established government brainwashing institutions, to the helms of which it appointed ideological and financial governors with immediate personal ties through the chain of loyalty.
- The installation of patron-client relationships serves to break in and domesticate not only the intellectuals, the employed elite and the main body of society, but also extends to the bottom of the social pyramid. Social groups living in disadvantaged regions, and/or most affected by the crisis are more susceptible to the threats of a practically stagnating number of jobs in the Hungarian economy, and to the reductions of unemployment benefits from nine to three months, with the prospect of its complete annulment within a couple of years. For those who have per-

manently got stuck in lasting unemployment even the reduced benefit is not available, as it is conditional upon a year of certified employment within the last three years. **Public work**, a central employment relief program adapted to the needs of political communication and financed in an unpredictable fashion, employed twice as many people in the month of the parliamentary elections in 2014, as in the month following it. Those who are employed in this program are not only exposed to the temporary, ad hoc nature of this work, along with the fact that they work for half the minimum wage, but they are also burdened by their employment and dismissal being a discretional decision of the local mayor, that cannot be legally questioned. In actual fact this is a *centrally institutionalized form of servitude* in which the rights of those employed do not even come up to the rights that were assured the servants with employment books between the two world wars. No wonder they have no choice but to endure assisting at government party rallies as bio decorations, or demonstrate as counter-demonstrators at anti-government protests, or work on the estates of the local potentates. This final notion in its full bloom was encapsulated in the interior minister's draft law—accepted by parliament in June 2015—that allows the landowner who would take on day-laborers between May and October, to report his need of hands to the local mayor, who would select the suitable day-laborers and then "submit the list to the district office, which informs the public works employee's supervisor, to let the person off his/her 'duties at work or being in available status' while the public work employee must take up the seasonal work, otherwise be banned from public work and benefits for the next three months. On the basis of this proposal the worker would not even be able to quit, if for example the work conditions were too bad, because by leaving they would resign the three months of public work as well."[90] The law however, also excludes those "from three months of public work, whose previous employment ended on the basis of common agreement, or if they quit of their own accord."[91] The "work-based society"[92] announced by Orbán in 2012, as opposed to the welfare state ("which would not return even in Western Europe, as it was not competitive") means in fact the institutionalization of conditions of vulnerability characteristic of servant labor. By 2018 Orbán aims to end "income-substituting benefits" (i.e., unemployment benefits)[93]—which will in the process take a cut of one quarter of the current sum per year—and replace them with public work.

- In the case of **property owners**, the tools of building patron-client relationships comprise of a broad scale of various constraints on their market and ownership rights.

At one end of the scale we find the *elimination of the system of fair competitive procurements*. The recession caused by the economic crisis provide the grounds for the establishment of state dependency: this is because the proportion of state contracts in investments grows, and if in parallel to this the normative rules of procurement are replaced by politically motivated discretional decisions, this will undermine a significant segment of the independent corporate positions. Raising the public procurement thresholds by multiples of the original value has made mass exemption from public procurement obligations possible. In the case of large investments the constant citation of the project being of "special interest" in terms of national-security or for national-economy opens the gate to individual exemptions on a mass scale. The nepotistic decisions with regard to the use of public funds are eased by further relaxation of already quite lax laws regarding conflicts of interest in the 2015 Budget Act. "Though the data regarding the winning bids and their implementation will remain public, those regarding the unsuccessful applications will not. In fact they must be deleted after the evaluation process has ended (virtually excluding the possibility of revealing abuses in retrospect, observe a similar solution in the case of the national tobacco shop licenses and agricultural land swindles), nor will data regarding the identity of the decision-makers have to be made public."[94] The abundance of arbitrary exclusion of lower-cost bids from public procurements and constraints on the possibility to appeal the decisions spur on the formative social process as a result of which businesses will either "voluntarily" stay far afield of the market of public procurements, or look for a patron embedded in the political family, so they can become subcontractors. This is how the chain of vassalage among the **court purveyors** expands.

A further tool for the inculcation of client relationships is to put **constraints upon owners' rights to dispose**, as for example in the case of sales of land, where the normative laws for preemptive purchase are compounded with a requirement of approval for the transaction by local land committees dominated by Fidesz cadres. By these means, firstly the owner of the land can be held hostage by the denial of approval for the sale, thereby forcing a decrease in the price, and secondly a quasi political organization can indirectly claim the right to name the new owner of the land. The nationalization of the savings cooperatives in the meanwhile has created the conditions for individually tailored political blackmail where the need for financial loans come into the deal.

Additionally the autocratic change in the conditions of earned ownership entitlements (e.g., system of state land-leases), or the **nationalization of economic activities** that had previously not been carried on through state monopoly or concessions, and their consequent expropriation and redistribution among new actors (e.g., tobacco shop concessions) also serve to establish the patron-client relationships.

And then at the other end of the scale we find the **takeover**, that is, the bloodless, but nevertheless coercive expropriation and/or redistribution of properties or businesses using the instruments of public authority—discussed later in detail.

5.9. The middle strata of the mafia state power hierarchy: service gentry and court purveyors—the "new national middle class"

The question now is whether the mafia state will be able to ensure the new autocratic regime's sustainability by—besides holding manipulated elections— establishing a chain of command that reaches down through the layers of society. The aim would be to ensure that the autocratic regime holds fast, relying on existing, deeper sociological processes than the previously discussed techniques, which were applied institutionally to restrict critical action and freedom of speech. Politically speaking, the form taken by the "central field of power" is an autocracy, yet the **social group at its center** is called—euphemistically and propagandistically—the national middle class. As in the case of the communist regime the adjective in the term "socialist democracy" was indeed a privative suffix, the qualifier of the middle class as "national" also functions alike. What is meant under "national middle class" is not a community of autonomous citizens better endowed with intellectual or material assets and a grip on power. On the contrary, the qualifier "national" refers to a social group known for a restricted ideology and values, which is fortified with privileges and organized into a martial order that allows entry or ejects its members on the terms of a revived nomenclature—that is however tied this time to the adopted political family rather than the party. Two pillars can be observed emerging in the formative stages of this envisioned national middle class.

One pillar could be called that of the "service gentry," and the other that of "court purveyors." The transformation of the whole institutional system is molded to these two orders, which provide the tools required for the operation of the autocratic system of rule. The *"new national middle class"* is in reality a *level of subordinated vassalage with restricted freedoms in the spheres of intellect and economy*.

5.9.1. The service gentry

As a first step, the centralization of administration was completed, eliminating all autonomies, be they regional, municipal, public or higher education, any form of scientific or cultural self-government, or for that matter public media. As it overpowered the spheres of liberal democracy that had been protected by freedom rights and autonomy, the centralized state demolished the institutional autonomy of the social strata composed of civil servants, intelligentsia variously employed by the state, as well as formerly independent intellectual groups who were not in public service, but had a broad influence on public opinion, and began either to recruit them into the orders at its own service, or to marginalize and ghettoize them.

To begin reclassifying the professional intellectuals in public service into the ranks of the service gentry, *first* a *comprehensive political cleansing* was carried out, often accompanied by campaigns of stigmatization and criminalization. The serial institutional mergers and liquidations that naturally also involved significant cuts in public resources only made the mass layoffs easier to justify.

The second step was to force the groups of intellectuals in public service to *join newly created professional chambers* controlled by the government. It is nevertheless a *mistake to cite corporations* in referring to the system of state employment under construction, for in their classical forms they were the supports of the establishment in the corporative regimes prior to World War Two reducing the conflict between "capital and labor" but at the same time retaining their corporate bargaining positions. In the current system the members of the arm of public service—the service gentry—do not possess any special privileges as a body, as their status only ensures them the advantage to fill the state positions as opposed to those who are excluded from it. The code of ethics compiles norms of expected behavior—i.e., loyalty—for dependent bureaucratic middle layer of the political family in the form of a catechistic manual. Though all those belonging to the service gentry *enjoy the advantages assured to them, they do not enjoy the freedoms that would belong to their feudalistic order*. They are not reincarnations of the age-old feudal "gentry," with rights that cannot be revoked, but a lot of public servants and newly made bureaucrats out of intellectuals drilled into the martial order of the rank and file.

In the mafia state the de facto situation of vassals of vulnerable social groups, exposed to individual despotism and forced into the chain of command, does not go with the legal status of vassals. This is what makes the otherwise often illuminating use of feudal metaphors only conditionally apt. At the same time however, in the case of some of the white-collar workers forced into various professional chambers by duress of the enforcement authorities, the situation of vassals does partly result in the rights of vassals as well. In contrast to the professional chambers of the civilized western world—that may similarly be compulsory—which essentially have roles in ensuring quality (including consumer protection, and a regulated market), *the chambers of the mafia state are loyalty warranting state organizations.* In the case of the legal bar for example, the clause referring to attorney-client privilege was removed, while a clause on "practicing office to the benefit of the Hungarian nation" was added to the lawyer's oath, which is rather absurd when it is considered that the lawyer may well on occasion have to represent a client against the Hungarian state. But the format of the code of ethics is also flexible enough to provide the legal basis for any sort of autocratic procedure.

The professional chambers are in fact transmission belts, they have no bargaining power, only serve as a formal framework of recruitment. But these forms of organization—i.e., the clan-like mafia concentration and its branches descending through the organization to those who fall outside the first circle of privilege, the body of public servants, meaning the "service gentry" and the order of "court purveyors"—are also quite *different from those of the earlier leftist totalitarian dictatorships*. The reason there was no need for such a role then was because outside of the party state there was really no other structure, while control and surveillance were in part handled by official labor unions. In contrast, where Hungary, and to various degrees in numerous post-communist regimes outside the European

Union are concerned, there still exist a number of fields that have not been reached, taken over by the organized upperworld. The system is not closed in a physical sense either, as the communist dictatorships had once been, indeed the country could not be left in those days, and the system had control over the totality of life. One need but only recall the legal formula of "social parasitism": the communist state not only determined what position an individual could fill, regulated not only the conditions of advancement, but also did not allow anyone to disappear from the system, everyone had a registered place in it. Total control covered the whole of society. In contrast, the post-communist mafia state only concentrates on the nodes of decision-making and trade transactions, and of course the networks that are woven around them across society.

The third step is the extension of ***direct oversight to the processes of recruitment*** currently still underway. Moreover, by means of the reorganization of public and higher education the control of long-term channels of social mobility are also tied into this system. The ***educating of the "new national" political and administrative elite*** is also going through a significant transformation. In training of the intellectual elite, secondary schools in church care have gained ground continuously since the 1990s. Pázmány Péter Catholic University has played an almost exclusive role in providing young lawyers for institutions of public service under Fidesz control—such as the prosecutor's offices. And now that Fidesz is in government, after the makeshift arrangements of the period in opposition, the time has come to establish an educational institution suited to the needs of the feudalistic career models in public administration. This was the objective of the new ***National University of Public Service***, established by merging the faculty of public administration taken from Corvinus University of Budapest, the Police College, and the Zrínyi Miklós National Defence University. So as not to leave a shadow of doubt as to the spirit of the institution being created, it was placed—at the cost of dislodging the Hungarian Natural History Museum—in the building that once housed the Ludovika cadet school prior to World War Two. This neatly symbolizes the military ethos of the order in the making, its character based on service and supervision. This is intended to be the place of training for all members of the single unified order of service gentry, be it for the secret services, the police, the army, or various levels of public administration, each ready for assignment as a link within the martial chain of command. Presumably the circle of positions and statuses within public administration open only to individuals with diplomas from this institution will be determined in the future. The steps to come can be logically deduced from the worldview of the autocratic regime. This worldview could be compared to a periodic table of elements for the logic of power, where sooner or later—as it becomes possible—the still empty cells are filled. For the moment, a monopoly has been established for the National University of Public Service to teach certain disciplines, by prohibiting them at other institutions. An example of such a measure is the ban on "science of state governance," with which they seek to weaken the departments of law at other universities, unheeding of loud protests. Of course it will eventually not be left to academia to decide what "science of state governance" really means, as it becomes a matter more apt for HR: in concrete terms it will mean the diploma given by the National University, without which certain fields and positions of public administration cannot be filled, but "only by public servants from the janissary school."[95] Passages of justification accompanying the draft legislation proposed in June of 2015 spell this out loud and clear: "the aim of the amendment [...], is to ensure that only the National University of Public Service can undertake higher education programs in state governance, public administration, policing, military sciences, national security, or international and European public services."

5.9.2. The court purveyors

The other pillar of the new national middle class to be established is the order of court purveyors, virtually the exclusive beneficiary of any purchases and investments related to the state, and the added liberty to expand the organized upperworld's influence on the funds secured from the European Union as development resources. This is in part why parallels drawn with various forms of the communist dictatorships are wrong: firstly because the state did not assist in the creation of private fortunes then; and secondly because the nomenclature was much less typified by the predominance of family relations. The mafia state on the other hand basically comprises the adopted family of recruits. This is Fidesz's "national family model." The mafia state transfers an increasingly large segment of the private economy under the command of the adopted political family. The means of achieving this are marvelously variegated.

Since the passing of laws regulating public procurements and priority public investments, which make discretionary choices among the economic actors possible, there is nothing left to hide, *as of this point in time mafia methods have become the lawful order of managing affairs*. Thus state contracts and—paradoxically—resources from the European Union make the accelerated and large-scale enlargement of the order of court purveyors possible. Some are admitted, others barred, as the fair market competition is replaced by state concessions or exclusions. Megacorporations affiliated to the regime come into existence in a matter of moments—as did Vegyépszer under the first Fidesz government and Közgép following 2010—forming tributary supplier chains of their subcontractors. Guides on banned partners assist the work of decision-makers on the lower levels. This is how as many economic actors as possible are drawn into state control and the chain of command under the order of court purveyors. This is no ordinary day-to-day corruption, which would and could not seek to oversee all resources exclusively. The logic of the mafia state is different: just as the organized underworld would not allow a rival to take protection money on its territory, the mafia state is also interested in eliminating the possibility of independent and especially critical businesses or institutions being nurtured by resources at the command of the state. For this reason, in the case of the resources overseen by or under the influence of the state there is no longer real competition, there is no sector neutrality, and even the legal framework and conditions for the practice of favoritism on the basis of incidental considerations has been established. This is an important stipulation in order to condition the business actors appropriately, and to compel them to accept the new rules. Neglect for the rules of the mafia state results not only exclusion and ruling out access to resources, but also may force naïve businesses into expenses that cannot be recovered.

5.9.3. Cementing the "new national middle class"

The stability and sustaining power of this social group is quite different from that of the isolated citizens. Those who gain positions through the mechanisms of power-based privileges already have something to lose—this is what ties them to the new order.

For members of the service gentry did not attain their positions by merit of their expertise, but on account of the unconditional loyalty that was demanded of them. This results in the slow demise of public service ethos and composure, when a public servant might believe that his/her expertise and political neutrality guarantee a stable position in public service. A position, claimed heretofore by merit, became a job delivered—and taken away at the drop of a hat—by political favor. The public servant thereby gains a vested interest in upholding the system, as any change would come with an existential risk. Grappling with the sense of vulnerability intrinsic to servitude, an urge for emotional identification with the system is allowed to grow, which means that the **proportion of enraptured followers of the government** in this stratum becomes stabilized.

Recent changes in the—heretofore independent—positions of the intelligentsia employed by the professional apparatus are essentially different from the waves of replacements that had taken place after earlier changes of government: partly because of their simply massive numbers, partly the measure in which the matter of loyalty relegates professionalism to the background, thirdly the martial discipline required to conform, and fourthly in the way that all positions that can be tied to the state are closed to those who are ejected, further boosting discipline within the ranks. In the last mentioned procedure, being registered on—real or virtual—blacklist means a political stigmatization that results in a ban from the whole sphere of public service. This type of prohibition on employment is familiar from the times under the communist regime, although there these bans were communicated through the channels of the party and the secret service.

Discipline among those who remain in the filtered system is also increased by a huge gap between their current incomes and what their skills would be worth on the free market. In the circle of court purveyors on the other hand, to be a winner or loser of a tender can be measured in fortunes. With the neophyte zeal of converts among the elder generations also considered, it would be a mistake to underestimate the **regime's capacity to cement the "national consciousness,"** i.e., the cohesion and loyalty of those adopted to the political family. Like the steel structure in reinforced concrete: the social coherence of the will of individuals is not a perceivable dimension for opinion polls, where ideology, program and existences clearly match up for the members of the order. They are portrayed as the national middle class, and they like to believe this about themselves, but actually they are only the recruits of the feudal chain of command ranging between the ranks of "sergeants and officers."

The consolidation of the mafia state means that the adopted political family may draw those who are obedient into the system—though at different levels of gratuity. The chances of its consolidation must therefore not be underestimated, for this is *a forgiving, inclusive regime*, though on the basis of standards different to the way this term is usually understood. There are family rules, conditions and rewards for a return into the fold. Many people who seem alien to the system can find a place in it: past communists, secret service agents, disoriented intellectuals, scared artists, and businessmen who once thought of themselves as independent...

5.9.4. The sin above all sins: disloyalty

There is only one sin in the mafia family rooted in the organized underworld that is always avenged: disloyalty. With the growing influence of the organized upperworld, the statement comes to apply to a continuously widening circle of—social, political, public, and economic—positions drawn into its sphere. Loyalty is the condition of both employment and being party to a share of the proceeds. Those who want to leave the system, or turn against it, may be penalized for things they could never be penalized for in a democracy, and the way they are penalized could never be pulled off in a democracy. Through the obstruction and liquidation of the institutions upholding democracy and the establishment of the patron-client system, tools—that would never be accessible in a functioning democracy—have become available to enforce silence and obedience. The tools basically affect existences, possibly in an all-consuming and lasting way. Thus the victims coerced under threat of their existences are silent—as familiar from criminology—for if they would speak, it would only visit more troubles upon them. And if they do speak, they can only be heard in media-bubbles that reach a small fraction of the populace.

The fact that *there is no peaceful means—by individual volition—of stepping out of the system* is another evidence of the mafia culture that reigns throughout government. Once inside the system, whether by wish or conscripted, the member is either discharged by the head of the political family, or if deserting, he will be chased down. No matter if he be the political family's appointed president of the republic, minister, or a member of parliament, he knows the consequences of opposition and of quitting. It is not merely the loss of some advantages, but the possibility of complete loss of existential means. Defection entails not only a shooting licence against the unprotected individuals but even a shooting obligation on them.

On the other hand, since only disloyalty counts as a sin, members of the political family who commit some other offence, whether against the law or decency, cannot be punished in the organized upperworld. Corruption, forgery of official documents, or—common—domestic violence do not matter. If public opinion pursues the offender more vociferously, or the case meets with an exceptionally serious international response, it may come to a sacrifice of the one responsible. Yet those individuals can still be assured of one thing: *the political family will always be there for them*. At most, the family will create a new existence for them—on the model of witness-protection programs—somewhere else, removing them from public view. Only, however, if the individual is loyal. This gives the regime its strength: they do not serve their own people up to "alien powers." And for those who know the disadvantages of confrontation and the protection that adherence means—while they experience the increasingly strong and extensive control of society by the organized upperworld—not only the possibility of confrontation is lost, but its rationale as well. It is no coincidence that Banfield's category *"amoral familism,"* describing the poverty-ridden conditions of a Southern Italy woven through-and-through with mafia culture, can also be used describe the rules of conduct determining the behavior of the adopted political family in the mafia state.[96] A lack of any responsibility or solidarity towards all those who do not belong to the family/nationality.

Meanwhile, all those who are not capable, or not willing to shoulder these conditions organized into the patron-client relations, and excluding any and all meritocratic competition would at most leave the country—if able to do so. Hundreds of thousands are already working abroad, many of whom are not necessarily doing so on material grounds, but because they do not want their professional or business careers to be determined solely by their loyalty to those in power.

The regime could not employ the tried and tested tools of dictatorship within the European Union anyway. Then isn't it more useful from its perspective if the upstarts are out of the way, abroad? And why would it care that the people who leave are the ones with skills that have value abroad? Why should the system be physically closed, if it is more stable this way? For this reason, while some believe that at some point the country must reach boiling point, it is highly doubtful that this will ever occur. After all, what is being carried on is a highly *subtle, utilitarian balancing act of reward and coercion*. The instruments of deterrence are applied appropriately. Though the mafia state may seem impetuous, it is not. It only uses the impetuous emotions of others with expedient rationality. It does not annihilate, it only expels—from autonomous intellectual existences, business ventures, the country... Unlike some eastern versions of the post-communist mafia state at present, where—the **coercion threshold** being lower than in the European Union—political rivals can easily find themselves in prison, and even assassinations are not considered rare.

5.10. Tributes exacted as economic policy: the system of special taxes

The mafia state perpetuates the concept of a power-compatible society by creating a new national propertied middle class organized into a clear chain of command from magnate to minor entrepreneurs. Its self-idealization is manifested as the main corps of the nation united by a faith in order and religious belief, free from deviancies. This target social group providing the backbone of Fidesz politics is indeed much easier to hold together through the value-system proclaiming "God, motherland, family" than was the case with the alternative liberals Fidesz had been in the days gone by: the digression of the country boys of the same college fraternity to the liberal capital long ago, is now seen as the indulgent excesses of young men straying from the strict and narrow path. As one of Fidesz's ideologists, Gyula Tellér explains: "The leading figures of Fidesz came from a rural educated, or semi-educated, ambitious social strata that held on to the classical, Hungarian conservative set of values. Not because they were trained, theoretical conservative, but because this was obligatory in rural society, they were reared upon these values. [...] Freed of the rules of neoliberal thought, the codes they had been brought up with suddenly came to the surface."[97] It would be a misunderstanding however to take their current rhetoric—though very possibly cynical—as mere veneer and mimicry. The growing fortunes of their families fits their social vision harmoniously, and in their conscience it even wins justification as they see themselves as the poor boy of the Hungarian fairy tales, who has come to claim his share. In the fairy tale of course it was easier for the youngest boy to win half the country as the prize of accomplished feats: his task was not burdened by all sorts of scruples about the rule of law, regulations on conflicts of interest and what not. Yet the economic policies of Fidesz can only be interpreted correctly if all of these factors are taken into account—in comparison with other practices where the personal involvement is less determinant.

The cyclicality of the **socialists'** economic policy was defined by **alternating periods of generous distribution and austerity measures**—a distorted continuation of the cyclicality that was observed in the communist command economy. All liberal efforts to halt this were in vain. The distributive politics that did not serve to spur the economy on, but merely to gather votes laid waste the resources that could have served as security for long-term, sustainable growth, while the austerity measures—lacking reform—did not serve the introduction of effective, rational economic models. The areas in which serious systemic reforms were effectuated prior to the advent of the Fidesz era in 2010 can be counted on the fingers of one hand: the establishment of the private pension funds, higher education and a partial public education reform, as well as the creation of the non-conscript professional army.

In the case of **Fidesz**, an economy subordinated to the purposes of power is determined by a **duality of politically targeted allowances and tributes exacted**. In the economic policies of the socialists the beneficiaries and the targets of austerity measures both appear as value-free statistical categories of society: if they could, they would give to everyone in a social group, but if they had to take away resources, they would rather aim them at impersonal institutions, always communicated in technocratic and not ideological terms. In the case of Fidesz however the withdrawal of resources and allowances are ideologically driven and communicated as such. Allowances (tax benefits, the development projects realized from the resources tapped from the European Union) have served the "healthy proliferation of the nation," the "sustenance of the nation," the reinforcement of the "national Christian middle class," etc., all delineating the political family in a broader sense.

With the **introduction of the flat rate tax**—redirecting income to the higher layers of society in a general, impersonal sense, tailored for the moment to a social layer, rather than individuals—Fidesz blew a 600 million forint (2 billion euro) hole into the national budget. It could only offset this partially with drastic cuts in the expenditures of the large distribution systems—municipalities, social welfare, health care, education and culture. Therefore with the aid of a thoroughly ideologically grounded reasoning the plunder of a part of private savings began.

In order to grab the private pension funds, heightened emotions had to be aroused, eliciting the message about private pension funds that they were "laying waste to our money through speculations." Since even such communications criminalizing the funds were not enough, the capture of a vast majority of the 3,000 billion forint fortune had to be ensured through intimidation, the blackmail of pension fund members, raising the threat of losing state guaranteed pensions and the installation of an array of technical hurdles to be overcome to stay members of the private funds. The money the state robbed from the funds was used in part to stop up the gaps in the budget and in part to decrease the sovereign debt.[98] The curiosity of how the matter of the private pension funds was suppressed is that in this case losses, being their own, were presumably far more palpable to the fund members than it had been in the case of other, indirect tributes exacted until then. Nevertheless the members of the funds were stripped of their savings without notable social dissent, paid off with the precarious promise of a future state pension.

5.10.1. Some forms of special taxes prior to 2010

Special taxes had appeared in Hungary already around the time of the regime change. The state imposed levies—which could in retrospect be called special taxes—created earmarked resources for the realization of particular sectorial objectives which could not be secured through the annual parliamentary debates over the budget. Yet the purpose, the reach and the measure of these funds was of marked difference to the system that unfolded after 2010.

One of these was the **National Highway Fund**, which functioned between 1989 and 1998, partly financed by taxes on fuel and intended to solve the problem of no stable, dependable financial bracket being available earmarked for the development and maintenance of the road network, also taking account of depreciation. Until then the financing of tasks related to road networks had moved in recurring cycles of huge advances and complete ruin. In order to create more freely expendable resources, Fidesz liquidated the Fund—during its first term in government—in 1999.

The creation of the **National Cultural Fund** in 1993 and the **Innovation Fund** in 2004 was motivated in both cases by the wish to create long-term, flexible funding for not only institutions but programs, with their boards of trustees providing the autonomous frameworks for the mechanism of evaluating applications for funding. The extra taxes financing the two funds were applied in the first case to the industrial branch of cultural content-carrier technology and in the second, on the medium and large companies of the corporate sector. Another fact that also warranted the creation of these necessity-dictated extra financial channels was that during parliamentary debates on the budget, resources were easily spun off by the powerful, if inert institutions with stronger bargaining positions, or the more immediate political advantages promised by raising public servant wages or pensions.

The **bank tax** set at 24 percent of profits made by financial ventures in 2005—compared to the 16 percent tax on other types of business—began to show signs of differentiation between sectors. On the basis of the so-called **Robin Hood tax** introduced in 2009 an 8 percent special tax had to be paid by large energy supply and trade companies to fund compensation of expensive tele-heating systems and the modernization of heating systems. It is apparent that this is a case of cross-subsidization, in which the socialist government—the liberals left the coalition in 2008—tried to help the poorer social groups of the housing estates, also attempting to give credence to the peculiarity of this tax, that went against the general expectation of taxes applying normatively, to everyone, by considering them temporary. According to their plans the bank tax would have been ended after two years, and the Robin Hood tax after three, had the 2008 global financial and economic crisis not stepped in. Though neither the compass, nor objectives of these taxes had been purposed to expel their subjects from the economy in the service of private interests masquerading as public interest, nevertheless the ideological, propagandistic names and justifications for these taxes foreshadowed the dangers, and destructive possibilities for the market that were inherent in the use of special taxes. Their claimed temporary character was also not too auspicious, if in comparison we consider the title of a piece in the journal *Veszprémi Napló* from 1983: "Officers of the Soviet troops temporarily stationed in Hungary to receive permanent condominiums."

5.10.2. The systemic escalation of special taxes after 2010

To begin with, the financial burdens imposed as special taxes so as to balance the budget did not only appear to be just ideology-based **punitive tributes**. Coming up against the prescriptions applicable to Hungary under the then current excessive deficit procedure that required the budget deficit to be lowered to below 3 percent of the GDP in step with a preset schedule, without these taxes the Fidesz government could not have set out to fulfill its one and only election promise: a large-scale and radical decrease in taxes. Without special taxes this decrease in income tax would have pushed deficit—recently brought down to 4 percent by the outgoing Bajnai government—up to 6–7 percent. It stood in Fidesz's basic interest to secure and to reward its primary potential support base, the "national middle class," and the introduction of the flat rate personal income tax would immediately deliver these political aims. The huge budget revenue fallout caused by this measure was balanced with the so-called "crisis taxes," which have developed into a widespread system. Fidesz simply continued to use the taxes and rhetoric inherited from the Gyurcsány and Bajnai governments, even keeping the confidence in their temporary character, with the difference that the system of "crisis taxes" was immediately broadened. Thereby the four types of crisis tax were directed especially at branches of the economy (financial sector, energy providers, telecommunications, and small retail chains) where foreign involvement was more pronounced. Taking advantage of the global wave of bank unpopularity in reaction to the 2008 credit crisis, the Orbán government emphasized the "punitive" nature of the special tax on the financial sector right from the beginning. (Even though the bank bailouts necessitated in Hungary were taken care of by the western parent banks, and cost the state nothing.)

It was clear from the start that Fidesz's economic policies are merely a play on a continuous struggle between the anthropomorphic forces of "nation-construction" and "nation-corruption": special taxes were imposed on the banks, telecommunications companies, energy provider companies, public utility companies, the multinationals that "sneaked their profits out of the country," the "hamburger makers" who sold "unhealthy" food. These actions command significant social support, as the post–regime-change experience of the ordinary people is that while the large systems of oppression (one-party system, state monopoly on ownership) were eliminated, the small systems of oppression and exploitation that determine everyday life continue to survive. Under the pressure of bureaucracy, public utility companies and banks, the citizen has only become more vulnerable existentially than before. This uncertainty and frustration became the *malleable emotions supporting and legitimizing the government's tribute exacting measures.*

Taxes on profit and "generally applicable standard contributions" to the budget by small businesses presently make up only 37 percent of state revenues from business organizations, writes István Csillag, former liberal minister of economy, and then continues, to say:[99] "The majority, 63% of state revenues come from tributes exacted of companies and groups of corporations through taxes tailored specifically to them, 'by name.' I need not sermonize for too long to point out that the only aim of imposing 'name-tagged' payments rather than the predictable payments under generally applicable conditions can be to gain unconstrained sway for autocracy, in the same fashion as those instances when generally applicable payments are let off in part or as a whole." Fidesz, "when it took power in 2010, promised to decrease the 52 forms of tax then applicable by one-third, yet they have actually increased their number to 73 by July 2014, according to the National Tax Office. If the new forms of taxation introduced for the budget in 2015 are added to the above figure, the number of channels of tax revenues seem to have nearly doubled."[100]

It is typical of the special taxes that their objective is never solely to raise budget revenues. After all, some of them result in negligible revenues in terms of the budget, and only impact negatively on the concerned target individuals or target companies. This is also why the ideology-ridden, spirited, stigmatizing government communication that accompanies them is so strong. The actual aims—not merely of generating revenues—may include simple, politically motivated penalization, expulsion from the market, making the position of the business less favorable than that of the competing companies connected to the political family, preparation for buyout or nationalization, the enforced realization of objectives related to life-style and ideology, or any combination of the above. What is essential however is that the given objective, beyond that of an interest in increasing the budget revenues, does not serve legitimate social objectives, but rather the aims of the adopted political family, its grip on power and accumulation of wealth.

5.10.2.1. agricultural support funds are—cial taxes

- One type of punitive tax introduced in 2010, was a **98 percent tax** imposed retroactively reaching back to 2005, on **severance pay given to public officials and state employees** under the socialist-liberal government—a measure that reeked of political revenge. The constitutional court undid the retroactive effect of the law, however it still applied to those effected by the layoffs following the change of government in 2010. With the wave of political cleansing calming down, the government moderated the level of the tax—which was insignificant in terms of revenue of the budget—to 75 percent, but also created means to compensate the disadvantages of the generally applicable tax on the basis of individual decisions when shifting their own cadres between positions.

- The **advertisement tax** was introduced after Fidesz's efforts to acquire the two major commercial televisions proved only partially successful. Though accompanied by a power struggle within the family, they succeeded in drawing TV2 into their own sphere of interest with a business deal that still remains suspicious, but they could not get the television channel RTL Klub. Of the tabloid televisions that had until then always been politically neutral towards governments the news programs on TV2 were as a result pressed into the service of government communications, while RTL Klub was not. The progressive taxes imposed as a penalty, to teach the channel discipline, or even extrude from the market, were calculated in such way as to make RTL Klub, with a 16 percent share in the total advertisement cake to pay 54 percent of the budget revenues from this type of tax. The tax on RTL Klub income is the highest at 15 percent. And though the tax on TV2's revenue is also 11 percent,[101] state advertisement sponsorship received by TV2 after it had been transferred to the political family compensated its losses plentifully, while RTL Klub receives no state advertisement. Moreover the law was amended in such a way as to ensure that the friendly channel TV2 would not have to pay the tax in 2014.

- A drastic increase in the **food chain supervision fee** in 2015 affects the food chains in Hungarian possession to an insignificant degree. "CBA and Coop will hardly pay anything, however the progressive rate of the food chain supervision fee may mean an even greater liability to discount chains and hypermarkets than the earlier crisis tax. [...] over revenues of 300 billion forint the **rate rises to sixty times what it had been**. Which could mean that, for example, the liability of the chain with the largest turnover, UK owned Tesco, may increase from roughly 600 million forint (2 million euro) to approximately 12 billion (40 million euro), so the largest shopping chains could be paying a combined 20–35 billion forint (65–110 million euro)."[102] The discrimination between Hungarian and foreign chains is made possible by the progressive rate of the imposed fee, which is zero when the annual turnover does not reach 500 million forint, and rises from a thousandth in many graded steps to 6 percent for a turnover above 300 billion. And though the business turnover of the Hungarian owned Coop and CBA—which latter organizes the so-called Peace March as well as other loyalty demonstrating rallies—together comes to three-quarters of the turnover at Tesco, their operation as a franchise practically exempts them from paying the fee, while in accounting terms, Tesco operates as a single concern.

- The food chain supervision fee is the umpteenth step taken by the government in its "national freedom fight" against the multinational food chains. The ones that had gone before did not achieve the desired effect. One of them was a similarly progressive *crisis tax*, or the law popularly known as *plaza-stop* introduced already in 2012, though taking effect only in 2015, making the construction or extension of shops covering premises of over 400 m2 conditional on case-by-case permits issued discretionally, as a favor. According to a statement from the ministry of national economy "224 requests for exemption have been submitted since the law came into effect, and permission was granted in 135 instances (60%) and dismissed in 89 (40%)."[103] This makes the government decision about which chain can and which one cannot expand its infrastructure wholly arbitrary. Yet the government is not satisfied with halting the expansion of the multinationals, it seeks to make their situation untenable, and to force them out of the Hungarian market. It is securing further devices for the process. They voted into force the closure of shops on Sundays (to be discussed below), and have prohibited the delivery of online orders between 10 pm and 6 am, as well as on public holidays and Sundays. In addition[104]

  ➤ from 2016 the discount stores and larger super-, or hypermarkets located in Unesco world heritage areas will be closed;
  ➤ the bus lines free of charge to shopping centers from the city center will be banned;
  ➤ overnight opening hours will be prohibited;
  ➤ the larger shops operating at a loss for two consecutive years will be closed, or their permit to sell basic foodstuff will be revoked;
  ➤ according to a draft regulation from October 2015 all shops larger than 400 square meters would have to employ at least one salesperson per 70 square meters, virtually doubling the current average staff.[105]

There can be few more plain-speaking examples of the way in which the mafia state operates than the attempted change of ownership of this type with the tools of bloodless state coercion, aiming to deliver the market and ownership positions thus liberated not only into "Hungarian" hands, but the hands of the members of the adopted political family, who are not autonomous businessman, but oligarchs and stooges under the direct supervision of the godfather. So as not to leave any doubt with regard to the aims of their series of actions, László Baldauf, president of CBA has gone so far as to announce that "currently our most important task is to grow by acquiring the shops of any companies that chance to withdraw from the country, as we have already done in the case of Profi and Match."[106] On another occasions he addresses the wider public in the role of the disciple: "I am a great admirer of Prime Minister Viktor Orbán, I even know him personally, I visit him in Felcsút. By god's grace the Prime Minister knows best what has to be done in this country to help the nation rise, and what he does, he does well."[107] While the battle to redistribute the market is fought with the weapons of state coercion under the "national" banner, it must be noted that the proportion of Hungarian foodstuff on the shelves of Tesco or Spar is no smaller than that of its Hungarian rivals. In fact Tesco ensures the export of approximately 65 billion forint (200 million euro) worth of Hungarian foodstuff through its non-Hungarian retail chain.[108]

- Since 2015 the **solar panel tax** has been introduced, which is to be paid after the significant environmental pollution caused by the product. The 117 forint (0.36 euro) to be paid per kilogram is twice that charged for accumulators.[109] This even startled Zoltán Illés, the now out of favor former state secretary responsible for environmental affairs in Fidesz's government until 2014, who called the government proposal inexplicable, in that it sets out that "*product tax must be imposed on solar panels, and even the main construction parts of wind power stations and heat pumps.* Only a person who has no inkling of the main correlations in sustainability can write down such a thing, and someone willing to do anything to satisfy the expectation from above to prove that: renewables are more expensive than nuclear energy."[110] It is not an accident why the government is going against the common sense solution even apparent in international trends. The last sentence of the foregoing statement gives the explanation, though only with addition of the distinction that the answer is not simply "nuclear energy," but "Russian nuclear energy." In other words, a business deal to be made with another autocrat, Putin, not a single element of which is subjected to any obligations of transparency or procurement standards, that is on a scale large enough that if it takes off, it would be settled, just like the "unbreakable Soviet-Hungarian friendship" in years past, and which can also make the political family as rich as need be for decades to come. The 3,000 billion forint (10 billion euro) **Paks Nuclear Power Plant** development would fit the above criteria. On the condition that the ailing Russian economy can pre-finance the deal. The matter also shows the geopolitical interests of Russia dangerously intertwined with the private interests of the Hungarian political family.

• Since 2010 the system of special taxes was essentially built on the **bank tax**, and the rest of the **sector-specific special taxes**. The bank taxes were introduced in a number of countries following the 2008 global financial crisis, but their scale remained far below that in Hungary. While its level moved somewhere between 0.02 and 0.2 percent of the GDP in other countries, in Hungary it even rose above 0.7 percent of the GDP. (See Annex 2.) Moreover, the continuous shortfall of 500–600 billion forint (200 million euro) in the personal income tax revenues caused by the flat rate tax and the obligatory wind-up of the sector-specific special taxes in the system along with the rapid depletion of the resources plundered from the private pension funds with the necessity of keeping both the budget balanced and the 3 percent national deficit on target at the same time made it acutely important for the government not only to keep the bank taxes in effect—breaking its pledge—but also to open a new major financial tap. The **financial transaction fee** introduced in 2013 filled the role. The two financial taps on the banks seemed apt for the role, because the rhetoric of the national freedom fight could convincingly be twinned with the historically "tested" anti-bank and banker rhetoric. The government even promised that the banks would not be allowed to shift the losses on to their clients, and could keep up its fighting stance on the pretext of ensuring this, with the result finally that a positive balance in the foreign capital influx depended solely on the required recapitalization of foreign-owned subsidiaries by their parent banks.

Though the tax revenues from the bank tax and the financial transaction fee together come to somewhere around an annual 400 billion forint (1.3 billion euro), the government continues obsessively to look for further areas that could be taxed. From 2010 the income from special taxes increased from 361 billion forint (1.2 billion euro) to 846 billion forint (2.7 billion euro) to 2014. (See Annex 3.) A sort of pyramid scheme can be observed in which there is a constant rise of the number of risky decisions that may unpredictably hit back both politically and economically. The most spectacular among them was the plan to introduce the so-called *internet tax*, where the absolute lack of preparation could be seen in the fact that the actual amount of income drawn away to feed the budget according to the parameters of the tax as they were given would have unrealistically, multiply exceeded, the government-planned revenues from the tax at 20 billion forint (65 million euro). At that time already no one was willing to believe that this would not actually burden the end users of the internet service; the issue generated the so far largest mass rally to have occurred against the Fidesz government. With this measure the government had picked a fight with a young populace that had until then been indifferent to politics, even as it lived with a great deal of awareness.

Types of special taxes according to their aims
(+ = insignificant; ++ = moderately significant; +++ = significant;
++++ = very significant)

Name of special tax	Role in increasing budget revenues	Discrimination against specific sectors	Discrimination within sectors	Expulsion, market acquisition	Political penalization
98% special tax on severances payments			+++		++++
Bank tax	++++	+++	++	+++	++
Financial transaction fee	++++	+++		+	
Insurance tax	++	++			
Accident tax	++	++			

Name of special tax	Role in increasing budget revenues	Discrimination against specific sectors	Discrimination within sectors	Expulsion, market acquisition	Political penalization
Energy sector special tax	+++	+++		++	
Environmental product tax on solar panels, and the main parts of wind power plants and heat pumps	++		++++	+++	
Telecommunications special tax	+++	++			
Advertisement tax	++	+	+++	++	+++
Special tax for retail chains	++	++	+++	+++	
Food chain supervision fee	+++	++	+++	+++	
Public utility tax	++	++		++	

5.10.2.2. Indirect special taxes

One also comes across "indirect special taxes" that companies are to pay not to the state, but to the consumer. This type of tax usually appears in the form of such depressed officially sanctioned prices that companies burdened with it are not only stripped of their profit, but also what would cover the costs of amortization and development. What is more, if the *forced administrative price* rate goes below the cost of operation, the measure must have a twofold objective: the exclusion of the company from the market, and to secure the votes of consumers served by the concerned companies. The most well matured logic of this kind could be found working in the *utility price cuts program*. While the "utility price war" in full swing since 2012 was the central campaign action for the coming parliamentary elections, it also served the purpose of bleeding the—largely foreign—owners and expelling them from the market. In this action the palpable gift (lowered utility bills) is visible even to the poorest, while the personified kindly caretaker (the government) is also clear. But for those who are not even capable of linking the two, the utility company issuing the bills has also been obliged to print the figures on the bills in highlighted type: advertising material delivered to three million homes on a monthly basis. Omissions in this regard have drawn hefty fines already. The logic of the market however raises obstacles to meeting such voluntarist requirements, and the costs of the taxes are passed on to the consumer along less dramatically perceivable by-ways. Yet the rise of costs elsewhere, or the decline in standards that appear in other areas are no longer personified, and their odium cannot be directed straight at the government. Were someone to try to do so, that would serve as another pretext to continue the thoroughly ideological national freedom fight against the "nation corrupting" actors of the economy, accruing further communications gains to the government. The final outcome of the action was legislation ensuring that utility services could only be provided further on by compulsorily nonprofit companies.

At the same time however, this also resulted in a trap: among the large gas providers EMFESZ went bankrupt, while GDF Suez, E.ON, and the Italian energy concern, ENI owned Tigáz, who were not willing to accept either the continuous losses or the roles of financial motors to the "utility price war" campaign returned their universal gas supplier license to the Hungarian Energy and Public Utility Regulatory Authority. Yet the necessities of the market acquiring nationalization have also brought the state-owned gas supplier Főgáz up against an insurmountable challenge: how to keep the consumer prices dictated by the "utility price war" lower than the actual expenditures incurred, while averting a downturn in quality of services and infrastructure. The only way this could be done would be if the direction of the money pump would change, and the losses would be continuously compensated from the budget. This, however, is prohibited by EU regulations. The consequences of this on the other hand may be that "with pressure from the energy authorities, government populism will have to be taken a few notches down."[111]

Similar government intentions can be observed in the market for electricity providers: "The company Elmű-Émász, directed by the German RWE is preparing to sell and hand over a number of its assets by the end of 2015, including the right to provide household electricity to the Hungarian state. According to the declaration of intent signed in May 2015 by the

Hungarian state and the German party, the electricity provider will hand over the right to universal electricity provision, which includes the household segment, to the First National Public Utility Ltd., will sell its customer service subsidiary, as well as 49-49 percent of its network operator. The latter umbrella subsidiary, Elmű Network Ltd. has lately announced in a company statement that it is decreasing its registered capital from 261 billion to 228 billion forints. The reasons for this may include the taxes on public utility pipelines imposed on network companies—both state and local government."[112]

Another form of indirect special tax was introduced on the demand of Fidesz's coalition partner, the Christian Democratic People's Party—insignificant in numbers to the extent that opinion polls are not able to estimate—that took the form of law after a long-drawn-out period of gestation in 2015, as the ***closure of shops on Sunday***. Only shops that have their owners or relatives serving at the counters and their premises cover less than 200 m² are exempted. This is another cunning way to cleanse the market and make room for crony Hungarian companies through state coercion. Critics of the action project a decrease in retail turnover, the layoff of employees in the tens of thousands, and a tax loophole of around 200–250 billion forint (600–800 million euro). Yet the measure affecting a large proportion of the volume of transactions in shops is not only likely to restrain economic growth, it also counts as an ideology-based, overbearing intervention in the lifestyles of citizens. The National Association of Entrepreneurs and Employers—sensing the widely felt antipathy for the government's suggestion "to attend church instead of shopping"—initiated a referendum on the matter, which the government tries to halt with all its procedural tricks.

5.10.3. State penalization of critical reactions called forth by special taxes

Efforts by companies to shift the cost of the diverse range of liabilities and special taxes onto the consumers gave government the occasion to bring further theatrical measures in the charade of protecting the people, and establish scores of institutions for autocratic political intervention in response. Among them are found the ***price commando***, a watchdog over the attempts of taxed multinationals to raise prices, ***wage and tax action teams***, to force private companies to compensate their employees for the drop in their incomes—resulting from the modifications to the personal income tax. Then the Government Control Office overruns the plundered pension funds in order to rob the remaining 60 thousand members—who withstood the blackmail tactics of the government—of their savings worth around 200 billion forint (600 million euro) in total. The more absurd the planned government action, and the less it can be fitted into any sort of market rationale, the more it takes on a moralizing-criminalizing character. Scapegoating and methodical character assassination—whether we are talking of an institution, or a person representing it—has become an organic part of governmental economic policy.

Some of the large commercial groups that have national or local monopoly—from the bank sector to public services—and consumers in Hungary (which means they cannot be moved abroad, exposed to be taxed by the political family through administrative prices or tributes), are being steered by the mafia state into its own holdings, or towards a takeover. On the other hand, where the market does work, the mafia state tries to artificially create a monopoly. This is how the organized upperworld acquires ownership and a secure income—through creation of monopolies, administrative price regimes, or guaranteed profits. While its ideology proclaims a labor-based society, in fact the revenues of the mafia state are based on the protection money it squeezes out of others.

5.10.4. The inverse of special taxes: strategic agreements and mutual benefits

Companies that can be forced to pay allowances are **made into tributaries, or eliminated and their place taken over,** while those that cannot be forced to pay allowances are offered **strategic agreements**: Audi, Coca-Cola, Daimler, GE, Microsoft, Richter, Samsung, Sanofi, Synergon, and so on.[113] Perhaps only Tesco is an exception to this rule, but it may so happen that while with one hand the government gives a "box on the ear," with the other it gently comforts. (Even churches or football clubs can be found among the strategic partners.) Much of what these partners produce is not sold on Hungarian markets, and so it is impossible to dictate an appropriate profit through laws, but at the same time they give jobs to Hungarians and pay taxes on their wages here. There is a limit to the patience of these companies: if the organized upperworld really gets on their nerves, they may simply move abroad, though the time such a decision takes to implement in a production-based company can be 4–5 years, until the given technology becomes outdated. They are not so easily blackmailed, and so the government makes partnership agreements with them. In their case the deal is based on mutual interests, and not bare force.

Péter Szijjártó, minister of foreign affairs and trade gave a statement in 2013, still as state secretary, to the effect that the number of strategic agreements could even rise to above 50, because *"the program has aroused the interest of corporations on account of the opportunity to regularly consult with government. This may give these companies a competitive edge within the corporate group when new sites for development are selected."* This speaks volumes. According to the anti-corruption website for investigative reporting, átlátszó.hu: "The closer ties were initiated by government on virtually each occasion, and most of the companies approached felt that this was an offer they could not refuse, or they would be left out of certain benefits, and perhaps even the axe of unorthodox legislation and tax regimes might descend on them. Word has it though, that in spite of this fear some companies were not afraid to show the government the door."[114] Government support for strategic partners can even be caught in action when the conditions for funding bids set.

5.11. Takeover—replacement of the economic elite

The regime change was what brought about by economic collapse within the communist bloc, which means that the economic crisis manifested in the demise of the eastern markets and a mass bankruptcy of state corporations was not the consequence, but cause of the change. Even if mass unemployment in the hundreds of thousands only came about after 1990, it revalued the careers, knowledge and skills gathered till then either positively or negatively. The regime change eliminated what had been until then, in the *Kádár-era, legitimate mechanisms of individual wellbeing* well expressed in the age-old Hungarian motto *"keep on scraping shorty, you'll get your share,"* at the same time the culture and consensual mechanism befitting a western value-system was not established, by means of which someone could acquire wealth and property in a legitimate way, which would be considered morally acceptable by others. This is why throughout the last two decades *political programs could be built on the wish for redistribution of wealth*.

Moreover, history has taken quite a few hectic turns from this point of view. Property relations in western countries developed through continuity over centuries, with the result that an established middle class could come about in an organic way. In contrast in eastern Europe, whole social groups have been stripped of their wealth on a number of occasions just over the past century—on racial or ethnic grounds, due to their social position or territorial changes—resorting them into new social classes, autocratically destroying and rearranging their means of eking out an existence.

The historical uncertainty of ownership relations never made it possible for a strong citizenry to take root in Hungary, with a sense of its property being safe through generations. The propertied classes have been upturned three times over the last century: on the first occasion it was the Hungarian population of territories who became citizens of successor states following World War One and the subsequent peace treaties, found themselves pushed out of their stable positions; then Hungarians of Jewish origin were robbed through the anti-Jewish laws and the Holocaust; and finally it was the communist regime that nationalized practically all private property. In each case the political forces carrying out these expropriations acted in the name of some sort of social justice. With these experiences Hungarian society learned socially to expect that the safety of property, and especially large property could be overwritten on account of other aims—based on higher principles.

This Hungarian historical tradition was not broken by the regime change, in fact it has become a not insignificant driving force behind political and social struggles, to see *who, starting from the egalitarian zero line, would become a billionaire, and who a beggar.* And in the *privatization that followed the regime change,* it was not merely the growing wealth of the new propertied class, but the way they acquired the money that particularly offended the sense of justice of those who lost out on the transformation. This opened the way for political trends whose aim, whether openly or in a hidden way, was to reshuffle the ownership situation. In Hungary, these political tendencies merged successfully with anticommunist rhetoric—aimed at the nomenclature that converted its political power to an economic one. With the electoral victory of Fidesz in the 2010 elections a turning point was also reached in this matter, because while the institutional system of liberal democracy and the balance of various political forces had kept the selfish instincts more or less, as far as possible within civilized boundaries, with the two-thirds of parliamentary seats the entry of the mafia state has by now opened a new chapter in this story, as concerns its very nature.

5.11.1. The alliance of Fidesz and the "Christian middle class"

Although most of the leaders of Fidesz did not come from a background of urban culture, they had western tastes, and they characterized themselves as "children of divorced parents" who would surmount the centuries long enmity of folk and urban culture, a traditional pest of Hungarian society. With their later march to the right of the political landscape though, taking up the space of the failing Hungarian right (Hungarian Democratic Forum and Smallholders Party)—they turned to a curious mix and match of folk ideology on the one hand, and the world of the Christian national middle class from between the world wars. But while the "folk classic" in its day— as György Konrád put it—promoted untouched peasant culture against the culture of the urban, secularized, independently employed intelligentsia, the anger of Fidesz's new folk culture is born of the suspicions and frustrations of the room-and-board college student, the child of ambitious small and middle communist cadre parents, harbored against the young successors of the liberal urban intelligentsia who had lived in Budapest for generations.

Fidesz was driven by the desire of the smallest boy to set off in search of the golden stock signifying wealth. The stock however could not be found anywhere, because the two evils, "commie" and "multi" had grabbed it first. In the course of his wanderings he met and married the historical, middle class Christian girl who had been stripped of her remaining wealth under communism, and had also been left out of the deals struck around the regime change. *He decided to serve the cause of justice being done to them, and get a hand on their fare share—whatever the cost.*

Fidesz could see very well how it was virtually a matter of course for those who had earlier been excluded from political power to attain it *in the course of the regime change*—through democratic elections—but the chance to get in on the privatizations was not open to everyone. The privatized state property partly landed with the former—largely depoliticized—manager elite (who used their political and network capital to gain control of the management and employee buyout programs) on the one hand, or foreign investors. Meanwhile the wealth that could be accumulated from privatizations of state property was depleting constantly. While a historical wisdom known to both the smallest boy and the middle class girl, according to which a marriage without fortune would be a short-lived affair. The only way to grab a fortune without state assets to be seized involved the redistribution of private fortunes—and solution quite impossible under the terms of the law.

While the Hungarian Democratic Forum was in government, and later in deals with the socialists the available fortunes were sizable, but the new owners were not granted significant economic influence to go with it. *In the first cycle of Fidesz government*, from 1998–2002 the few remaining state properties could be acquired even by companies short of capital with the help of loans—covered by state or state associated banks. Political contacts helped to buy them below the going rate. CD Hungary could be mentioned as an example, involved as it was in the privatization of the real estate fortunes of the diplomatic corps managed by the foreign ministry. The winning bid for the real estate holding came in at half the price of its actual value, from a crony company that had only 1 million forint (3,500 euro) in capital stock, and was able to get a loan to cover practically the whole price of the buy up—about 18 billion forint (60 million euro). The other way to build major corporations from naught was by winning mega-contracts—even as foreign competitors were swept off the field—though when the political support stopped, these companies became fragile. A leading example of this kind of company was Vegyépszer, that was not even able to fully exploit the opportunity offered by its political embeddedness in spite of all the government support helping it along, as it lacked a practiced corporate organization and culture. The first path, based on the wealth that could still be privatized was running out, while the second path, the establishment and operation of greenfield, party affiliated companies proved too rugged.

Moreover the strong two-thirds institutional checks constituted by the distribution of seats in parliament during the first cycle of Fidesz government managed more or less to keep the all-engulfing hunger for power within bounds, stalling attempts to replace the proprietary elite by powers of state. Though there were no inherent, moral constraints to the hunger for power and wealth even then, institutional ones still prevailed. It is nevertheless true that the governing political elite started an all out offensive with the full arsenal of state power, as a mafia state, to gain new positions and achieve a change of owners in certain segments of the economy, but these efforts of the time did not still aim for the total domination of whole sectors, aimed merely at getting hold of certain companies. The change of owners was explained by the Fidesz ideologist András Lánczi as follows: "It was clear until 2010, on the political right that the regime change was not yet complete. Between 2006 and 2010 a recognition had matured about the fact that the change of elite, which had been skirted, could not be avoided. Something had to be done about the way privatization had been run, a review was necessary. The deal after 1989–90, in which every position was held by post-communists or their liberal allies, in all fields, from politics, through the economy to culture, had to be upturned. If this was not going to happen, Viktor Orbán and the Hungarian right would once again only have an episodic role."[115]

5.11.2. The unique nature of property expropriation by the mafia state

The mafia state differs from other autocratic systems in its principles of wealth redistribution as well. The historical **south European corporative autocratic regimes** or the **Horthy regime** in Hungary did not replace the economic elite. The expropriation of Jewish fortunes formed an exception to this rule—which was not in fact carried out everywhere—but no new layer of owners was brought about, the plundered fortunes simply further enriched the existing Christian middle class. The expropriation of goods was *"normative" on racial grounds*, and not arbitrary on an individual, case-by-case basis. And on the other side, in **dictatorships of the Soviet type** all property was expropriated, so the loss of property was *"normative" on a class basis*. The elite formed there was purely of a political nature. Their remuneration—as discussed earlier—was not in wealth, but in better provisions: higher pay, better living circumstances, allocation of flats or holiday homes, the possibility of shopping in stores operated in a system closed to others, access to things in short supply and various other privileges. But however keenly these appeared as desirable advantages and privileges in the eyes of those who were not offered them, they could not result in the amassment of significant fortunes.

However, the situation is different *in the post-communist mafia state: expropriation of wealth is not normative, but arbitrarily incidental.* Anything that catches their fancy they will take. In a significant number of former Soviet republics people around the nomenclature, mainly party and secret service cadres gained positions of power, as well as being in a situation at the time of the privatizations that they could exploit to gather personal wealth. If independent businessmen did appear in the breaches of the privatization dumping, they were either integrated into the organized upperworld controlled politically, or if not, serious consequences were to follow: scores are settled in such societies of the wild east even with murder, though sometimes long prison sentences or—for the sake of international acceptance—the offender could get off lightly, with "voluntary" exile for the conflict with the powers that be.

5.11.3. A change of the owner elite and ensuring surrender

In the time elapsed since 2010 Fidesz has passed the phase of offensive tactics in its progress towards installing an autocratic establishment: with its two-thirds majority it overran the institutional system of liberal democracy and left it in shambles, eradicating autonomies. The lawless private violence typical of the organized underworld, the classical mafia was replaced in the mafia state by the legalized, bloodless coercion of public authorities, which, apart from preserving power in the hands of the adopted political family, also serves to increase its wealth. By now *the mafia state is redistributing wealth through the instruments of legalized robbery*. In parallel with a systematic replacement of the elite that had evolved in the phase of alternation of corrupt regimes, there is a central subordination and replacement of the economic elite being carried on with non-market tools of coercion, organized into the adopted political family's chain of command.

This is not the process of primitive accumulation of capital, because in that case a flow of capital takes place between a premodern and modern sector, or the agricultural and industrial sector accompanied by a change of owner. In the case of the mafia state however there is no momentum of modernization, only the controlled change of owners of already accumulated capital. Yet the new circle of proprietors do not become true businessmen, because in terms of their social function they are only exactors of tributes—empowered by the head of the family and fortified by political monopolies—who appear in the cloak of businessmen.

The mafia state forces private fortunes into its sphere of interest through tools of legalized state coercion, redistributing them within the circles of the adopted political family. It also differs from the "usual" forms of corruption, because in this instance apart from the illegitimate rechanneling of current revenues, there is also the forced redistribution of property/property rights underway.

The institutions of public authority participating *in the redistribution of private property through administrative coercion* and its redirection into the sphere of interest of the adopted political family are the parliament, the government, the tax authorities, the prosecutor's office, and the police. They join in various combinations to carry out the actions, which enable the transformation of the owner elite through the means of state coercion, from legislation that shows preference or discriminates certain businesses in a targeted fashion, to tax office exemptions or the opposite, harassment, and even politically ordered selective law enforcement by the prosecutor's office and the police. The inventory of tools for upsetting stable ownership shows a wide range: from punitive taxation to removal from the market through legal means, or from nationalization to threats issued through public authorities in support of a buy-out bid by a preferred company. To dodge the competition law a legal provision for "national strategic significance" was developed, which exempts the buyer of either state or private companies from investigation by the Office of Economic Competition (i.e., whether the merger is or is not a threat to competition). If potential target companies for takeover would like to avoid coming into the sights or influence of predatory eyes, they would either hide their incomes and send them to safe havens outside the country, or would piece apart their successful businesses and resettle certain parts abroad.

5.11.4. The offer that could not be refused

The prototype of the **partial replacement of the economic elite** could be encountered even in the first period of Fidesz government (1998–2002).

One example is the renationalization and then re-privatization to friends of the formerly state owned, then privatized pawn-store chain, BÁV Rt., which was pressured through by blackmail with the assistance of the tax authorities, the police and the Hungarian Development Bank. The tax authorities visited a variety of businesses owned by the proprietor of BÁV Rt. unwilling to sell his company, the police conducted night raids at a hotel owned by the same person, until he understood that all of his businesses could be destroyed. Since the buyer representing the political family did not at the time have enough capital to purchase BÁV Rt., the Hungarian Development Bank bought it up, so it could then re-privatize it to the preferred new owner at the appropriate price, granting a loan on friendly terms to go along with it. There was naturally no benefit to the state in the whole deal. The state only played the role of the "brutal enforcer" and "involuntary creditor."

Another large-scale action—that was left incomplete—was an attempt to plunder a branch of the business interests of MOL, the leading Hungarian oil and gas company. In this case the state forced the gas branch of MOL into a lengthy period of only losses by imposing administrative retail prices. In response to its complaints the company was told, if they could not handle it, the state would be happy to take over the business. That would have been followed by a re-privatization to people to cronies— the process would have been greased with the aid of a large loan from the Hungarian Development Bank. Had the deal been accomplished, the prices would surely have been let to raise again. The transaction only fell through in the end, because of the electoral defeat of Fidesz in 2002.

After 2010 reinforcement of the "new Hungarian middle class" fell into place with fairy tale-like ease, in harmony with the development of the new layer of propertied individuals around Fidesz, and to a degree also reaching into the world of politics. In order for an offer of takeover by the organized upperworld to be an offer that could not be refused it must bear at least *four potential threats*: (1) unlimited command of legislative authority, (2) a secret service, prosecution office and police loyal to the head of the political family, (3) tax authorities willing to carry out the politically selective actions, and (4) complete control of state procurements and EU funding bids. *This is what makes the offers by the mafia state, though bloodless*—in a quasi legal fashion—*still effective*.

The most important technique in the repertoire of expropriations is the *takeover*, either by state transmission, or directly. In such cases, rather than excluding private businesses and building up their own new business in its place, the organized upperworld takes over existing companies by coercive means. Later research may give more exact data about the scale of changes in the ownership of profit-making market leader businesses, the deliberate and centrally directed change of elite.

5.11.4.1. Ways of looting individual owners

An offer that could not be refused may be directed at the partial or complete takeover of a company at the market price, its price by the account books, or even for free, depending on the level of cooperation shown by the owner or their personal blackmailability, and the likelihood of the state being able to block the activities of the company. If the owner is *Hungarian, and not a member of the adopted political family*, threats from the state enforcement apparatus may in itself be convincing enough. The regular tool in this case is also the **takeover**, not bothering with the building of new companies—as in the first term of Fidesz government. Instead, the existing ones are taken over, the owners blackmailed to hand over or sell part or whole of their companies. But of course they can offer a price so convincing that the phase of nationalization—which is difficult to justify—can also be left out, and the company can go straight into possession of a member of the organized upperworld. This is especially frequent in the case of companies that have the right infrastructure, expertise, and capacities to draw EU funds and large state orders effectively, and where time is of the essence. The choice of which way to go about it, depends on the balance of forces and how prone the business is to blackmail. In the case of foreign-owned companies the price paid from public coffers can even exceed market value of the purchase, as in the case of the shares of the Hungarian oil company MOL that were in Russian hands, or the gas stores of the German E.ON. In other instances an unhindered pullout is offered in exchange for the property, on other occasions again the big guns of legislation are leveled at the stubborn business owner. As in Las Vegas, when the mafia makes an offer for a casino... Except in Hungary, neither the severed head of a horse placed in the bed nor the barrel of a gun has to be faced by the victim—this is not the style of the mafia state, there is simply no need. No corpses to see on the street. *In the mafia state the musclemen collecting the cash are replaced by the repurposed parliament, tax authorities and prosecutor's office.*

In case of resistance from the owner, the parliament can be mobilized to eliminate the unacquirable business from the market with the proposal of a quick amendment. Individual cases of such initiatives—comprising the illegitimate actions of public authorities—are highly revealing as regards the nature and mechanisms of this sort of coercion from the mafia state. This is the organized upperworld, where the seemingly independent actions of different institutions of public authority are strung onto a single thread of one or other illegitimate "project" under the political family.

- The owner of a **company for open air advertisement, ESMA**—who incidentally sympathized with liberal and left wing political forces—was not willing to "sell" the company with the rights to advertising on lamp posts along the streets of Budapest to one of the adopted political family's chief oligarchs, in spite of a government request. The response was not long in coming: the men of the tax authority appeared at the companies of the owner. Since this had not been persuasive enough to seal the "deal," the parliament passed a motion by a Fidesz MP within the following weeks that prohibited all advertising on pedestrian sidewalks within 5 meters of the road, on grounds of road safety. The field of ESMA's operation was basically banned with this action of parliament, its value cut down to nothing. It was however somewhat of a problem that the ban also applied to the advertising boards of the company MAHIR, which was supposed to have been favored by the takeover. Finally, with the aid of a motion by another Fidesz MP an amendment was made to the law, exempting the latter company from the prohibition. Then after a few years of unwelcome respite and corporate decay, the company was bought by the new favorite oligarch and stooge of the godfather, István Garancsi, because as a result of the Orbán-Simicska war, the adopted political family had to establish its own open air advertising surfaces to compete with those that belong to the oligarch disgraced in the meantime. In the aftermath it comes as no surprise that in June of 2015 the parliament wiped out the passage of law with the ban used to eliminate the original owner of ESMA from the market, with a paragraph hidden in the budget Act.

• Using an industrial-environmental catastrophe, the breach of the red sludge dam of the **Hungarian Aluminium Production and Trade Company** (MAL Rt.) as an excuse, the parliament accepted with great urgency an amendment by means of which almost any type of company could be brought under state supervision for any length of time including the management rights if an emergency situation is cited.

• On lower levels **decrees, rulings by municipal and other authorities may mean the threat backed up by public force**. For example, a permit for the use of public space may be withheld until the offer for change of ownership is accepted. This is what happened in the case of the so-called **National Gallop**, a horse race and festival held annually since 2008. The municipal authorities of Budapest were in charge of issuing the permit for use of the site of this three-day event—drawing a crowd in the hundreds of thousands, and managing about a hundred jockeys, each entered by municipalities—a representative, historic and symbolic square in Budapest. After the Fidesz victory in 2010, and the municipal elections following in the autumn, the National Gallop did not get a public space permit until the company that held the rights to the event and managed it was not sold to the—coach driving champion—Lázár brothers, devoted followers of the government. Because of the delay created by the process of "persuasion," rather than the usual May-June date of the event, it could only be held in the autumn. The Lázár brothers are also part owners of the CBA "national" food chain store, which has been favored by the government in a variety of ways. In 2013, CBA called upon its employees to participate in the above mentioned loyalty demonstrating Peace March in a letter, citing the following grounds: "It is important that all of us, true patriots with a sense of national pride, support our own most exceptional Hungarian politician, Viktor Orbán. [...] since only united can we set a limit to, and categorically refuse the tricks of the post-communist, liberal scoundrels who have turned traitor to our country on every occasion possible, and serve the interests of foreign multinationals."[116] Naturally the forced change of ownership also opened the gates to growth in state sponsorship and support to the galloping festival.

- But depending on the nature of each acquisition the various elements of blackmail through public authorities can be mixed—like in a cocktail—to suite the occasion. Let us take the example of the *freely distributed daily, the* **Metropol** founded in 1998, and producing runs of 400 thousand copies. The newspaper owned by a foreign interest was kept up from private and state, or municipal advertisements, and distributed in public areas in Budapest, especially underground passages and entrances to metro stations. If the advertisements from the public sphere are frozen and the private advertisers are scared off, and maybe even the distribution in public areas under municipal control and the stations under the Budapest Transport Company is legally blocked, the profit-making venture will soon only make losses, and lose value. This message was clear to the owners when they received an offer for purchase from a member of the circle around the top oligarch of the time, Lajos Simicska, in 2011.[117] Since the owners were foreign, in order to avoid diplomatic conflicts the deal for change of ownership—though not voluntary—was priced at market value.

- The majority shares of a *leading Hungarian company for overground construction*, doing well in terms of market competition, called *Market Építő Zrt.* was owned by a company called Wing Zrt., belonging to the Wallis Group. István Garancsi, Viktor Orbán's latest oligarch and stooge favored in opposition to Lajos Simicska made an offer for the shares of Market Zrt. owned by Wing Zrt. The seriousness of the offer was underscored by heightened investigations by the tax authorities targeting Wallis Group. It was important to secure the company not only because of the string of developments to be channeled to the company, but also because the projects were to be overpriced. The profit must not flow to the wrong place. The deal was finally struck. An amount was even paid for the shares of the company.[118] It is of course a question, how the market value of sold goods can be established in such circumstances. A transaction impelled by means of coercion from public authorities can only be called a "sale" with limitations, since the expression assumes a voluntary decision, which is not the case—neither here, nor in other similar deals. Establishing the "market value" of the shares is just as difficult, because the market of investments in development is not operating by the rules of competition based on performance, but is determined by political network capital. The value of the majority shares of Market Zrt. will be different if a significant portion of real estate development investments by the state and the EU are deliberately channeled to it in the future. Of course this can only take place if the ownership of the company is transferred to the political family, and even within the family to the right people. Its value is quite different again if in addition to private developments, the state contracts over the last few years are taken into consideration. However, the offer of purchase actually indicated that the situation could not be maintained in the then current ownership structure. The value of the company would naturally be different again, if the state consciously turned its back to the returning clients of the company, but did not wish to "scare them off." If an owner refusing the offer then becomes the target for complete destruction, the value of the company, which would have to be categorized in the prohibited zone for private investors as well, will be a different matter. Having taken account of the actual room for maneuver the previous owner finally sold the majority share held by Market Zrt. to the new favorite oligarch at a depressed price. Perhaps in return the remaining interests of Wallis will not be harassed further. (Another overground construction company, the Magyar Építő Zrt. was bought up—as previously mentioned—for similar reasons, using similar techniques.)

The few examples above were only meant to give a sense of the wide variety of **single cases in company ownership changes enforced with state** *pressure*, the means depending on the type and size of the company, the reason for the change of ownership, etc. Though the proclaimed ideology is to establish a "national middle class," it is clear that the changes of ownership are not being carried out along the foreign-Hungarian axis, but along the cleavage between those inside the adopted political family and those outside. For if the interests of the political family so demand it, they have no qualms about robbing fellow Hungarians of their property, or a part of it. Not even the support of the Fidesz membership, the party, or sympathy with Fidesz means any protection if the interests of the higher regions of the political family require the plunder of a company.

In cases requiring forced changes in ownership the prosecutor's office, tax authorities, the Government Control Office or any other overseeing authority may be mobilized. Any one of them is capable of completely shutting down a business. And since a significant segment of businessmen are also at home in the grey zone of the economy—if only on account of the particulars of eastern European social development after the regime change—they can be caught out, or blackmailed to various degrees. The legal retaliations that can be applied to them can stretch from fines to imprisonment. Thus the mentioned ***politically motivated, prescribed selective inquiry shown by state apparatus ensures all reasons necessary to persuade*** the party who shies away from the deal, so the deal can be finalized.

The online news portal *Civilhetes* states the following as a commonplace notion among the populace. "Businessmen familiar with economic life in Hungary say that Fidesz has gained control of three to four hundred private companies by force and blackmail since it came to power. Though the media is largely occupied with details of the tribulations caused to banks and public utility service providers in foreign hands, meanwhile, in the background, an alarming phenomenon has descended upon the world of business activities, as the owners of prospering Hungarian businesses are approached by lawyers claiming affiliation to Fidesz, making an offer for the purchase of the company at a fraction of its real value, achieved often at the cost of decades of hard work. The stealing of these companies, structurally supported by the authorities can already mean a threat to family businesses with a turnover of a few hundred million forint, any downtown restaurant and better visited hotel among them. If the owner does not wish to give up their business with a major loss, the authorities soon make an appearance and make it impossible to manage with various measures. Whether the offer is accepted is only a matter of time. Often even the original price offered is not kept when the owner is seen to crumble under pressure, for the buyers claim that the means of persuasion also had a cost."[119]

There is clearly a wide range of solutions for securing acquisitions: some owners are paradoxically able to increase their income after losing a share of their company due to the state contracts and bids that are guaranteed by the new (co-)owner who is a member of the political family. Others are paid at market value or below that, but can keep their other interests. Yet others are obliged to give up their property or a part of it in exchange for a chance to avoid being criminalized by the authorities. And since football must be loved under the new regime, some will have to adopt a football team as well. Who can tell whether this is a gift or punishment? The operational channels between business and politics are kept vital through the eager activity of the prosecutor's office and the tax authorities. The arbitrary, political selection between those who can be rightly accused of corruption and the example of those who are defamed with the accusation on no basis, only further strengthen the readiness for the *"national cooperation" between the organized upperworld and the players of the economy*.

5.11.4.2. Ways of looting economic branches, networks and groups of owners

A particularly effective way of redistributing wealth is tendering rental or concessional rights of certain business activities, or simply turning them into concessions.

- Observe an example of this in the case of the *state agricultural land leases*, when a multitude of people professionally engaged in agriculture were robbed of their hoped for future property, even as the properties they had worked were delivered into the hands of others who, in vast majority, were not of the given neighborhood or profession. Moreover it was generally known that many of them would only take EU allowances after the land they had been given, making an income on it without any input of either expertise or material.

  According to József Ángyán, resigned state secretary for the ministry of rural development under the Fidesz government between 2010–2014, the level of established corruption is such that "it is no longer a state official or decision-maker who is bought off, but the given interest group—functioning the way a mafia family would—that places their own man in the legislative or government decision-making position with the task of handling the affairs of the family."[120] He continues: "Where larger, and still larger public funds still remain to be plundered, or blocks of public property to be shoveled off, they place, in addition to their man, a handler of the sort we have learned about from the secret services. He is the one who keeps in touch with the godfather, conveying the orders, often whole decrees or draft laws, and carrying information back. While in the case of a state that functions normally it is the government institutions that operate network structures, when it comes to the state captured by bands of robbers it is the mafia networks that operate the government institutions."[121] In his opinion, the simplest way of building fortunes in the present system is to get hold of the development support resources meant for agriculture—this is what provides the backdrop to the government manipulation with agricultural land leases.[122] At any rate, these suggestions are confirmed by the fact that the greatest beneficiaries of the dynamically broadening array of agricultural support funds are—once again—the oligarchs (See Annex 4).

Meanwhile, in June 2015, the government passed an amendment to the law in order to ensure that the family circle that has become leaseholder to the state land by these nepotistic means can gain their ownership as soon as possible. A farmer in Fejér County put his finger on the heart of the matter when he pointed out that the local farmers "found it hard to swallow even the results of the strangely controlled land lease tenders, as the government had taken away the opportunity of farming from a whole generation by handing the leases to people who had nothing to do with the given locality or its agriculture. If the lease hold is converted to ownership, the ban that would last for a generation would remain permanently in place: people not only in a few villages, but over whole regions stretching across counties will have to renounce revenues from agriculture for people living locally, all they can have to do with lands around them would be as day laborers."[123]

This did not take long: the state has announced its intentions to deliver 400 thousand hectares of state-owned land into private hands at a fast pace from the end of 2015 onwards. And though according to the original plans only local residents professionally involved in agriculture would be allowed to place bids at the land auctions, this rule was diluted by a stipulation that people who have completed a specific course in agricultural management, "Aranykalászos gazdatanfolyam"

(Golden stalk agricultural management course) can also place bids. It is no surprise that relatives of politicians have secured such a certificate in large numbers, since it is a means to acquiring further fortunes. The auctions begin with the lands leased to the Simicska-Nyerges joint oligarchy, which will be a symbolic indication of whether an oligarch disinherited by the Godfather can secure state owned property.

Another amendment introduced in November 2015 also makes it possible in cases where anyone other than the leaseholder acquires the land, for the owner to raise the rent periodically, in spite of the valid lease contract.

In other cases the redistribution is not about possession of property itself, but a position from which tributes can be extracted, when the state taps the private sector under a second tax regime. But since according to the rationale of the system *the political family must be built, extended and fed on the middle and low levels as well*, always new segments in areas that were formerly operated sector-neutrally by the market, have to be occupied and repositioned as direct state tribute exactors of sorts.

- This is what happened in the case of the rights to sell tobacco products, in the case of the so-called *tobacco shop concessions*, when for the first time, on false health protection grounds—state monopoly was imposed on the retail of tobacco products, and once the previous small shop owners had been driven out of their means of making a living, the new clientele were provided higher profitability through legislative means. At the same time—having been stripped of their right to sell tobacco products, and so their businesses devalued—tens of thousands of rural, small food and newspaper shop owners and other small property holders were ruined. Altogether about thirty thousand shops were stripped of their right to sell tobacco products. In this case the mafia family had appeared in all of its organized structure and candid self-assurance. When it came to the distribution of large fortunes the deals between a counted number of actors took place behind closed— at times government—doors. In contrast, the tobacco shop concessions were run past the whole network of the adopted political family, reviewed by Fidesz-led municipalities and the rest of the government clientele. "Basically what is important is that the people chosen must be committed to the political right, [...] so the socialists don't win," said the Fidesz mayor of Szekszárd at the meeting where he and the Fidesz councilors reviewed the list of those applying for the tobacco shop concessions.[124]

The case of tobacco shop concessions is a great demonstration of what typifies the mafia state, in part because this is not classic corruption, where many independent, small cases of corruption are carried through within the large application procedure in a decentralized and unsynchronized way, but to the contrary: as centrally planned by the adopted political family, a group of people are divested of their property—i.e., a concessionary right—legalized by a parliamentary amendment of law, and then comes the centrally directed robbery by selection of the new owners who belong to the family. The first phase of the process is also an example of market-acquiring nationalization, when it is not the property itself, the shop that is taken away, but the right to sell a range of products there. Obviously the case of the tobacco shop concession is not a bunch of individual "scams," but the coordinated functioning of the mafia state, which only aimed in small part to satiate the oligarchs of the adopted political family, largely being aimed towards its "small shareholders." Before the rearrangement of the retail market of tobacco products the guaranteed trading margin was 3 percent. The new law had already stipulated the margin at 4 percent, and following the manipulated selection process the parliament raised this to 10 percent with another amendment. While the annual profit margin in comparison to the invested capital for shops only selling cigarettes and tobacco products moved between 10–20 percent until the redistribution of the concessions ratio, the profit rose to 90 percent in 2014, after the reorganization of the market through government intervention.[125] In other words, the revenue generated from raising the levies on tobacco products—contradicting the declared ideological aims—is not directed into the health care system or prevention programs, but ensures the profitability of shops granted by the state to the lower ranks of the adopted political family. This guaranteed deal did not even serve the kind of social goals that go back to the praxis between the wars, when the state supported disabled war-veterans, war-widows, or war-orphans from the income of these concession rights. Of the 5,415 winning bids only 280 went to people with disabilities.[126] But the action did not leave the small food and convenience stores, especially in villages undisturbed, every twentieth had to shut

down in 2014—due to the major decrease in income, deprived from
the right to sell tobacco.[127]

The redistribution of tobacco retail rights was followed by the
nationalization of the wholesale rights as well. János Bencsik, a Fidesz
MP disciplinarily penalized with a fine of 300 thousand forint (1,000
euro) for his vote against the amendment gave a statement about
this, as follows: "I would have very much liked to show my support
for the third tobacco Act with my vote. It hung on very little. All that
it would have required was for the tobacco trade to become a state
monopoly indeed, and the profit it generates to serve the greater
good. The version now accepted however offers the possibility for
the state to pass on these rights, now in its possession, to a private
company without a tender for bids. The legal formula I am against
promotes the possibility of hunting for allowances. The hunting of
allowances meaning, in a nutshell, when rather than producing value
a given social-economic actor invests its resources in excluding other
actors from certain market opportunities with the cooperation of the
state."[128] Prophetic words, for indeed, "without a public tender, as the
only applicant, British American Tobacco and Continental Group
owned Tabán Trafik Zrt. were given the exclusive right to wholesale
of tobacco by the government. The co-owned business of these two
companies, shortly to be registered, will be supplying tobacco to all of
the 6,300 Hungarian tobacco stores. [...] To our inquiry about why a
public tender was not arranged for the state monopoly, [János] Lázár
[minister for the Prime Minister's Office] replied that: in the case of
public funds it is indeed usual to call for bids, however in this case
'there is no call for bids, because there are no public funds involved,'
showing ministerial largess in overlooking the matter of a fee for the
concession. [...] The success of Continental did not cause any surprise
among market observers. The company from Hódmezővásárhely,
with strong ties to the network around the governing party was
not only one of the big winners of the tobacco shop tenders, but
as a result of a small technical glitch it had also been revealed that
earlier it had even participated in drafting the tobacco concessions
law."[129] Meanwhile, "market experts estimate the expected profits
of the 'national tobacco distributor' to come to between 5–12 billion
forint (16–39 million euro), as it will not have competitors, and the
government majority has even granted it exemption from local busi-

ness tax. Meanwhile the concession fee is ridiculous: this year the co-owned company will have to pay 10 million forint (32,000 euro), and in the following year a 100 million forint (3,200,000 euro), while the concession fee of 600 million forint annually, which still seems symbolic compared to the fantastic deal they are getting, will only be expected from 2021 onwards."[130] At the same time the companies given monopolies on supplying the tobacco shops, all closely tied to the family, try to charge large rival companies overly high rates for delivery. In fact they try to make them pay "protection money." If they refuse, they are unable to deliver their merchandise to the tobacco shops, which once again serves to boost the earnings of the two companies who have the concessions for wholesale and can deliver their goods for retail without any obstacles. (In parallel to the foregoing, the CEO of the state beneficiary Continental Tobacco Corporation, János Sánta—presumably upon request—has bought a 49 percent share of the publisher of the new pro-government daily, *Napi gazdaság*. "With his entry, a new media empire presumably more loyal to János Lázár is beginning to take shape, while Árpád Habony, chief councilor to the prime minister continues to build his own separate unit, the Modern Media Group, which *seeks to occupy* the field of tabloids and online content,"[131] so these can challenge Lajos Simicska's media empire.)

After the revenues of tobacco trade have been diverted to the family network—when the situation seems propitious—under the cloak of some general health related ideology they can proceed along the same lines with trade in alcohol and medicine.

- And since the autocratic system under study has been defined as a mafia state, it is only appropriate to illustrate the mechanism of change of ownership carried out by state coercion on the example of slot machines and casinos. The operation of the **slot machines** (the one-armed bandits) generating a tax revenue worth somewhere around 70 billion forint (230 million euro) was overseen on behalf of the authorities by the state-owned Szerencsejáték Zrt. It is worth examining the rearrangement of this branch of business step-by-step, as it was integrated into the political family's circle of interests:

Step one: The reregulation of the operation of slot machines primarily placed in catering industry premises took place in 2011, when the monthly tax per machine was raised from 100 thousand forint (330 euro) to five times that amount with an unexpected amendment motion in the parliament, and the operators were obliged to change their existing machines to server-based machines by October 2012. As a result of the measure, the operators handed in 60 percent of the slot machines within a month of the amendment being passed.[132] Their numbers decreased further over the next year: from 22 thousand to 2 thousand.[133]

Step two: In October 2012 the operation of slot machines, as well as game rooms and electronic casinos was banned by means of an amendment pushed through parliament in the matter of a couple of days, only casinos were exempt, and allowed to continue operating them. The ban also affected the approximately one thousand businesses that had invested in the server-based slot machines in line with the amendment that had been introduced a year earlier. For according to the government "the earlier measures had only achieved their objective in part, trying to ensure that those who lived in the most disadvantaged situations did not dump their money into slot machines, while on the other hand, serious national security risks had also been raised in regard to the activities of those with interests in the gaming-industry."[134] Government intended to make up for some of the losses in tax revenue that followed from these actions by taxing online gambling.

Step three: The casinos were exempted from the ban on operation of slot machines, and the maximum number of machines that could be installed in one premise was set at 300. Then in 2013, the maximum number of casinos that could be operated in the country was set at 11.

Step four: "Amending the law on gambling in the middle of November 2013, parliament decided that the minister for national economy could sign concession contracts for the operation of at most five casinos without making a public tender, but taking an exceptionally high concession fee, with those contractors whom he considers reliable. [...] The other important change in the November amendment was that the gaming managers could deduct the amount of the concession fee from the tax on the games. The Las Vegas Casino, one of Andy Vajna's interests is best served by this change: thanks to the amendment he can pay 1.6 billion forint less to the state budget. In 2012 the Las Vegas Casino had paid 1.1 billion forint in gambling taxes at a rate of 30% on the net income of 3.8 billion forint, as well as 791 million forint as fee for the concession. Thus altogether 1.9 billion forint was paid to the state. According to the new regulations they should only have to pay about 300 million forint in taxes."[135]

Step five: In May 2014, of the 11 casino concessions that can be issued, five in Budapest were granted by the ministry for national economy to Andy Vajna's Las Vegas Casino Kft., while two were issued to Gábor Szima's Aranybónusz 2000 Kft. for the eastern Hungarian cities of Debrecen and Nyíregyháza. All of these were issued in spite of the fact that the state-owned Szerencsejáték Zrt. had also applied for the casino operator concessions. It seems they had proved less "reliable." As previously recounted, Andy Vajna, the former film producer is the government commissioner who disposes with the state support for the production of Hungarian films, and a close confidant of Viktor Orbán. Gábor Szima on the other hand, had been involved in the gambling business earlier, he once owned the Debrecen football team, his role with the team now filled by his son. "According to the ministry of national economy they will pay 4 billion forint in concession fees and 1 billion forint in VAT towards the state budget."[136]

Step six: Yet parliament, in parallel to distributing the casino concession, made it possible for the casino owners to deduct the concessions fee from the gaming tax, and even made it VAT exempt.[137]

Step seven: "With the involvement of Andy Vajna and Gábor Szima, the large international companies operating online casinos and card game websites—such as PokerStars or Bet365—can legalize their presence in Hungary. This opportunity is made available to the businessmen close to the government by the amendment, which was handed in by the cabinet to parliament as part of the omnibus bill on changes to the tax regulations for the following year. One item of the proposal would make it possible for the concession fee that is to be paid on the gambling games, to be paid by someone other than the owner of the concession—a third party. This makes it possible to pay the fee from a foreign, perhaps offshore type of company, out of funds whose origin is not clean for example, and on top of this the owner of the permit is still allowed to deduct it from the gambling tax to be paid to the budget accounts. Furthermore, according to the proposal, online card game websites and casinos can only be operated by people who have Hungarian concession for the operation of casinos— i.e., currently Vajna and Szima."[138]

Step eight: The taxes paid by the casinos owned by Andy Vajna and Gábor Szima—unlike tax regulations on retail units—"are based on self-declarations, because the National Tax and Customs Administration of Hungary does not really have an overview of the slot machines. On the one hand, the integrated online inspection device of the tax authorities was not fitted into these slot machines, which would have collected and recorded the data created in the course of its operation, and secondly there is no mention of the server-based network. So in this age of online cash registers the state is completely in the dark where the income of casinos is concerned."[139] While "various parties involved in this industry estimate that the income generated at Andy Vajna's five casinos in the capital should be around 15 billion forint."[140]

Step nine: All that is left is to launch the legislatively guaranteed money laundering machine called the Stability Savings Accounts which enables poligarchs, oligarchs and stooges to deposit disposable laundered funds under state protection.

This is how the adopted political family of the mafia state manages gambling and acquires casinos: expulsion, establishing monopoly, favoring friends in concessions, special tax benefits, state supported money laundering. And not a drop of blood has been spilled.

In the course of reorganizing leaseholders of state agricultural land, many former lease holders are stripped of their main means of living, and the areas that had been tilled by these people are handed over to a number of others. Though in their case the number of lease holders also decreases, it does not do so drastically. In the case of the tobacco retail stores, the number of new concession holders falls to a fraction of the numbers who had sold tobacco previously, but the number of winners is nevertheless in the thousands. Especially if compared with the many losers and couple of winners of the right to operate the "one armed bandits."

Yet the case of the land leases, the tobacco stores and the casinos is not a singular phenomenon of these times: the political, economic and communications networks that weave through society like parallel "vital blood and nervous systems" with the multiplicity of different genres and functions they represent are being scrupulously assessed for further structured integration into the realm of the adopted political family. Including the financial and bank sectors, the sphere of media and infocommunications, the networks of public utility services which normally have local monopolies, and the list of vital networks only continues, each ready to be tapped for some more resources to be utilized in building a privileged, closely tied, and well paid group within the patron-client system of the regime. But these significant sets of properties are too large for simple acquisition by the political family. For their partial or complete takeover the political supervision of the market of state commissions is not enough. In their case either a state monopoly has to be created through legislative means, or an expulsion of the previous owners and transfer of the property using public funds by way of an interpolated nationalization.

Naturally, the plunder of private property and its diversion into the channels of the political family, when claiming legitimacy rely on a fake anti-market ideology that stigmatizes the victimized entrepreneurs as speculative profit-hunters. Mainly it's the nation that forms that emotional community, whose interests the mafia state pleads when it loots properties of the greatest possible variety. Its primary and ideologically most easily legitimated instrument of takeover however, is nationalization.

5.11.5. Types of nationalization defined by function

Nationalization, as practiced in the mafia state—expropriation of private property through instruments of public authority—is in its function fundamentally different from both its practice in state capitalism, and the communist command economy, which was based on state monopoly of property. In state capitalism, though non-economic objectives also appear among the motivating forces of the regime, the operation of the nationalized property nevertheless fits into the rationale of the market. In communist regimes on the other hand, the whole of the economy is operated in an irrevocable and homogeneous way under the ownership of the state—and the dominance of politics. In the mafia state however, nationalization simultaneously serves to increase the wealth of the adopted political family, provide regulated remuneration for those built into its chain of command, and to keep society in check.

It seems pointless to try to explain the government's pursuit and practice of nationalization by the declared causes and objectives by Fidesz, or its faith in the greater effectiveness of state property. It is also pointless to offer a critique by contending that state property is less effective, unwilling all the while to take note of the actual aims and functions of nationalization under Fidesz. For it is obvious from the following listing of main forms and functions emerging in the way these nationalizations are carried out that they show no connection whatsoever with the interests of the national economy:[141]

1. *Cold nationalization, nationalization of certain market elements of the economic environment*: the state expropriates the market environs of a given economic sector without directly nationalizing the businesses involved in it. Tools involved:
   - state authority determining prices (utility price cuts);
   - special taxes (bank tax, advertisement tax);
   - regulation/restriction of field of activity through decrees (plaza stop);
   - stipulations with regard to the operator of the business (e.g., from 2017 the majority share of the business operating a pharmacy has to be in the possession of the pharmacist or the state);
   - consumers are prescribed compulsory suppliers/service providers (e.g., schools are prescribed a particular state school book, the predetermination of where catering benefits for employees can be used, appointment of where Baby Savings Accounts newborns receive can be opened; or for example MTI's—the Hungarian news agency—circle of responsibilities were extended, so that it not only produces news items, but exclusive rights to producing news programs for public media providers).

   These measures—serving to bleed owners of businesses dry, to prepare permanent or transit nationalization of a business, to ensure the subordination of the players in the sector—personalize and impose a politically directed chain of command on market relations that are otherwise, on the whole, typified by impersonal connections and economic determinations. Cold nationalization does not necessarily turn into permanent nationalization or transit nationalization, but carries the potential of many ways to make the businesses pay tributes. In addition it is also a phenomenon accompanying the extension of the orbit of the adopted political family over economic positions, and the wealth accumulation within the organized upperworld. As the remaining set of state property capable of being privatized is meager the classical techniques of privatization do not apply any longer for the political family.

2. *Bandit nationalization, the nationalization of private assets:*
   - ➤ *one-time* action carried out with state threats, deception, and robbery using legislative means (this is how—as mentioned earlier—over 3,000 billion forint (10 billion euro) savings belonging to private pension fund members was taken away; but the nationalization of the sports establishments of ELTE university might also be cited);
   - ➤ the *constant*, continued taxation of already taxed revenues (banking transaction tax, copyright dues partially taken away from the collecting agency Artisjus, which is entrusted with managing them).

3. *Market acquiring nationalization, the nationalization of an economic activity or the right to it:* in this case the state does not strip the owners of businesses of their property directly, but monopolizes the economic activity by
   - ➤ either making the continuation of an activity *conditional on a concession* and redistributes those (as in the case of tobacco retail);
   - ➤ or when *only companies in state or municipal possession* are permitted to carry on certain activities (such as local public transport, water management, waste management, metal trade; or when the online communications within government and administration are transferred to the state owned Hungarian Electricity Company from German owned Magyar Telekom since 2012; also the state takeover—by way of a special law—of the underground facilities of strategic gas reserves and the right to construct them in the future, as well as the state's right of preemption in the case of already existing reserves; private companies that write bids for funding can no longer be commissioned by the state since 2014; in the case of developments undertaken from EU funds only state architect offices can design schools, hospitals, and anything that will belong to the state);
   - ➤ or a given activity is *made the sole province of a newly established state company* (e.g., state monopolies made out of managing highway tolls, the cellphone purchase of all travel tickets, parking,

and any service provided by a company whose shares are even partially held by a municipality or the state);

➤ or a given economic activity is *channeled to the state* (e.g., the state will handle the Baby Savings Accounts and the Start Accounts instead of commercial banks, with a separate type of bond grounded for these; but even weather forecasts, the gathering of meteorological data will be the sole task of the state, which does not pay for the analyses provided by the private meteorological companies).

4. *Competency nationalization, central appropriation of municipal responsibilities*, as a result of which a given economic activity or responsibility is diverted to a central state organization (nationalization of Budapest municipal public utility providers; nationalization of the municipal hospitals and hospitals delivered by the municipalities into the care of trustees, along with the outpatient treatment systems integrated with them; childcare institutions and homes for disabled, psychiatric patients and addicts maintained by the municipalities were also delivered into the hands of the state; the professional municipal firemen's brigades became the national fire brigade; as did the properties of the county governments as well as the institutional systems of health care and education). But the state can take over the local government entitlements through "market" means as well: "the public service of waste disposal can only be carried out by a company with a majority of its shares held by the state or the local government; these companies in public possession have been made loss-making by the introduction of new taxes; if public services go into an impasse, the disaster management authorities can appoint a new required provider, so that a situation endangering environmental safety and public health cannot come about. A new phenomenon: a new state public service provider has appeared on the market, which has begun to take over the market left open by the companies obstructed through government measures (in the same pattern observed on the energy market)."[142]

5. *Bargain chip nationalization, publicly funded acquisition of the decisive stocks of shares in private companies*, in various areas and motivated by diverse interests, but generally intended to improve the positions of the government in later political or economic bargaining:

> ➤ overpriced acquisitions of stocks belonging to less easily black-mailed foreign (Russian, German) owners, usually part of a broader business move (MOL, E.ON gas reservoirs);
> ➤ market acquiring nationalization through bargain chip acquisitions (GIRO Zrt., which handles retail and company transfers);
> ➤ acquisition of companies of "national" symbolic nature (Rába, Dunaferr, MAL Zrt.);
> ➤ a state corporation buys the majority shares of one of its "subtenants" (as MÁV did with its railway catering company, the Resti Zrt.);
> ➤ land acquisitions (the state buys back real estate properties on the Hajógyári island in Óbuda for 4 billion forint; it also provides 2 billion forint in one-time support to the municipality of Székesfehérvár, to buy back the airport of Börgönd);
> ➤ the harbinger of a bandit nationalization ending in transit nationalization (Takarék Bank);
> ➤ a necessary step in an alibi nationalization, in which Budapest Municipality is stripped of one of its corporations in "return" for budgetary support that is already due to the city (Budapest Waterworks).

6. **Transit nationalization, the taking of a private company into "temporary state care":** by means of this interim phase of nationalization private fortunes are forced into the ownership orbit of the adopted political family. The nationalization may be facilitated by prior actions of cold nationalization, forcing the owner to surrender and eventually leave the market. A state loan may be ensured to oil the re-privatization within the adopted family (as for example in the case of BÁV Zrt. already discussed). A similar future is in store for the nationalized savings associations, and the acquired banks, such as Budapest Bank, or the MKB Bank according to the declared aim of the government.

The **re-nationalization of properties mainly in foreign possession** through **transit nationalization** to be handed over later to the preferred circle of private owners, an effective way of creating distributable property after its depletion. This is normally accompanied by the ideology of "national freedom fight." A proclamation goes first, stating that a larger proportion of Hungarian ownership must be achieved in the key sectors, and with that the exclusion of the legitimate owners begins. Naturally the tools used to drive these owners away are the quasi legal tools ensured by unobstructed power: special taxes, plaza prohibitions, inexecutable construction regulations and other obstructive measures by municipalities and state. If even this is not enough, it may be followed by an ordered disparaging media campaign, and at worst a forced re-nationalization. Depending on the financial powers of the foreign owners and their international influence the range of actions stretches from simple hounding out of the Hungarian market, through purchase below or above the market price, to forcing them out of the market. And if the future owner-beneficiary needs capital in the second, re-privatization phase of transit nationalization, it is ensured at no risk by the Hungarian Development Bank among others. For this bank has been legally freed from the obligation of prudent activity, and its losses are compensated from the budget. As a result the loan offered to the company chosen as owner can even actually be a gift: in the final run the purloining of budget resources, a sort of state directed laundering of money is an illegitimate tapping of the payments by taxpayers.

7. *Alibi nationalization, the nationalization of losses—the privatization of profits:* beyond acquiring wealth and income of the adopted political family it may also serve political and ideological goals.

> ➤ *A one-off money-pump,* exemplified by the consolidation of the Postabank (1998–2000), when the state, fearing for the safety of the savings deposited there by clients, capitalized the bank which had become loss-making, and transferred the bad debts to a winding-up institution. This institution sold the "defaulted loans" and companies to the debtors (or their representatives) at—presumably—a fraction of their real value. A similar pattern could be observed in the acquisition of the majority shares of the MKB Bank in 2014 from the Bayerische Landesbank owned by the Bavarian government. Both cases could also serve as examples of transit nationalization, with the difference that in the case of a basic transit nationalization prospering companies are hunted down, unlike in the above instances where a broken company is consolidated, capitalized on public funds, and then passed on at a cut price to the clients of the adopted political family.

➤ *The continuous money-pump,* a procedure best be demonstrated in the liquidation of the private school book market: in the first step the ministry of education was legally authorized to introduce school books to the market bypassing the accreditation procedure. In the second step the retailing of schoolbooks was divested from the private publishers, and made into a state monopoly. As the third step the state schoolbook retailer itself was given the right to publish schoolbooks. In the fourth step, the right of schools to freely select textbooks was taken away, and hereon they could make their selection from the limited list of publications issued by the ministry. Through these measures they ruined the schoolbook publishers, liquidated the schoolbook market, and diverted the profits from the largely budget-financed commerce in schoolbooks into their own pockets through the printing capacities owned by adopted family members. This alibi nationalization shows an organic link between the political aim of ideological indoctrination of the pupils, the propaganda objective of lowering prices, and the economic goal of wealth accumulation of the adopted political family. A similar rationale is followed in the transformation of public utility corporations into state **nonprofit companies** in the framework of the "utility price war," where these companies similarly function as interfaces helping to funnel budget resources to select subcontractors.

The various types of nationalization can be combined in whichever way appropriate to the complex goals in each instance (e.g., bargain chip nationalization cum alibi nationalization). It can also occur however that they qualify as something else with the passing of a period of time (e.g., cold nationalization followed by transit nationalization, or a bargain chip nationalization can be qualified later as a transit nationalization).

5.12. The rationale of power versus the irrationality of public policies

Though the logic of power may result in **mindless measures** on the level of professional administration, those who attempt to a critique of these on the terms of a rationale dictated by public good, trying to shore these up with a line arguments have no idea with whom they are engaged in debate. To prove the irrationality of individual Fidesz actions—such as the tobacco concessions, or the redistribution of agricultural land leases, or for that matter any of the various steps of nationalization—usually public policy arguments can be heard. This is reminiscent of what it was like to watch football games on the tiny opaque screen of a Soviet mini television set introduced in 1970 on the occasion of the 100th anniversary of Lenin's birth: since the ball was not visible, it looked like the 22 players were scampering around the pitch senselessly. But when it was possible to watch the game on a larger set, the ball became visible, and it gave meaning to the movements of the players. In Fidesz's "public policies" the ball is the power/wealth accumulation factor—this gives sense to the game. The shortsighted "professional discourse" does not take account of the fact that there is an additional—power/wealth—component in the equation that describes the system, and moreover that is the definitive variable. It looks like two-dimensional creatures, posing as "professionals," trying to interpret a three dimensional world. Meanwhile the political family only laughs sardonically at those who look for the classical rationale of public policies, at the nitwits who have still not got the slightest clue of what the game is about.

For this reason any argument about the measures taken by the mafia state and the way it operates, which relies on public policies in the narrow sense is intellectually ridiculous and disarming in political and moral terms, because it does not reckon with the most important factor of all: the rationale of power, to which all public policy considerations are subordinated. *For par excellence public policies only exist under democratic conditions, where private interests do not take the place of public interest.* For the issues of public policy to have a chance to once again become actual public policy issues, there first must be a change of the regime and a restoration of the institutional system of democracy must take place.

At the same time however what the regime does is consistent in political terms, because the adopted political family sends a clear and encouraging message to those who wish to be guided or must be guided, while their adversaries see a threat—helping them understand the new rules. Meanwhile the authentic information never reaches the purview of wider public opinion in an undistorted form. This therefore is the course of rational action according to the logic of the construction of the mafia state. "I will do it, because I can afford to do it." This of course does not mean that the regime can close the books on each of its actions with a profit margin. In the tobacco shop case for example, perhaps the balance is not positive, because it might backfire, if thousands of dispossessed shopkeepers in the country tell the hundreds of customers visiting them every day why they have to go to another shop to buy certain goods. Moreover the awareness of the wider public in regards to the operation of the mafia state is gradual, and one or another measure may elicit a more profound understanding, or even a turning point in political consciousness. For this reason the regime, in order to minimalize risks, must continuously keep measure of whether the withdrawal and institutional manipulation of freedom of expression and free elections has reached a level that ensures the will of the electorate cannot overturn the expanding mafia state.

NOTES

1. Krisztina Ferenczi, *Narancsbőr—Az Orbán-vagyonok nyomában* (Budapest: Tény 2014 Kft., 2014); See also András Becker, "Orbán's Wealth and Oligarchs," forthcoming in: *Twenty-Four Sides of a Post-Communist Mafia State*, edited by Bálint Magyar and Júlia Vásárhelyi.
2. An apt expression coined by Tamás Frei in his *2015—A káosz éve és a magyar elit háborúja* [2015 —The year of chaos and the war of the Hungarian elite] (Budapest: Ulpius, 2013), 18.
3. https://en.wikipedia.org/wiki/Lajos_Simicska.
4. https://hu.wikipedia.org/wiki/Sz%C3%A9les_G%C3%A1bor_%28%C3%BCzletember%29.
5. https://hu.wikipedia.org/wiki/Baldauf_L%C3%A1szl%C3%B3.
6. https://hu.wikipedia.org/wiki/L%C3%A1z%C3%A1r_Vilmos_%28fogathajt%C3%B3,_1967%29.
7. https://en.wikipedia.org/wiki/S%C3%A1ndor_Cs%C3%A1nyi_%28banker%29.
8. https://hu.wikipedia.org/wiki/Demj%C3%A1n_S%C3%A1ndor.
9. https://en.wikipedia.org/wiki/J%C3%A1nos_L%C3%A1z%C3%A1r.
10. http://hvg.hu/itthon/20130812_Lazar_Csanyi_Sandor_uzsoras/.
11. https://hu.wikipedia.org/wiki/Princz_G%C3%A1bor.
12. https://en.wikipedia.org/wiki/Lajos_Simicska
13. http://444.hu/2014/09/01/uj-klan-lep-simicska-lajos-helyebe-mikor-veget-er-a-csatajuk-orbannal/.
14. Pál Dániel Rényi, "Orbán Viktor vs. Simicska Lajos - Csak egy maradhat talpon" [Viktor Orbán vs. Lajos Simicska—only one can remain standing], http://magyarnarancs.hu/belpol/csak-egy-maradhat-talpon-91576.
15. https://en.wikipedia.org/wiki/Zsuzsanna_N%C3%A9meth.
16. https://en.wikipedia.org/wiki/Mikl%C3%B3s_Seszt%C3%A1k.
17. Rényi, "Orbán Viktor vs. Simicska Lajos."
18. Ibid.

[19] Eleni Tsakopoulos Kounalakis, *Madam Ambassador. Three Years of Diplomacy, Dinner Parties, and Democracy in Budapest* (New York: The New Press, 2015), 253.
[20] "You believe Viktor Orbán's people got the paper's leadership to abandon ship? – What else could have happened here in your opinion? I am telling you, you can publish it, Orbán is a fucker." http://index.hu/belfold/2015/02/06/simicska_lajos_orban_egy_geci/.
[21] http://www.mfor.hu/cikkek/Iden_mar_11_milliard_forinttol_esett_el_Simicska_.html.
[22] http://444.hu/2015/06/24/szasa-kinyirja-a-kozgepet/.
[23] http://www.origo.hu/gazdasag/20150916-ujra-ringbe-szallhat-a-kozpenzekert-a-kozgep.html.
[24] http://hvg.hu/w/20150930_Nemzeti_Elonytelenseg_Rendszere.
[25] http://www.blikk.hu/blikk_aktualis/1440-hektar-allami-foldet-vettek-vissza-simicskaektol-2345277.
[26] http://www.blikk.hu/blikk_aktualis/mtva-simicska-lajos-orban-viktor-szerenc-seszombat-haboru-lotto-musor-2342961.
[27] http://sztarklikk.hu/kozelet/simicska-oda-ut-ahol-igazan-faj/175289.
[28] Péter Erdélyi and Péter Magyari, *"Új klán lép Simicska Lajos helyébe, mikor véget ér a csatájuk Orbánnal"* [A new clan will take Lajos Simicska's place, once their battle with Orbán is over], 444, September 1, 2014. http://444.hu/2014/09/01/uj-klan-lep-simicska-lajos-helyebe-mikor-veget-er-a-csatajuk-orbannal/.
[29] Péter Szakonyi, ed., *A 100 leggazdagabb, 2014* [The 100 richest people in Hungary in 2014] (Napi.hu, 2014), 101.
[30] http://atlatszo.hu/2014/06/03/a-joisten-a-szerencse-es-orban-viktor-szeme-lye-igy-vagyonosodott-meszaros-lorinc/.
[31] http://444.hu/2015/11/03/hany-meszaros-lorinc-ad-ki-egy-csanyi-sandort.
[32] http://magyarnarancs.hu/kismagyarorszag/foldek-asvanyviz-pekseg-teszta-hotel-lista-meszaros-lorinc-osszes-uzleterol-96943.
[33] Ibid.
[34] https://hu.wikipedia.org/wiki/V%C3%A1radi_Andr%C3%A1s_%28juh%C3%A1sz%29.
[35] http://www.mfor.hu/cikkek/A_legtobb_TAO_Felcsut_zsebebe_kerult_tavaly_is.html ; http://atlatszo.hu/2013/07/09/orban-fociakademiaja-a-legegyenlobb-civil-szervezet-tavaly-3-milliardos-bevetele-volt/.
[36] http://gepnarancs.hu/2015/02/felcsuti-fenyben-ragyog-a-magyar-epito/.
[37] Ibid.
[38] https://hu.wikipedia.org/wiki/Garancsi_Istv%C3%A1n.
[39] http://index.hu/gazdasag/2014/01/27/mol/.
[40] http://nol.hu/belfold/20130816-garancsinal_lakik_orban_gaspar-1406873.
[41] https://en.wikipedia.org/wiki/Andrew_G._Vajna.
[42] http://www.origo.hu/gazdasag/20140506-a-kormany-het-kaszinora-adott-ki-engedelyt.html#.
[43] https://en.wikipedia.org/wiki/Mih%C3%A1ly_Varga.
[44] http://hvg.hu/gazdasag/20150601_Olcsobb_lesz_az_adocsalas.
[45] http://444.hu/2015/07/09/tenyleg-zsenialis-ahogy-a-kormany-segit-a-buno-zoknek-penzt-mosni/.

[46] András Földi, *A római család jogi rendje* [The legal order of the Roman family], http://www.rubicon.hu/magyar/oldalak/a_romai_csalad_jogi_rendje/, 1997.

[47] Ibid.

[48] Ibid.

[49] http://hvg.hu/itthon/20140710_Terminal_Etterem_Pap_Karpati_Tiborcz.

[50] http://444.hu/2015/03/11/igy-kaptak-tiborczek-szabad-utat-a-milliardokhoz/.

[51] http://444.hu/2015/12/01/tud-hatekony-lenni-ez-az-allam-ha-akar-tiborcz-istvan-csak-egyetlen-honapig-nem-indulhatott-kozbeszerzesen-de-most-korrigalta-a-kormany-ezt-az-apro-hibat.

[52] https://hu.wikipedia.org/wiki/Stadler_FC.

[53] *EU Anti-Corruption Report*, Brussels, 3.2.2014, COM(2014) 38 final, ANNEX 17, HUNGARY; http://ec.europa.eu/dgs/home-affairs/what-we-do/policies/organized-crime-and-human-trafficking/corruption/anti-corruption-report/docs/2014_acr_hungary_chapter_en.pdf.

[54] Dávid Jancsics, "A friend gave me a phone number"—Brokerage in low-level corruption, *International Journal of Law, Crime an Justice* (2014), http://www.sciencedirect.com/science/article/pii/S1756061614000500.

[55] http://index.hu/belfold/2015/06/12/de_akkor_ki_akarta_az_ugyvedi_bevetelek_ujratitkositasat/.

[56] Katherine Stovel and Lynette Shaw, "Brokerage," *Annual Review of Sociology*, 38 (2012): 139–58.

[57] https://hu.wikipedia.org/wiki/Hajd%C3%BA_J%C3%A1nos_%28rend%C5%91r%29.

[58] https://en.wikipedia.org/wiki/L%C3%A1szl%C3%B3_K%C3%B6v%C3%A9r.

[59] https://en.wikipedia.org/wiki/J%C3%A1nos_%C3%81der.

[60] http://hvg.hu/velemeny.nyuzsog/20130123_Nem_artatlannak_valo_videk#39i70bg; http://hvg.hu/cimke/UD_Zrt.

[61] https://hu.wikipedia.org/wiki/Kenedi_J%C3%A1nos.

[62] http://www.xn--infordi-lwa8n.hu/hir/belfold/hir-400579.

[63] http://nol.hu/belfold/a_jogvedok_strasbourgban_tamadjak_a_terrorelharitok_jogositvanyait_-1429269.

[64] http://hu.wikipedia.org/wiki/Simicska_Lajos.

[65] http://nepszava.hu/cikk/1015154-napokra-leall-a-nav-informatikai-rendszere.

[66] http://hvg.hu/gazdasag/20140423_Mire_kell_Matolcsyeknak_a_nagy_adatbank/.

[67] http://444.hu/2014/03/03/meghalt-a-welt-2000-alapitoja/; http://index.hu/.gazdasag/2014/03/03/az_allammal_uzletelt_masnap_meghalt/.

[68] Apt expression used by Sándor Révész, in Sándor Révész, "Polip büró" [Polip buro], *Népszabadság*, December 7, 2013.

[69] Imre Vörös, "A 'Constitutional' Putsch in Hungary between 2010–2014," forthcoming in: *Twenty-Four Sides of a Post-Communist Mafia State*, edited by Bálint Magyar and Júlia Vásárhelyi.

[70] Ibid.

[71] http://tenytar.blog.hu/2014/11/28/lex_baratok_es_ellensegek_torvenyhozas_az_uzleti_erdekek_szolgalataban.

[72] Instances belonging in the category of certain types of nationalization. Researchers associated with the Ténytár (Fact-base) participated in the compilation of examples.

[73] http://ataszjelenti.blog.hu/2015/10/08/onkenyes_alkotmanybirosag.

[74] Viktor Orbán, *MTI*, 2 February 2011.

[75] Max Weber, *Economy and Society, An outline of interpretative sociology*, translated by Ephraim Fischoff, Hans Gerth, et al., and edited by Guenther Roth, Claus Wittich (Berkeley, Los Angeles, London: University of California, 1978).

[76] Ibid., 228.

[77] Ibid., 232.

[78] Ibid., 218-9.

[79] Ibid., 240.

[80] http://444.hu/2015/05/20/ujabb-hatarozott-lepeseket-tesz-a-kormany-az-atlathatatlansag-iranyaba/.

[81] Weber, *Economy and Society*, 229.

[82] Ibid., 232.

[83] József Hegedűs and Gábor Péteri, "A helyi önkormányzatok államosítása" [Nationalization of municipal governments], in *Magyar polip*, eds. Bálint Magyar and Júlia Vásárhelyi, 351-352.

[84] After a delay of decades, in the spring of 1998, the construction of the new National Theatre began in Budapest on the proposals of the liberal minister. The winning design won the overwhelming approval of the 15-member jury in a competition of the most submissions ever in the history of Hungarian architecture, with 71 architects. A few months later, upon taking government, Fidesz halted the well advanced building works to erect a building considered below criticism by the architects, designed by the house architect of the government commissioner for theatre without any competition, adding years of delay and on a completely different location.

[85] http://index.hu/gazdasag/2014/08/28/igy_szorja_a_penzt_az_mnb/; http://index.hu/gazdasag/2015/01/21/250_milliard_a_forint_a_matolcsy-tanokra/.

[86] Ádám C. Nagy, "The Taming of Civil Society," forthcoming in: *Twenty-Four Sides of a Post-Communist Mafia State*, edited by Bálint Magyar and Júlia Vásárhelyi.

[87] http://index.hu/belfold/2015/06/29/valamiert_iszonyu_surgos_lett_az_infotorveny_modositasa/.

[88] Seven political scientists had to grade 150 persons selected by the editors on a scale of ten, according to the estimated measure of their social-political-economic influence. The first 40 individuals were made public, with the scale called "Befolyás barométer" (Influence barometer), in *A 100 leggazdagabb 2014*, edited by Péter Szakonyi, *Napi.hu*, 114-118.

[89] http://index.hu/belfold/2015/06/03/panikban_az_ugyvedek_a_magyar_allam_lehallgatasatol_felnek/.

[90] http://hvg.hu/itthon/20150612_Pinter_uj_otlete_napszamosnak_lehetne_ige.

[91] Ibid.

[92] http://www.fidesz.hu/hirek/2012-10-19/orban-nem-joleti-allam-hanem-munka-alapu-tarsadalom-epul-kepek/.

[93] http://index.hu/gazdasag/2014/11/13/szocialpolitika/.

[94] http://atlatszo.hu/2014/11/22/januartol-konnyebb-lesz-lopni-megint-lehet-majd-kozpenzbol-tamogatni-a-partkozeli-szervezeteket-es-a-csaladot/.

[95]   http://nol.hu/belfold/kozszolgak-csak-janicsarkepzobol-1540453.

[96]   Edward C. Banfield, with the assistance of Laura F. Banfield, *The Moral Basis of a Backward Society* (Glencoe, IL: The Free Press, 1958).

[97]   http://mandiner.hu/cikk/20150702_orban_viktor_valositja_meg_a_ rendszervaltast_interju_lanczi_andras_teller_gyula.

[98]   http://hu.budapestbeacon.com/kiemelt-cikkek/nyugdij-reformot-az-allama-dossag-csokkentesere-es-koltsegvetesi-lyukak-betomesere-hasznaltak-mag-yarorszagon/.

[99]   http://www.galamus.hu/index.php?option=com_content&view=article&id= 430480:a-diktatura-bore-1-430480&catid=9:vendegek&Itemid=134.

[100] http://www.galamus.hu/index.php?option=com_content&view=article&id= 430480:a-diktatura-bore-1-430480&catid=9:vendegek&Itemid=134.
       The full list of taxes introduced since 2010 can be found in the following blog: http://tenytar.blog.hu/2014/11/05/2015_a_megszoritasok_eve_ime_az_ uj_adok.

[101] http://mediapedia.hu/reklamado.

[102] http://index.hu/gazdasag/2014/11/06/kiskereskedok/.

[103] http://444.hu/2014/12/18/a-magyar-allam-egy-resze-ugy-szervezi-a-mukodeset-hogy-minel-konnyebb-legyen-korruptnak-lenni/.

[104] http://index.hu/gazdasag/2014/11/06/kiskereskedok/, http://www.vg.hu/ vallalatok/kereskedelem/megerositettek-tilos-lesz-az-online-vasarlas-is-vasarnap-441680.

[105] http://index.hu/gazdasag/2015/10/28/ujabb_szivatas_a_tesconak_es_az_ auchannak_kotelezo_letszamnoveles_a_hipermarketeknek/.

[106] http://fn.hir24.hu/gazdasag/2014/11/19/itt-a-nagy-parharc-cba-vagy-tesco/.

[107] Ibid.

[108] By courtesy of Pál Juhász.

[109] http://hir.ma/belfold/a-vilagon-elsokent-napelem-ado-a-napot-is-megadoztatjak/ 473080.

[110] http://nol.hu/belfold/pelikan-elvtarsak-az-orban-kormanyban-1510531.

[111] http://hvg.hu/gazdasag/20150424_Orosz_rulettre_kapott_felhivast_Orban.

[112] http://nol.hu/gazdasag/sinen-az-elmu-emasz-vetel-1568285.

[113] http://2010-2014.kormany.hu/hu/nemzetgazdasagi-miniszterium/strategiai-partnersegi-megallapodasok.

[114] http://atlatszo.blog.hu/2013/07/30/milliardos_palyazatok_a_strategiai_part-nereknek1.

[115] http://mandiner.hu/cikk/20150702_orban_viktor_valositja_meg_a_rendszervaltast_ interju_lanczi_andras_teller_gyula.

[116] http://nepszava.hu/document/6/original/Felhivas%20Oktober%2023-ra. pdf?utm_source=mandiner&utm_medium=link&utm_campaign=mandiner_ 201501.

[117] http://hvg.hu/gazdasag/20110704_megapolis_metropolis_fonyo_karoly.

[118] http://index.hu/gazdasag/2014/09/17/megvette_a_fradi-stadiont_epito_ ceget_orban_milliardos_baratja/.

[119] http://civilhetes.net/velemeny/elvette-a-fidesz-a-ceget-belehalt.

120 http://nol.hu/belfold/foldharcban-veszitettek-1508211.
121 Ibid.
122 Ibid.
123 http://nol.hu/belfold/ingyenbirtok-a-holdudvarnak-1552969.
124 http://hvg.hu/itthon/20130509_trafik_Szekszard_Fidesz_hangfelvetel?utm_
    source=mandiner&utm_medium=link&utm_campaign=mandiner_201502.
125 http://hvg.hu/gazdasag/20151112_Ezert_erte_meg_a_trafikmutyiMultimil
    liomo.
126 http://nepszava.hu/cikk/644749-hallo-itt-a-trafikmutyi-hangja-beszel.
127 http://hvg.hu/enesacegem/20150603_Tomegesen_zarnak_be_a_boltok_a_
    trafikok_m.
128 http://444.hu/2014/12/18/300-ezret-kell-fizetnie-a-fideszes-kepviselonek-aki-
    haromszor-sem-ugy-szavazott-ahogy-elvartak-tole/.
129 http://nol.hu/gazdasag/valami-nagyon-gyanus-az-orbank-kormany-alomuzleteben-
    1539525; http://propeller.hu/itthon/3118393-kihuzta-gyufat-kormany-
    nemzetkozi-dohanycegeknel.
130 http://nol.hu/gazdasag/habony-emberevel-erositenek-1541333.
131 http://valasz.hu/uzlet/lazar-janos-dohanyos-embere-a-napi-gazdasag-uj-
    tulajdonosa-113652.
132 http://feol.hu/gazdasag/a-felkaru-rablok-kivegzese-1123941.
133 http://hvg.hu/itthon/20121002_Megszavaztak_a_nyerogepek_betiltasat.
134 Ibid.
135 http://hvg.hu/gazdasag/20131209_Tobbezer_felkaru_rablo_lepi_el_Magyarorsz
136 http://www.origo.hu/gazdasag/20140506-a-kormany-het-kaszinora-adott-ki-
    engedelyt.html.
137 http://www.napi.hu/ado/varga_ezert_kap_milliardos_adokedvezmenyt_
    vajna.585449.html.
138 http://nol.hu/belfold/vajna-a-neten-is-mindent-visz-1497253.
139 http://www.vg.hu/gazdasag/felepult-a-vajna-birodalom-448456.
140 Ibid.
141 Associates of Ténytár assisted me in compiling the cases illustrating the various
    forms of nationalization.
142 http://nol.hu/belfold/falank-az-allami-kukaholding-1570425.

6. The legitimacy deficit faced by the mafia state and the means to overcome it

6.1. Domestication of the media

Fidesz *does not rely on the dictatorial form of censorship, all encompassing and administrative*. It does not even apply the cautious, hand-guided censorship of soft-dictatorships (such as that of the late communist regime in Hungary) that graded material according to which is to be "supported, tolerated, prohibited." This worked under the conditions of exclusive state ownership, including the media. At the time, only the samizdat publishers of the anti-communist dissident movement persecuted by the authorities—directly reaching no more than a couple of thousand readers—remained outside the compass of state controlled publicity. Following the regime change, a mixed media ownership structure came about, overseen later by Fidesz using a variety of repressive means.

6.1.1. 2010–2014: Media control in the period of establishing the mafia state

Fidesz brought the *state-owned public media under its control* through the immediate means of authority (commissars, direct orders, censorship). It *depoliticized* (through threats in the form of arbitrarily imposed sanctions and the advertisement tax) the *major private televisions* (RTL Klub, TV2). It ghettoized any media with a critical voice (official persecutions, scaring away advertisers). Meanwhile, with state assistance (financial support and illegitimate coercion) the political family *built its own private media empire*.

The first president of the *Media Council* and the *National Media and Infocommunications Authority* established by the new media Act of 2011 was an Orbán favorite, and the second was the political family's legal advocate for the media organs close to Fidesz. By way of decrees, the president decides about the distribution of the stocks at the command of these organs (frequencies, concessions, permits, etc., artificially minimized to allow more room for the state monopoly), about the rules of the media market (criteria for public media, rating of programs, some of the restrictions on advertisement, etc.), and about imposition of penalties. With preferences and punishments meted out on the grounds of flexible regulations, it is fully within the president's discretion to award or strip a subject of frequencies, exclude a candidate from a round of applications or hand out financial penalties that would make the further operation of a private actor impossible. Meanwhile the state itself is a market participant through the *Media Support and Asset Management Fund*, and no less than its largest as the public service provider that includes the national news agency, a range of television and radio channels, and a continuously growing state-provided budget of altogether 80 billion forint (app. 260 million euro).

The new regime has nationalized the *public media and the Hungarian News Agency* not only in terms of ownership, but also in terms of content, a transformation leading from *public service to government service*. Its assets and employees have been gathered into a fund under the Media Council, imposing strict censorship, filling all positions with loyal cadres after thorough rounds of political cleansing, and even making room for journalists from the media run by the extreme right. *By providing state news free of charge* the government has undermined, practically liquidated the market for independent news providers, and thus indirectly the regime sets the agenda for the news programs of private media as well.

Fidesz supports loyal media with *subscriptions and advertising orders from state and municipal authorities, institutions and corporations*. At the same time the regime obstructs the freedom of the press by diminishing the revenues of private media mainly through withdrawing state advertisement and scaring off private advertisers by blackmail and threat. It manages to get the media that served as a home to voices critical of the government closed by these means, or at least force their retraction into small pockets of limited audience. If not able to shut down a medium by administrative means, seemingly economic tools may be used to evict the renitent media from the market. Of course this has the effect of depoliticizing other significant private media channels as well by cautioning them to self-censorship.

The issue does not stop at whether any channels are left for freely voiced opinions. A major part of the problem is that the regime was able to jam critical voice into ghettoes. Those who were already staunch opponents of the government merely converse amongst themselves, leaving a limited viability for a change in the proportion of loyal *versus* critical voices in the larger audience. A continuously decreasing number of critical channels that come to play the role of **communication rubber rooms** for the opponents of the regime are descending into a daily secular liturgy of counting the beads of often totally unreflective rage. At the same time the government—giving way to its instincts—strikes the critical media channels down through a redistribution of radio frequencies, or relegates them to the ghetto of the few intellectual consumer groups, or perhaps just starves them out. The intense involvement of those chatting among each other on the social media—which are not so easily regulated—might elicit a false sense of masses displeased with government, when in fact only the same people are exchanging views among one another in the same groups. **The mafia state is not doctrinarian:** it is not afraid of words, it can handle criticism—so long as it does not have outreach.

The media octopus, however, as Mária Vásárhelyi puts it,[1] is **not only brainwashing, but also money laundering.** Not only are the clients of the adopted political family the biggest subcontractors of state media, they are also builders of the frequency networks, the beneficiaries of state funds for the media, the receivers of state advertisement, the state funded buyers and founders of media firms. They are the ones to take over the places of the market players who were ejected by means of illegitimate state coercion. While Berlusconi built political power with the help of his media empire, Fidesz builds a media empire with the help of political power. After all, the winds of fortune change, and the media empire in the hands of the political family may help to pull through the lean years—as it had before 2010. Better not leave matters to chance.

The structure and operation of the media empire that has come to belong to Fidesz since 2010 is based on the cycle presented in the following diagram:[2] (1) the political family positions its cadres where the operation of state media, budget resources and state advertisement are decided; (2) these people redirect a vast majority of state advertising and commissions to the political family or media loyal to it; 3.) these simultaneously do the ideological brainwashing of public opinion and the delivery of state resources into private pockets through overpriced procurements and shares of profits; 4.) with the full turn of the circle, oligarchs of the political family delegate cadres to the key positions ensuring smooth operation.

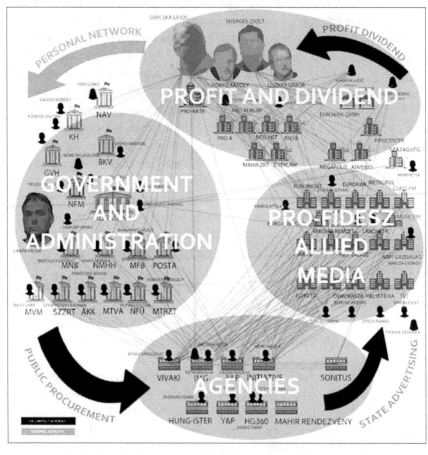

(Acronyms found on the diagram: NAV: National Tax and Customs Administration of Hungary (NTCA); GVH: Hungarian Competition Authority; KH: Public Procurement Authority (PPA); NMHH: National Media and Infocommunications Authority (NMIAH); BKV: Budapest Transport Corporation; NFM: Ministry of National Development; MNB: Hungarian National Bank; MFB: Hungarian Development Bank; MVM: Hungarian Electricity Company; SZZRT: Szerencsejáték Zrt.; ÁKK: Government Debt Management Agency; MTVA: Media Support and Asset Management Fund; NFÜ: National Development Agency; MTRZT: Hungarian National Tourist Office.; IMG: Inter Media Group; B&P: Bell & Partners; Y&P: Young & Partners)

The relatively balanced, non-partisan distribution of state advertising that reflected some self-restraint with regard to the balance of political forces applied until 2010, was drastically overturned after the elections—see Annex 5. Then during the 2010–2014 government term a *significant expansion of the media portfolio owned directly* by the oligarchs close to Fidesz was achieved. At the outset the media in their possession reached a rather small audience (printed press included *Magyar Nemzet*, *Magyar Hírlap*, *Heti Válasz*, and the electronic media channels were *Hír TV*, *Echo TV* and *Lánchíd Radio*). Only the national chain newspaper, the free, advertisement-based weekly *Helyi Téma* was an exception, as it had a wide circulation. The objective was for the political family to gather a significant segment of the media consumed by the vast majority of the populace simply not interested in politics. This was behind the acquisition of *Metropol*, another free, advertisement funded national daily with the highest print runs. Yet the real breakthrough would have been the acquisition of the two major, nationwide commercial television channels. These two channels had only adapted to the Fidesz media politics passively until then. Though the Media Act prescribes the programming of at least one 20-minute block of news a day, these had the genre of depoliticized crime news reports at these televisions.

Fidesz efforts were rewarded with success in the case of TV2,[3] though they failed at acquiring RTL Klub. Where acquisition was not required to enforce a more "understanding" tone and pure political pressure sufficed, as in the case of the largest online news portal Origo, state advertising funds that had stayed previously at 250 million forint (app 800 thousand euro), grew to a billion forint (3.2 million euro) soon after. While state advertising with TV2 comes to 10 billion (32 million euro), the more widely watched RTL Klub only receives half a billion (1.6 million euro): "state advertising grew to triple its previous figure with TV2, where the amount came to 10.6 billion in 2014 (about 35 million euro). Put differently, every third forint of taxpayer money spent on state advertising went to that commercial channel. RTL Klub received much less, a tenth of TV2's revenues, the difference growing in the second half of 2014 to 22 times the lower figure."[4] The only complication for the addition of TV2 to the assets of the adopted political family was caused by the Orbán-Simicska conflict. Because while the maneuver had been initiated by the Simicska arm of the political family, which had monopolized the media contacts, by the end of the takeover, Orbán wanted to place his new confidant and stooge at the helm of the new acquisition as owner. "Leaders of

Fidesz knew that Simicska had negotiated of a purchase of the TV2 channel. Our reports show that Viktor Orbán had been updated on Thursday about the chaotic situation evolving around the purchase of TV2. One of the leading politicians in Fidesz had said that they would wait out a few weeks to see whether Vajna or Simicska would come out as winner of the legal battle for TV2. The government decisions on the distribution of state advertisement expenditures and the introduction of a cable provider tax vital to the survival of the channel would be delayed until then. We have reports that Vajna bought TV2 in the hopes that it would be able to take a major cut of the 25 billion forint state bracket for advertising even this year. Due to the chaotic situation, the validation of the government decree that qouls increase the revenues of TV by as much as 6 billion forints will be put off."[5] This admission also means that a parliamentary, government, and a state agency's decision is openly made dependent on whether TV2 can be brought into the field of interests of the adopted political family through a new stooge. This provides bases for the prosecution of numerous provisions against organized crime. And though for a while it seemed like Simicska had beat Vajna to the acquisition by an pre-emptive option for purchase, it soon became clear that the organs of public authority that had played a major role in the initial stage of the transaction (Company Registry Courts, Hungarian Competition Authority—GVH) would place Vajna into position of ownership. To give its decision further weight the GVH also initiated a comprehensive examination of RTL Klub at the same time, to see if it abused it market superiority.[6] And even if Simicska takes the complicated legal case to foreign courts, he would not be made owner of TV2 years later even if he did win the case. At most, the Hungarian authorities that had taken illegal actions would be forced to pay reparations. In the event, costs incurred would not be paid by Vajna, but Hungarian taxpayers.

The **open air advertising corporations** related to the adopted political family of Fidesz (Publimont, MAHIR Cityposter, EuroAWK) operate along similar lines.

6.1.2. Media control in transformation after 2014, under conditions of the established mafia state

The system described above was grounded on two key figures: top poligarch Viktor Orbán and top oligarch Lajos Simicska. While the first ensured that the right people were in the right administrative positions, the right parliamentary, municipal, and administrative decisions were brought, and budget resources channeled to operate the media empire, the latter managed the optimal distribution of these resources within the empire and the operation itself—as either owner or coordinator of the given media.

The repeated electoral victory of Fidesz in 2014, once again ensuring unbridled political power, gave Viktor Orbán the opportunity to—as previously discussed—wind up the dualist control of the political family and make his own exclusive role as leader explicit. The key moments of Lajos Simicska's demotion within the adopted political family so far as the media was concerned were the following:

- The establishment of the **National Communications Office** in October 2014 meant a further two-way centralization. On the one hand, it compulsorily unifies and monopolizes the communications carried out in all the state and government administration, institutions and corporations partially or completely belonging to the state. On the other hand, the office, in the role of an agency, handles the market orders and contracts entailed by these organs. This means that while incapacitating autonomous market mechanisms, the regime also "nationalizes" its own inner circle, and eliminates possibilities of already limited horizontal separate deals within the family. The task may seem impossible, nevertheless the aim is to determine the communications messages of all state institutions and corporations centrally, and to do so not only in a general sense, but to directly control them, as well as deciding about the benefits to be offered to participants of the media alone. It practically liquidated the few private media agencies—affiliated with the political family, and primarily Lajos Simicska—through which they had decided about state advertising in media both in their hands, and not. The concentration of the power to define communications financed by the state in the hands of the top poligarch also means that the communications strategy of the regime switched into **permanent campaign mode**. Oversight and supervision of communications by state institutions is only one aspect of the new order, their activity is also kept under inspection and influenced by means of this parallel channel. This centralization indicates a further limitation of the already limited autonomy of state institutions.
- The actions that brought the media agencies belonging to top oligarch Lajos Simicska and other friends into a dependent position and then

repressed them were paralleled by the—previously mentioned—process in which **the privileged position** of media belonging to the political family so far as distribution of state resources and advertising were concerned **came to an end**.

- At the same time the main aim of introducing the selectively progressive advertisement tax was to **punish and possibly exclude RTL Klub from the Hungarian media market**, after the largest commercial television channel had resisted aggressive takeover attempts by the government. The international background of RTL Klub made it possible for the company to take up the challenge: it changed the depoliticized tone of its news program to extremely critical of government, which doubled the viewer ratings of the program within a couple of months, and made it the leading news program in the Hungarian media market. RTL Klub became one of the most powerful forces behind Fidesz's loss of one-third of its supporters within three months in the autumn of 2014, by helping government critical voice cross from the tiny ghetto of the opposition media that draws an audience of only a few hundred thousand. Indeed the politics of Fidesz had not changed over this period, merely the contextualization of the communications reaching the wide public had transformed. In the course of the media war it had fought with RTL Klub, the government raised the prospect of legally prohibiting the way television channels had found to compensate for the losses incurred through the progressive tax regime, planning to raise the fee charged from cable providers for the content they provided. Fidesz was finally forced to desist from amending the law to this effect, in fact it quickly agreed with the leadership of RTL Klub about ending the progressivity of the advertisement tax before the arrival of Angela Merkel in Budapest in February 2015. This deal moderately allayed the government critical tone of the news programs at the channel.

- From 2015 onwards Fidesz has concentrated on the **expansion of state owned media**. The direct budget support for state media and the national news agency has grown from 47 billion forint (approximately 150 million euro) in 2010 to 80 billion (approximately 260 million euro). The M1 channel of the Hungarian Television has been changed to a news channel. By doing so they made the political services provided until then by the Simicska affiliated Hír TV. Channel M2 became a children's channel during the day and a public tabloid television for young people from evening until the morning. The channel that had earlier been Duna TV, focusing on Hungarians living in the neighboring countries, took over the programs of M1 as M3. In 2015 they launched an additional sports channel (M4) and a regional channel for Budapest (M5) is under way, as well as a thematic channel (M6).

The main issue of note about the changes compared to the previous term of government is that it has expanded *state owned media* from its role as a public service media into a cost-immune media enterprise with a profuse dumping of programs targeted at all genres, age-groups, and audiences, and controlled directly by the regime, without any mediation. It either took over the *major commercial televisions* (TV2) or tried to eliminate them with the coercive tools of public authority (RTL Klub). It also *quasi demoted the political family's own private media empire*, and replaced the controls vested in the body that represented the family with the direct one-man control of the poligarch. (The following diagram outlines this situation.)[7]

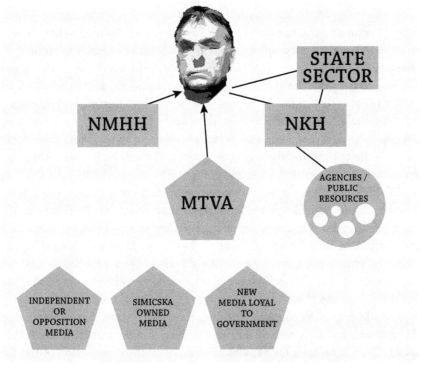

MTVA (Media Service Support and Asset Management Fund)
NMHH (National Media and Infocommunications Authority)
NKH (National Office of Communication)

The new private media loyal to government is managed by the newly established Modern Media Group Zrt., whose two owners are Árpád Habony, who makes a secure living from unknown sources while a confidant of the prime minister, and Tibor Győri, of the Prime Minister's Office where—as they put it ironically—he was the "state secretary of Orbán related affairs." According to the news portal 444 "Viktor Orbán's two Rasputins descend upon the Hungarian media market with a company they co-own,"[8] built on resources that are rather murky, since neither owners— the "unemployed" Habony, or the employed Győri—can possibly possess the capital needed to launch such a company. But one could also note that it is all in the name, since in 1998, one of the companies close to Fidesz that were made to vanish with significant public debts was accidentally called Modern Media. The new media empire loyal to the government comprises an opinion and finance portal on public life, a semi-tabloid weekly distributed free, and perhaps a radio station to be launched soon.[9]

"Viktor Orbán declared in an interview: a country's sovereignty is conditional upon a predominantly domestic ownership of the media that secures its influence over public opinion, but this condition is not yet fulfilled in Hungary. The only real motivation for the law eliminating the media agencies was to clear out the space between individual advertisers and individual media owners. To exclude all bothersome factors that deal with professional considerations (such as where it is worthwhile to advertise), or inspection (whether the advertisement was in fact conveyed to the public). These companies—the optimizers, the media agencies, and the sales houses—compose the system of checks and balances in the media industry. Without them it is difficult to verify whether the advertisements were actually placed, irrespective of how popular the medium is. The clearing out of the space did not mean hunting down the companies, instead they dropped a nuke. To rewrite the regulations for a branch of industry that works in periods lasting a year, while the year is not done, effects the field similarly to a nuclear attack: all participants in the field will be occupied for a long while now with clearing out the debris and the corpses, harboring anger for each other and grieving. Meanwhile under the mushroom cloud, the construction work on building the government-affiliated media empire has commenced with incredible speed. There is no time for decades of work, as in the cases of *Mahir, Hír Tv,* and *Magyar Nemzet,* or the others [owned or controlled by Simicska]. Nothing organic about this construction, its execution is based on brute force and the law: prohibit, ban, cut off, and permit another. These are the key words."[10]

6.2. Manipulation of the electoral system[11]

One of the decisive conditions of democracy is that the government could be replaced by free elections. If this possibility is not ensured, or has been drastically curtailed, the issue is no longer merely that of a distorted or incomplete democracy.

Between the two world wars the stability of the dominant regime in Hungary was ensured by administrative limits on electoral rights (electoral census, the absence of secret ballot in rural areas until 1939). The right to express an opinion in political matters was essentially—if somewhat sheepishly—held to be a privilege of the middle-class gentry. Seeking for parallels to the mafia state on the other side, drawing a comparison with totalitarian regimes would be completely misleading: for totalitarian regimes had virtually a one-party system. After World War Two, the power monopoly of the communist party was ensured with a ban on the operation of any other party, and by the fact that only delegates of the transmission belt of the communist party, the Patriotic People's Front—the organization that handled the elections itself—were allowed to run in the elections. But since their power was built openly on force, it was not necessary to worry about manipulating details of electoral conditions and chances. Between 1939 and 1943, in Italy, the traditional, multi-party parliament was in fact dissolved under the Fascist regime of Mussolini, while in Germany, from the mid-1930s onwards, not even manipulated elections were held. In the Soviet Union, elections were held with one party and one delegate to vote for. *In the totalitarian regimes everyone was under all-round surveillance and mobilization.*

The mafia state however employs a mixed technique of mobilization and demobilization. Since 2010 the conditions for free and fair elections have been in constant decline. This not only meant the situation with the freedom of press—as described in the foregoing—but also that of other pertaining rights. The *right of association* can at times only be practiced at the price of wrangling with the authorities, the *right to assembly* has been impeded, and *right to strike* has been virtually made impossible (aspects of these issues are discussed at the respective parts of this analysis). The regime has failed to attend to a stable and transparent *party financing mechanism*. Moreover government parties have decreased the budget allowance for political parties—hypocritically claiming popular demand—while at the 2014 elections they openhandedly supported the mass appearance of short-lived phantom "business parties" intended to disorient voters. At the same time, billions of public money are spent on party propaganda disguised as government information. The appropriation of the financial and communications environs of the elections by Fidesz in itself makes the electoral odds extremely unbalanced.

In the case of the declassed—that is, the *people pressed onto the periphery of the adopted political family or thrown out of it*—the regime uses the combined tools of repositioning by blackmail and vulnerability in such a way as to make turning openly against the autocratic powers not quite worth the battle, or too risky in the final run. As if it were a large mixing board, on which the tunes of "reward-disregard-penalize" were tailored to individual people or organizations. While the cases of arbitrary actions of the government form the everyday subjects of public conversation, there are rare instances of open resistance to them or efforts to get legal redress. People still have something to lose, and at the same time there is little confidence in the independence of the institutions providing legal remedy. Individual risk is far too great. These are the *techniques of demobilization and pulverization* that autocracy, unlike dictatorship—operates with. The analysts are more or less clear about these mechanisms, and are calculating whether in the circumstances that have been brought about by the manipulation of the electoral law a situation could present itself at all, where the government might possibly be defeated. Yet the growing proportion of those disillusioned, disappointed, confused could also be misleading, because they are more of a statistical quantity than an organic social fabric. (Reasons of the absence of a cohesive opposition are touched upon below.)

The aim of the process is unequivocally clear: first the *free and fair elections* become *free but not fair* elections, and then as a result conditions can be achieved where the means are available to ensure that if the regime so requires, future elections can be shifted into the category of *contested elections*.

6.2.1. Changes to electoral law after 2010

The most direct and final tool for the permanent installation of power however, is to manipulate the election law and the law for electoral procedure, that is, to de facto falsify the will of the electorate.

- With the extinction of the bipolar (right versus left, liberal) political structure following the regime change, an extreme right party, Jobbik taking around 15–20 percent of the national vote became a long-term fixture, which excludes the possibility—both in structural terms and in terms of values—of adding up all protest votes against Fidesz. This is the essence of the Fidesz strategy of the central field of power, which, as an analogy of the interwar pattern of party structure, constitutes a dominant governing force in the middle of the political scale flanked by an extreme right and some parties to the left. Furthermore, the political forces to the left of Fidesz are fragmented, the possibilities for their cooperation are limited. Well aware of this, Fidesz *introduced single-round elections* in place of the two-round elections that had been in place before. Therefore the democratic opposition actors that are not only fighting Fidesz but also rivaling one another, are forced to make their coalitions in advance, that is, to share the cake before they had a chance to match their strengths by the voters.
- *The restructuring of campaign financing*—while normal operations of parliamentary parties are sorely underfinanced—served the purpose of releasing an armada of insignificant *"business parties"* upon the electoral field. While the opposition parties were forced into preliminary coalitions by the electoral system, the plentiful availability of campaign funds gave adventure-seeking rogues the incentive to pick up the funding in the name of parties that practically did not exist. The relaxation of rules of candidacy served the purpose of allowing as many parties as possible to delegate individual candidates, and have them included on the party lists. For if a party was capable of delegating a candidate to one quarter of the single-member constituencies in 2014 it received 149 million forint (about 500 thousand euro), and if it could do so in all of the single-member constituencies it received 597 million forint (about 2 million euro) in campaign funding from the national budget. Allowances addressed lists and not parties, resulting that the coalition of democratic opposition parties could receive an amount as if they were one single party. The real function of the business parties was to disorient voters, fragmenting the government-critical votes. "Such parties pocketed nearly 4 billion forint of taxpayer's money, and the fate of 90 percent of the amount is not known, *so only 10 percent of the amount was spent on the campaigns in an accountable fashion. [...] Moreover, since none of the business parties won a*

single mandate, probably not even the State Audit Office will be con-
ducting investigations at the fake parties, as that could only be done
on the basis of filed complaints, and a complaint could only be filed by
another party that had run in the elections if it had concrete evidence
of misappropriation of public funds."[12]

- *The decrease in the number of members of parliament from 386 to 199*,
along with the simultaneous introduction of the one-round election
system in which relative majority wins the mandate favors the strongest party in relative terms. Its consequences became more excessive
by decreasing the compensatory effect of the votes for party lists by
granting the party winning most mandates in the single-mandate constituencies further compensatory bonuses. By these means the *dispro-*
portionality of the electoral system was exacerbated. (It was no accident that earlier, in 2009, Fidesz was not willing to support a motion
bringing about a parliament of 200 seats, because that solution wished
to ensure increased proportionality along with the cutback.)

- The drawing up of the larger electoral constituencies decreasing their
number from 176 to 106, and the continuous gerrymandering was
used as a tool in the creation of an *electoral geography* favoring the
parties in government. (On the basis of the new borders for the electoral constituencies Fidesz would have won every election since 1998,
including both 2002 and 2006—which it lost.)

- The introduction of *preliminary registration* would have been intended
to keep the layers of society that essentially lose out on the status quo
and are more ready to listen to social populism away from actually
being able to cast their votes, thereby decreasing the electoral swing
effect that is achieved purely by financial promises. Their efforts in this
regard failed however, due to negative reaction at home and abroad.

- Accepting Bertolt Brecht's ironic advice "to dissolve the people
and elect another," Fidesz indeed carried out a partial *virtual replace-*
ment of the population: while ethnic Hungarians living across the
borders from Hungary—mainly Transylvania in Romania—who took
advantage of the opportunity to have a dual citizenship are largely in
the government camp in terms of votes, those Hungarians who have
emigrated for shorter or longer periods belong generally in the opposition. The earlier could vote by a simplified procedure and simply mail
their votes. Moreover the loyal, government-funded civil organizations
across the borders could collect the ballots by the tens of thousands

without any oversight, on the basis of lists of addresses available only to them, and could eventually deliver them by hand, rather than post, to the organs handing the elections. At the same time the hundreds of thousands of Hungarian citizens working in Western Europe or the USA virtually had no means to exercise their right to vote: perchance they were able to vote by taking a trip of hundreds of kilometers, going to expenses of hundreds of dollars and standing in line for hour upon hour. This was the way government replaced a few hundred thousand government-critical voters with a few hundred thousand government supporters.

- Voters could register as members of an ethnic minority, but in this case they could not vote for a party on the national list, only the established ethnic organizations included on the **minority list**. Instead of strengthening minority rights, this resulted in the discriminative withdrawal of the political rights of hundreds of thousands, which had the most distorting effect in relation to the Roma people.
- With the **elimination of the campaign silence**, Fidesz, with its ample resources and the lists, databases of the party director Gábor Kubatov at hand (discussed earlier), could transform the elections into such a **central led logistical mission** that—lacking means—it was impossible for the opposition to mount a comparable mobilization in response.[13]

Even if the will of the voters had changed in case of a significant drop in popularity, the new election law could keep Fidesz in power due to its central political position and the biased revision of the electoral system.

6.2.2. The Prosecutor's Office as part of the campaign staff

Two factors external to the electoral system, yet with a significant influence on the outcome of the elections are usually highlighted: party-campaign financing and access to media. Both of these have been discussed earlier. Yet a third issue, the role of the **Prosecutor's Office** in criminalizing the opponents of Fidesz is wrapped in embarrassed silence even by international observers. Even though there is nothing new about the practice of the Prosecutor's Office putting a representative of Fidesz's political opponents on trial. It leaks information that vilifies the opponents to Fidesz supporting media carefully in keeping with the campaign schedule, while sometimes qualifying the cases as state secret so the accused is not allowed to even defend themselves in public. In certain cases public opinion is preconditioned with a pre-trial detention, house arrest or a photograph of the accused being led through court. The scoops are well-timed, while the cases can stretch out for years without a sentence. Their public presentation follows the seasonal variation of the most varied campaigns. Such *selective law enforcement adjusted to campaign objectives* can equally target innocents, others who can be blackmailed when the case is brought against them with lesser affairs, or parties actually guilty. At any rate, a significant proportion of the cases never reach the trial phase, or the accused are acquitted. The targeted individual is nevertheless successfully discredited. In these actions the real aim is not to bring justice, to have the individuals jailed, but to expulse them from the political scene, and/or to discredit and smear the political organization they represent.

Following the Prosecutor's Office however the *court has also been able to function as a government campaign tool*. The symbolic date to begin the trial of the police leaders who took measures in the anti-governmental demonstrations of autumn 2006 not only against those occupying the Hungarian television headquarters and setting it alight, but also against peaceful protesters was set on the anniversary of the date socialist prime minister Ferenc Gyurcsány's famous "lie speech" was leaked. The prosecutor's proposal of a suspended sentence is in itself indicative of the fact that the show campaign of disgrace serves identity building and voter base strengthening. In the "happiest mafia state" (paraphrasing the happiest barrack in the socialist camp, the label Hungary used to enjoy) there are only show trials for the moment—no prison sentences. In this case there is no target individual, but a "target cause," which means that the essence of the procedure is the symbolic importance of the identity-forming narrative of the accusation. Other cases—such as the approval by a former socialist prime minister of an exchange of real estate properties that could be tied to a casino development deal, or the case of spying by a former socialist minister overseeing the secret services—were motivated by personal revenge. In these cases a prison sentence was in fact at stake—unsuccessfully for the moment.

6.2.3. Establishing the institutional means of electoral fraud

But if all of the above had failed, *the law for electoral procedure ensures the possibility of fraud* as a final lifebelt.

- The obligation to prevent and combat the electoral fraud and impartial rulings on cases of legal redress was omitted from the new law.
- The law practically ensures a government party majority of elected and delegated members on all levels of the commissions supervising the electoral procedure. The "independent," "non-partisan" members of the commission are delegated either by the parliament with a two-thirds majority controlled by Fidesz, or the municipalities most of which have a marked pro-government majority.
- The private service provider for the IT systems of all the previous elections—to the satisfaction of all the political forces—was nationalized, so it has come under direct government control. The electronic procedure for vote processing has been interrupted by new stations in terms of the law, which creates uncontrolled possibilities for manipulation of the results.
- On grounds of protecting the ethnic Hungarian population abroad (with dual citizenship) the government is not willing to disclose the list of voters, or even their number country-by-country either prior, or after the elections. Thereby—in a unique fashion for Europe—the existence of votes in their hundreds of thousands cannot be verified. The National Election Commission, which has a Fidesz majority, publishes the results of the mailed votes of the Hungarians abroad, and no form of social verification is possible.
- The law leaves it up to the minister in charge to determine what parts of the comprehensive results of the elections will be made public, and how the electoral protocol containing the results is expected to cohere in mathematical-logical terms.
- The president of the National Election Commission—appointed for a nine-year term—decides about giving or denying the accreditation for the international observers without any justification, and there is no room for appeal. In terms of the regulation the international observers are prohibited from putting any questions to the representatives of the parties, the candidates or the voters. They are only allowed to address inquiries to the election commission.

These passages of the law making **election fraud** possible indicate that if need be, they can also be used. ***Not as an end in itself, but expediently when required.*** Similarly to the way it is done in post-communist states on the occasions when—as reported by international observers—a part of the elections are rigged. On the basis of the election law and the law for election procedure, as well as the tools of disenfranchisement and manipulation cited above not only the fairness of the elections can be called into doubt, but also its freedom. These methods are not those of the communist dictatorship, when the elections in fact were changed into the mere casting of votes as only one candidate and one party were allowed to stand or, if there were a choice of two candidates, they would represent the same category of a carefully arranged social tableau: two miners, two university professors, or two weavers competed between one another. Yet the exercise of these rights was quasi compulsory for the citizens—in order to demonstrate the commitment of the dictatorship to democracy. In contrast the mafia state, working behind the scenes of a democratic setup, manipulates and distorts the major aspects of the election system: the freedom of self-definition for the candidates, the resources the campaigns can rely on, the channels of access to voters, the impartial activity of the state enforcement authorities, the voter participation and especially the value of individual votes.

6.2.4. The 2014 spring parliamentary elections and autumn municipal elections

The manipulation of the electoral system can be seen as a sort of reversed salami-slice technique (piecemeal destruction of opponents): there was no trick serving the purposes of Fidesz, which they would not stoop to, irrespective of the number of votes it would bring. This is how the unfair advantages gained through the manipulation of the electoral system could lead to a two-thirds, constituent majority a second time, in the 2014 parliamentary elections. While in 2010 a 52.7 percent of votes were required for the majority ensuring absolute power, by 2014 a 43.6 percent was enough to secure 66.8 percent of the seats in Parliament. According to the 2010 rules this would have ensured only 59 percent of the seats.[14]

Thanks to changes in the election rules including a restructuring of the Budapest body of representatives, in the autumn of 2014, in spite of its decreasing support Fidesz has not only been able to hold on, but to grow its majority in the municipal leadership. While the new electoral system ensured that Fidesz had 61 percent of the Budapest body of representatives in 2014, according to the previous, 2010 electoral system—with the same number of votes—it would have taken only 39 percent of the seats in the body of the representatives.[15]

6.2.5. Means of curbing election results retrospectively

Fidesz had already questioned the cleanness of the 2002 parliamentary elections after having lost them, while its own government apparatus had actually managed them. Of course they were satisfied with the results of the 2010 and 2014 elections.

It was a different case with the municipal elections, where Fidesz could not get control over some municipalities even though it had secured a sweeping victory in the country. Let us disregard in the following the sort of appeals that requested the recounting of the ballot or protested the results with reference to a violation of the election law, for these are means that fit into the democratic procedure, even if at times they may have been used unnecessarily. There were however measures that sought to change the results of one or another non-government municipality by means abusing legislative power. Just a few exemplary cases are cited below:

- In the 2010 municipal elections in Felcsút, the prime minister's birthplace, an independent candidate won the position of mayor against the Fidesz candidate. The parliament passed a decree in the following stating that anybody with a tax backlog cannot become a mayor, and as a result due to a small amount's debt to the tax authorities the winner was stripped of his position. The repeat election was finally won by the stooge belonging to the adopted political family. Then in the following this legal constraint was withdrawn.
- Again, in 2010, the city of Esztergom elected an independent mayor in the municipal elections, while Fidesz held the majority in the body of representatives. The majority stripped the mayor of a significant portion of her authority on the one hand, and on the other made put such obstacles in the way of the municipal government's operation as to make direct government intervention in the life of the city possible.
- It could be seen in advance that the prospective structure of the Budapest self government would be dysfunctional, and governing the city would become even more exposed to the diverging interests of the 23 districts than before. The Fidesz candidate voiced his fear in this regard, and proposed the necessity of a Lord Mayor's right to veto decisions of the municipal body. Fidesz, however, waited for the results of the elections to come in, and only changed the law when its

own candidate had won. Obviously an opposition Lord Mayor would not have been given the reasonable authority necessary to make the city function. Though it is possible to look at the matter from the opposite angle: the members of the Budapest body of representatives were legislatively stripped of certain rights after they had been elected.

If Fidesz were to lose the next parliamentary elections, it would still be a valid question to raise: in how much would Fidesz then be able to make the competencies of the new government—formed of the will of a majority of the voters—virtual, through the agency of its cadres fixed firmly in their positions of public authority. One need but only think of the Fiscal Council dominated by Fidesz, not approving the budget, which would allow the president of the republic to call for new elections, as stipulated in the new constitution. While external to the election law, this is a way to not only question the results of the election, but nullify it.

NOTES

[1] Mária Vásárhelyi, "The Workings of the Media Octopus—a Brainwashing and Money Laundering Mechanism," forthcoming in: *Twenty-Four Sides of a Post-Communist Mafia State*, edited by Bálint Magyar and Júlia Vásárhelyi.

[2] Permission for the use of the diagram under discussion was granted by Attila Bátorfy, journalist at kreatív.hu. (See also under the following link: http://www.kreativ.hu/databanya/cikk/hogyan_mukodott_orban_es_simicska_mediabirodalma).

[3] http://vs.hu/mind/osszes/itt-a-kapcsolat-a-fidesz-es-a-tv2-eladasa-kozott-0120.

[4] http://abcug.hu/milliardokat-nyom-az-allam-az-origonak-es-tv2-nek/; http://magyarinfo.blog.hu/2015/02/05/itt_vannak_a_szamok_igy_befolyasoljak_orbanek_a_mediat.

[5] http://nol.hu/belfold/nagy-testver-a-tv2-t-figyeli-1569911.

[6] http://nol.hu/belfold/raszalltak-az-rtl-klubra-1574503.

[7] Permission for the use of the diagram under discussion was granted by Attila Bátorfy, journalist at kreatív.hu.

[8] http://444.hu/2015/04/15/habony-arpad-elolep-az-arnyekbol-es-mediacezar-lesz/.

[9] http://valasz.hu/itthon/eldolt-habony-lesz-az-uj-simicska-111628.

[10] http://hvg.hu/velemeny/20150609_A_media_elfoglalasanak_haditerve.

[11] For more on the electoral system, see the detailed discussion in Kim Lane Scheppele, "Legal But Not Fair (Hungary)," last accessed 13 April 2014, http://

krugman.blogs.nytimes.com/?s=Scheppele&_r=0; http://tenytar.hu/elemzes/kampany_es_valasztasi_rendszer_tanulsagai#.VMlVddKG9tM.

[12] http://tenytar.hu/elemzes/kampany_es_valasztasi_rendszer_tanulsagai#.VPoK2XyG9tO.

[13] http://444.hu/2015/02/20/szecs/.

[14] http://tenytar.blog.hu/2014/04/22/ezzel_az_eredmennyel_2010-ben_messze_nincs_ketharmad.

[15] http://tenytar.blog.hu/2014/10/20/budapesten_meg_tobbsege_sem_lenne_a_fidesznek_a_regi_valasztasi_rendszerben.

7. Legitimizing the mafia state: the ideological arsenal

7.1. Ideology-driven vs. ideology-applying system

Rather than driven by ideology, the mafia state relies on ideological templates of various sorts, and their use is determined by political expediency. It is as inconsistent in its policies as it is consistent emotionally. And its strength consists precisely in this: it defies rational criticism. "The epitome of my politics," Viktor Orbán explained in an interview in 2006, "can be summed up as follows: *reality without ideology*. (...) As it is true of any broad alliance, Fidesz is not held together by ideology but by common goals. People with various lifestyles and value systems are able to work in Fidesz, work for the victory of Fidesz, because they are bound together by common goals. It is not an organization based on one single coherent system of principles or an ideology—such an organization is incapable of expanding beyond a certain point. Fidesz has no such boundary, and therefore support for the party has no maximal value that could be determined in advance."[1]

The **weakness of rational criticism** consists in the fact that critics try to take the concepts used in the communication of the mafia state at face value rather than interpret them in the actual context of their meaning in society—concepts like nation, Hungarian, value-producing work, work-based society, speculative capital, bank, etc. This critical stance is unwilling to face the fact that these concepts have a different meaning in the language of the government and their followers: the nation / Hungarians = us, i.e., the members of the adopted political family, the non-foreign, the non-Jew; value-producing work = work that produces profit for us; speculative capital = work that produces profit for others; banks = those who exploit people; work-based society = he who does not work neither shall he eat, i.e., forgoing social solidarity, etc. Therefore, such criticism is **stuck in the basic stance of government criticism** rather than system criticism, or in other words, what it articulates is merely a **criticism of policy issues**, the presupposition of such criticism being that the criticized system and its critics both have the public good in mind, they only differ in their idea of the ways to achieve that. These two pillars of compulsively "politically correct" criticism—i.e., the narrow, literal interpretation of the language of the mafia state, devoid of its context, and the supposition that those in power have the public good in mind—confine liberal intellectuals to a subculture of martyrs who are "not understood." The intellectual superciliousness of these critical intellectuals who speak from the perspective of a Western set of social values when trying to point out the contradictions and the irrationality inherent in the messages and the politics of the mafia state betrays their misunderstanding of the new system and its operation. And the result is that they do not even start to scratch the mafia state with the linguistic inventory available to them.

The **weakness of ideological criticism**, on the other hand, consists in the fact that it looks at the system as if it was ideology-driven; what's more, as if it was driven by a coherent value system. This critical approach assumes that a descriptive model which explains the system by a sheer will to power and a desire to accumulate wealth lacks seriousness, as those in power do have certain ideas and values. We do not mean to say, of course, that this form of autocracy exhibits itself in a sheer desire for power and riches, without any ideological clothing. It is clear, however, that the mafia state is not the realization of a coherent value system or ideology chosen before coming to power, or of a system driven by any idea of the public good. What is it, then, that lends it an illusory "ideological" coherence?

As we have mentioned before, the power of the mafia state is based on an illegitimate extension of the competences of the head of the patriarchal family to the whole nation. The household of the head of the family includes blood relatives and adopted relatives; high- and low-ranking servants of the household and the land; and individuals who provide various, loosely related services. The head of the patriarchal family disposes of people, possessions, and statuses. Human history can be regarded as the process of gradual emancipation of the family and the servants under the command of the patriarch as these people were becoming less and less embedded in a system of dependencies. (The last phase of this process—which seems rather slow in coming—involves the declaration of the rights of children and the sanctioning of domestic violence, developments which would eliminate the last remnants of the patriarch's monopoly on violence within the family.) The mafia state is implementing the opposite of this process by eliminating the autonomous status of people belonging to various groups of society, and trying to subordinate them to itself, in accordance with the traditional patriarchal family model. The "ideological" coherence of the system consists in the *cultural patterns of the nature of a patriarch's domination,* as well as those ideological templates that are built on and are in accordance with those patterns, even if they are picked up from various value systems.

Of course, not all ideological panels fit the cultural patterns of this type of power. For example, those ideologies and set of ideas which stress the autonomy and the freedom of the individual (as long as the exercise of freedom does not impair the freedom of others) are alien to it as the role of the patriarch is easier to reconcile with elements of collectivist ideologies that allow domination over the household. However, not all collectivist ideologies can be reconciled with this function. The class-based and internationalist collectivism of the communist system of ideas is not suitable for the ideological legitimation of the patriarchal patterns of power. Therefore, the state mostly ends up picking bits and pieces from the ideological inventory of right-wing authoritarian systems. However, those value reflexes that it tries to activate in people it has drawn under its rule are not necessarily associated with modern dictatorships. "The thinking behind conservative (political) texts is dominated by a situation well-known in life: the conceptual metaphor that the state is 'a (strict) head of family.' In other words, it punishes and rewards its 'children'—citizens—according to their deserts; it does not tolerate deviation from the norms; it means to interfere with our private life, and so on. This family model is well-known to most people, even if they are lucky enough not to have been brought up in such a family, as they have surely encountered it in books and films, or have such a relative, teacher, or boss. There are countless clichés that call forth this model: from 'this is not the way to speak to your father' and 'do not talk back to me' to 'I'm the one who will tell you what you wear as long as I'm paying the bills'— right-wing parties prefer authority that stems from position rather than performance; they like to tell people how they should live, act, and think, and all this in the interest of the nation-cum-family and the citizen-child."[2]

The emotional coherence of power is ensured by the cultural pattern of this patriarchal family model, to which various ideological templates can be appended that may seem eclectic in other contexts. In this pattern, though power is commanding, it has a certain jovial artlessness and a personal, family-like nature. Its ritualistic, self-exhibiting acts are very different from the military parades of fascist or communist dictators in uniform, where masses of people were molded into impersonality, and from the impersonal protocol of the leaders of the Nazi party or the politburo of the communist party on the grandstand. On the contrary: the godfather spends time jovially talking to members of his 'household'—oligarchs, stooges, stewards, and farm hands—in the VIP box of his stadium, with shirt sleeves rolled up. If he is consistent in anything, it is surely in the maintenance and communication of this pattern of power rather than in ideologies or ideas.

7.2. Target-ideological templates: God, homeland, family, work-based society

The most important *ideological templates* of the legitimation of power are arranged around the concepts of *"God, homeland, family,"* the function and mode of use of which show, however, that the system is not ideology-driven, i.e., it is not determined by these concepts. When Orbán's critics define the ideological motives of his regime with categories like nationalism, religion, or a conservative focus on family, they are in fact attempting to interpret the system by starting from a traditional interpretation of these categories. That, however, has not much to do with the actual nature of the mafia state.

7.2.1. Nationalism, antisemitism, racism

By establishing the political nation, 19th century nationalism made all the citizens of a nation equal before the law, and it was on that basis that it struggled against other national endeavors. *The nationalism of the mafia state*, however, is not directed against other nations, but against those *within the nation* who are not part of the adopted political family, who are not subordinated to that family as vassals, and the family's opponents. In other words, all those who are not part of the godfather's "household" must bear the consequences for that. In this sense, the nation corresponds to the adopted political family and their appendages, from the head of the family down to the servants, i.e., public workers. The Hungarian adopted political family invented a national collectivist ideological framework for their own personal self-interest, in the name of a false social justice.

The winners—those who are part of the "central power-field"—can easily decode this language: "the nation" is in fact a euphemistic term for the adopted political family. After all, they cannot say that they are grabbing fortune for themselves. They know very well that when the godfather cites the interests of the nation, he actually means them, the adopted political family. The nation is guiltless, as it is the family itself, and those who are admitted to the fold will be protected and absolved of all their sins. Be they secret police informers compromised in previous regimes, communist apparatchiks or common criminals—all their sins will be forgiven if only they are loyal to the adopted political family. The power of belonging to the adopted family is guaranteed by the protection by the patron and the main threat, the inverse of that—the exclusion. Personal excellence of any kind will not protect critics of the regime from stigmatization and criminalization by the authorities, politically selective law enforcement, or the media of the mafia state.

For want of better, those adherents of the regime who have no share in riches and privileges are offered a sense of national community and a gratification of positive and negative biases: the exclusivity of "true patriotism" and the right to despise the enemies of the nation ("the alien-hearted," "traitors," and "bankers"; for some people this is basically equivalent to "Jews") and parasites of the nation (Gypsies, homeless and unemployed people). These are enthusiastic fools whose reward is the sense of being among the chosen ones and the legitimation of their disdain, sometimes hatred, for others.

7.2.2. Ideological pyramid scheme

This does not mean, however, that the leaders of Fidesz are antisemites. Their targets are not "Jews"—rather, they regard **antisemites as a political target audience.** Their problem with banks is not that they are "Jews" but that they are not *theirs.* They are not racist either—they just want to **win over people who have racist inclinations to their camp,** too. They do this consciously, pragmatically, without emotional turmoil. And on the way, they make morally unforgiveable concessions to that audience. It is this encoded but obvious antisemitism that informs **the language of Fidesz,** which labels its political rivals as "those alien-hearted," "destroyers of the nation," or "bankers' government"; their *favorite historical and literary figures*, including Miklós Horthy, the governor of Hungary between the two world wars, or antisemitic writers such as Albert Wass, József Nyírő, and Cécile Tormay; and their *symbolic gestures* like the inclusion of these writers in the national curriculum, the (re)naming of various public places or the awarding of extreme right-wing persons with national prizes and their appointment to leading positions in cultural institutions. In its relation to antisemitism and racism, Fidesz is utilitarian and cynical, because it needs that audience as well.

However, an inevitable consequence of this *ideological pyramid scheme*, aimed at winning over extreme right-wing voters, is the *legitimation and reproduction of antisemitic and racist feelings and discourse, as well as the increase in number of people who share these feelings*. (In this respect, the policy of Fidesz differs from the post-World War I policy of their role model, Prime Minister István Bethlen, who perhaps did not take strong and effective action against massive antisemitic feelings and movements but at least it was not him to transfer these onto the political field.) With the institutionalization and the strengthening of the extreme right (in spring 2015, the extreme right-wing party, Jobbik won a constituency seat in a by-election for the first time) the political field, hitherto divided into two, was divided into three, with the "central power-field," as Fidesz's communication is wont to call the party, doing their "peacock dance"[3] between two "extremes," the extreme left and the extreme right, offended at the former for questioning their commitment to democratic values, and at the latter for questioning their commitment to the nation. At the same time, Fidesz ironically comments on the unproductive struggle of the two "extreme" forces, where both are focused on the other. The "peacock dance," however, is not ideologically driven: a committed antisemite or racist would refuse to take one of its steps, a committed democrat the other. But the essence of the dance is precisely that its aim is not at all ideological—it is purely political and tactical.

Those to whom the regime cannot offer anything tangible should at least be given the joy to envy "the Jew" and despise "the Gypsy." This feeling binds them to the household of the family, i. e., their "nation." This term means various things on various levels of the hierarchy of the adopted political family: for the upper échelons of the political family, it is an ideological framework to legitimize their "national rule"; for the "serving gentry" and the "court purveyors," it means admission to the family and a "national certificate" that allows them to do their business; and for "believers" who have no share in the possessions, a "national consciousness-altering drug."

Any intellectual critical of the government can become a "Jew" who is alien to the nation, anyone poor can become a "Gypsy," exposed to the madness of an antisemitic and racist mob. The competition of Fidesz for antisemitic and racist voters with the extreme right—the number of whose followers is actually *increased* by this competition—by removing the obstacles to hate speech creates a dangerous situation. While of course the mafia state does not enact racist laws (making comparisons to fascism or Nazism unwarranted), their policy, which consciously brings up ominous reminiscences, increases the tendency of lynch culture to ease social tensions. The often ambiguous behavior of the police makes stigmatized groups and individuals even more helpless in front of racist and antisemitic aggression.

Refugees not considering Hungary as their final destination, who arrived in negligible numbers before 2014, have the same function. The broad aversion felt for them has grown to fear, at times hatred, as a result of a massive government propaganda which is trying to divert people's attention from the real reasons of their loss of popularity with stigmatizing and hate-mongering rhetoric. Rather than embarking on the road to democratic development, North African and Middle Eastern countries whose dictators were toppled have fallen into chaos, poverty, and violence. As of now, Europe has not found adequate political and economic answers to the flood of refugees that seriously effects Hungary as a transit country since spring of 2015. Orbán exploited the tension between the anxiety of citizens and the inadequacy of institutions when he sent out a questionnaire (at the expense of state budget) to all adult Hungarian citizens in the spring of 2015 as part of the "national consultation," with questions that highlighted the alleged link between terrorism, refugees, and unemployment—a typical instance of *incitement by the government*. The dramaturgy of this was the following: the series of questions begins with a terrorism alarm, and links that to the impotence of European immigration policy. Then the growing number of illegal immigrants crossing the Hungarian border is mentioned—immigrants who "jeopardize the jobs and livelihood of Hungarian people." Therefore the government urges action against the "lenient policy of the EU," including detaining and returning illegal immigrants to their country of provenance. As long as *"economic migrants"* are in Hungary, however, they "themselves should cover the costs associated with their time" in the country. With a populism that amounts to cynicism, the concluding question points to a possible solution of what is a real dilemma for Hungarian citizens: "Do you agree with the Hungarian government that support should be focused more on Hungarian families and the children they can have, rather than on immigration?"[4] This xenophobia is not ideologically driven; it is merely exploited for pragmatic reasons. Again, the language use is a way of stigmatizing immigrants in a sophisticated way: the Hungarian expression used for "economic immigrants" (*megélhetési bevándorló*) is not a value-free word. As Miklós Haraszti has pointed out,[5] the connotation of the word *megélhetési* is "parasitic, profiteering." It is used with the intention of hate-mongering, as in the expressions "*megélhetési gyermekvállaló*" (those [Gypsy] families who have children solely for the sake of child care benefits), "*megélhetési bűnöző*" (criminal out of poverty, code for Roma criminals), or even "*megélhetési politikus*" (a corrupt, opportunistic politician). The questionnaire was followed by the government's anti-immigration billboard campaign, with posters addressed to "economic immigrants" in Hungarian, within the Hungarian borders, conveying messages like "If you come to Hungary, you cannot take away Hungarians' jobs" (with the verbs in the informal form—*jössz, veheted*—used with friends and family or with people of lower rank). And if such warning were not enough, the government has closed the Serbian–Hungarian, and later the Croatian–Hungarian border with a 175-kilometre long and 4-metre high fence and hints at the possible construction of further walls if required. The influx of refugees was unhindered to begin with. Their amassment at the central train station in Budapest, and the well-considered inaction of the government authorities (such as the disaster management authorities) and the Budapest municipal government created unbearable conditions, merely to make it clear to the population: this is what would happen if the government did not protect you. With the building of the fence by the border, and the redirection of the flow of refugees Orbán demonstrated how effectively he had handled the situation, protected the Hungarian, and not only Hungarians, but the whole of Europe in fact.

In spite of the populist government campaign, opinion pols by TÁRKI, a social survey company show that "July 2015 data for xenophobia are once again at the same levels as in 2014 (which is lower than the levels measured before the campaign), which means it is high, but has not grown further as a result of the national consultation, the poster campaign, or the recent flood of immigrants arriving from the direction of Serbia, and receiving much attention in the media. However the number of those critical of foreigners has grown, and the proportion of those friendly towards them, decreased. Among those critical, the proportion of those who would refuse refugees entry has gone down, but Arabs would still be turned away by three-fourths (76%) of this group. Xenophobia is higher than average (39%) in those areas where the presence of refugees is most visible/troublesome, and where people feel the asylum seekers are apt for an expression of their prejudices against aliens."[6] The Paris terror attacks may however result in an increase of xenophobia, since the government propaganda obviously identifies the refugees with the terrorists. The government pushes the communications on the issue of migration full force simply on account of the fact that social approval of its measures in this area meet with far greater social acceptance than the popularity of Fidesz, while other areas are usually far less popular than the party as a whole.[7]

However, if those "foreigners" are sound businessmen, even if they belong to the criminal underworld, then the political family creates an opportunity for their stooges to do private business, breaking the state monopoly of issuing passports, so they could trade in passports valid in the EU. Those who buy "residency bonds" are granted a Hungarian passport and citizenship for 250,000 euro, with the stooge company's dividend amounting to 29,000 euro—a total income of 65 million euro up to February 2015.[8] From January 2015 the minimum price of the entry ticket has been raised to 300 thousand euro, while the agency charges an "administrative" fee of 40–60 thousand euros on top of this for its services. However, "according to a 2013 law, only intermediary companies designated by the economic committee of parliament, presently led by Antal Rogán (Fidesz) are entitled to subscribe these bonds to the Government Debt Management Agency. The foreign investor receives a bill issued by that company."[9] "Only counting the discounts the middling agencies have pocketed 25 billion forints until now, with the sum rising by another 37–40 billion if the administrative fee of 45–60 thousand euros is added. Thus the selected companies, among which there is only one registered in Hungary, will have earned 60 billion forints (200 million euro) since 2013. The highest earner is registered in the Cayman Islands, while the others are registered in Malta, Cyprus, Liechtenstein and Singapore."[10] The government's claim that Hungary does not need economic immigrants[11] is especially hypocritical in light of the fact that in 2014 the number of Hungarians employed in Western countries ran to at least 300 thousand, and their remittances grew twelvefold between 2008 and 2014, to 127 billion forints (approx. 410 million euro).[12]

The latest development in this ideological pyramid scheme was Orbán's declaration that one of the demands of the extreme right was now elevated to the rank of government program. Namely, the demand—echoed last year by János Lázár, Minister of the Prime Minister's Office—that "the question of *death penalty* should be kept on the agenda in Hungary, and we must let it be known that we will stop at nothing when it comes to protecting our citizens."[13] This in spite of the fact that Orbán knows all too well that manslaughter rate has decreased significantly compared to the decades before the abolishment of death penalty in 1990. He is also aware of the fact that the reintroduction of death penalty would go against our international commitments, and would therefore be unfeasible. However, this is not the real reason behind his rhetoric: he is counting on popular, visceral feelings, and in case this idea fails, he will still have the ideological benefit of increased anti-EU sentiments.

7.2.3. Religion

The religious commitment of the adopted political family is similarly pragmatic. Its function is, first and foremost, to transfer the legitimation of power from an accountable, democratic base to an unaccountable, authoritarian one, and ideologize the deeds of the godfather as guided by providence. Secondly, religion provides an unfalsifiable language for the ritualization of public affairs. Thirdly, it ensures that the power of Fidesz is socially embedded even in politically less accessible regions and social groups. And finally, it serves as an instrument of ideological indoctrination in education. *The link between the Church and the political power is businesslike, in a very secular way.*

This is how Orbán, who was an atheist in his youth, became an adherent of the Reformed Church, and he is also absolutely willing to take part in a Catholic procession, or to let go the Muslim murderer of an Armenian Christian, in the hope of striking a deal with the autocratic leader of Azerbaijan. The fact that he deprived the church which baptized two of his children of its previous status when its leader was critical of his policy, in spite of the decision of the constitutional court, is further proof that his religious policy is not ideologically driven. This is a veritable Thomas Becket story indeed. The idea behind his attitude is clear, but it is driven by power rather than by a Christian commitment.

7.3. Instrument-ideological templates: the System of National Cooperation and the national freedom fight

The moral responsibilities of the adopted political family—similarly to its historical prefiguration, the patriarchal family—are extended only to members of the family and the household. In terms of "us and them," "us" no longer means all the citizens of the nation, and "them" is no longer equivalent to members of other nations. On the contrary, the meaning of "nation" is narrowed down to the adopted political family, and all the other people are "them," even if they used to be considered as natural members of the nation when defined in a different sense. But now they have also become aliens for whom the adopted political family bears no moral or financial responsibility.

7.3.1. The System of National Cooperation (NER)

According to the declaration of parliament following the parliamentary elections of 2010, "in spring of 2010 the *Hungarian nation* once again gathered its vigor and realized a successful revolution in the voting booths. The National Assembly declares that it acknowledges and respects this revolution fought within the framework of the Constitution. The National Assembly declares the inception of a *new social contract* in the elections held in April whereby Hungarians decided on the creation of a new system: the System of National Cooperation. With this historical deed the Hungarian nation has committed the newly established National Assembly and the new government to *resolutely, uncompromisingly and steadfastly direct the work with which Hungary is going to build the System of National Cooperation.*"[14]

7.3.1.1. *The substantive, value-based justification of the NER— "the new principle of justice"*

The System of National Cooperation is actually nothing but the abrogation of the rules of liberal democracies in the name of the "revolution in the voting booths," and the proclamation of a policy aimed at establishing Orbán's illiberal democracy. As Gyula Tellér, the ideologue who has had perhaps the greatest influence on Orbán, wrote,[15] in the western model of democracies established after the 1989 regime change, "even after more than twenty years, it is still basically the internationalist successor groups (elites, parties, voters) of socialist power—who have preserved their positions or are intent on regaining power—who are confronted by civic and national forces striving for a regime change. (...) This struggle, which should have been settled in the moment of the regime change—in fact, *that* should have been the regime change itself—is a real life-and-death struggle which has still not been settled, as both parties represent a more or less equal force but radically different and mutually exclusive interests and conceptions about society." And he continues that "the basic principle of the new system is rather simple. It is communitarianism (...) as opposed to (neo-) liberal doctrine. (...) The nation is an organic structure which serves to determine public interest, to carry out our common tasks that stem from it, to solve them by relying on a common culture, common institutions, a common language, and the knowledge of a common past—a structure which expects its members to be motivated enough to preserve the community and participate in solving our common tasks, and which provides them with the necessary means for that purpose."[16] "The first indispensable element of the national system is distribution according to a 'new justice,' giving (extraordinary) reward for (extraordinary) efforts and performances that benefit the nation, launching en masse the cycle of 'reward–performance–reward' which would open up the possibility for recruitment inherent in this cycle (...) The second indispensable element of the national system is **the new principle of justice** and the mutual support and protection of those who profit from distribution based on this new principle and those in government who ensure this. From cycle to cycle, the government power supports and shapes those who perform well, and from cycle to cycle, the latter renew the government power which helps shape them; in other words, they launch and operate a 'performance–power–performance' spiral."[17] "This structure, which resembles patron-client politics, is merely a contingent element for the government which builds the national system— a sort of political 'womb' in which the new, well-performing part of society is being shaped and where it is allowed to grow."[18]

Or, in the words of András Lánczi, another ideologue of the NER: "How we evaluate the realignment of property after the regime change is a decisive question. There was a phase of spontaneous privatization immediately before the regime change, when those who were close to communist power were able to acquire state property. Although this was a brief period, lawful privatization made it possible for a great number of comrades to gain property through various channels. (...) It is all too well to claim that this is a new America, (...) but (...) [what is happening] here does not look at all like the foundation of America. Let no one be misled by the claim that what is going on here is 'theft' or 'corruption.' Not at all—this is a political revolution with economic consequences."[19] And this is happening because "the national bourgeoisie [must be] created by force," as Gábor Bencsik, the director of the extreme right-wing weekly *Magyar Demokrata* claims. "Of course, if you look at it from America, this is crony capitalism. Personalized tenders, rigged competitions, fixed aids. But there's no other way. Without this, Hungarian economy will never be strong."[20]

This is quite a simple formula if we substitute the adopted political family and their interests for nation and national interest (in this collectivist ideology), and the relationship between those who are involved in this circle of mutual support for the relationship of patron and client. Though actually, the categories in these ideologies used to legitimize the regime are surprisingly similar to, at times identical with, the categories of our description here. This, however, leads us to the justification of the mafia state in terms of handling power.

7.3.1.2. The justification of NER in terms of handling power— "the art of friendship"

The ideas of Tilo Schabert—a political scientist and Secretary General of the International Council for Philosophy and Human Sciences of UNESCO between 1995–96—about power and the exercise of power as "the art of friendship" bring us closer to understanding the logic of Fidesz's machinery of power. It is "an open secret in political science circles,"[21] writes Gergely Tóth, a journalist of the news site *Index.hu*, "that the organization of the NER was based on [Schabert's] book *Boston Politics—The Creativity of Power*. Schabert's oeuvre has at least two great admirers in Hungary: András Lánczi and Gábor G. Fodor, both members of the three-person advisory board of the Századvég Foundation—the institution that became the most important government think tank after 2011 with lightning speed though not without antecedents." "Schabert's book is the best and deepest description of how Viktor Orbán relates to governance," Gábor G. Fodor said in an unwittingly revealing interview.[22] Let's see the essence of Schabert's theory of power as summarized in five points by Gergely Tóth.[23]

- *It is easier to control a person than an institution*

According to Schabert, the greatest contradiction inherent in modern politics is that while the system of common law divides power and keeps it in check through various institutions, the government always needs to concentrate power to achieve its own aims. Therefore, the government has a predilection to act by avoiding *institutions* which resist the logic of power, and shape policy through *persons* who are willing to become clients, and therefore to be committed and manipulated. Paradoxically, the person-centeredness of government often manifests in the proliferation of institutions, but this is only the surface: according to Schabert, government institutions do not have much to do with real power.

- *Power structures must be loosened*

According to Schabert, the real structure of government cannot be described as a structure of institutions; he prefers to borrow a term from the Renaissance and call it the *Court*. In the Court, the *Autocrat* is the only fixed star, with the "second government"—consisting of persons who constitute the network of power rather than of institutions—revolving around it. The borders of the Court are blurred, with formal and informal positions constantly shifting, but there are some archetypal figures as well. It is an iron rule of the Court that the Autocrat must immediately loosen every single power structure that evolves outside of him.

- *Friends everywhere*

The Court and the organizations, institutions, and networks controlled by the Court function as an invisible employment agency. Schabert, however, provocatively claims that this is *not* corruption or nepotism as political power needs friends understood in the antique sense of the word—people who invest in power, both in the personal and in the material sense. Actually, the more such friends the Autocrat has, the better, as he is less indebted to one single person. Stressing the value of a relationship based on personalness and trust, Schabert repeatedly declares that modern political theories make too much of publicity, whereas real politics—that is, sheer power—always needs to be obscured.

- *Conflict rather than order*

Rather than establishing order, a real leader always strives to keep up chaos that he alone can see through and that permanently engenders new issues and new conflicts.

• *Power creates new and good things*

The power of the Autocrat, however, is not despotism or mafia government but—in Schabert's words—*creative government*. This is the most exciting idea of his theory as he claims, contrary to our civic conditioning, that highly politicized governance is in fact that much talked-about *good governance*. According to this theory, the tensions kindled by stratagems and conflicts have an effect similar to atoms clashing with increased frequency: they boost government activities with creative energy. This intensity must be the "chassis of politics" that runs public services, otherwise reforming ideas will remain mere fantasies.

The government think tank Századvég published a selection of Schabert's essays, including an essay on Kevin White—the mayor of Boston for sixteen years between 1968–84—his party and his power techniques.[24]

These essays can be read as a description of the genesis and the operation of Orbán's power practice: they describe "the 'natural' evolution" of a "party of friends," i.e., a "personal party," "from being an interest to being a *political* party and from being a family connection to being a web of widely extended connections,"[25] "transposing the political aspirations of a few friends into an effective political organization, forming a government."[26] "The core of this structure was the 'political family.' It consisted of not more than three dozen persons; its character as a 'family' sprang from the prevalent mode of relationship between these persons. (...) And they formed a family that was thoroughly 'political'; almost all of them held a position (or several positions) in the governmental structure established by the head of their family, Kevin White; the few others served the party in 'unofficial' but nevertheless political functions. The political family reproduced the cosmos of the interests of Kevin White—and these were the interests of the party. Besides the connection of Kevin White's family and old friends, the political family included: members of the court (...); pollsters and political consultants (...); developers and other persons active in the business of urban development (...); journalists (...); a fundraiser and a versatile politician..."[27]

Schabert, however, complains that "what existed necessarily as an instrument of governing" was depicted by Kevin White's critics and journalists "as a product of machine politics in its pure, i.e., 'dirty' form. What was animated by the art of friendship was described as a cancer of corruption. What was a quest for a chassis of politics in a city of fluid shapes was construed as a flagrant example of bossism."[28] Indeed, this model of governance was already present in republican Rome where "the personal parties of the patrician families dominated the public life."[29] In these parties, "the head of the patrician family established himself as a patron (*patronus*), protecting a throng of clients by using the political weight of his party, to which the more clients were likely turned, the more influence—that is followers and friends—it accumulated."[30] "After all, a party is a community of friends with a tail added to it," András Lánczi continues this train of thought, adding topical relevance. Gábor G. Fodor seems to be joining the same conversation: "And these friends will strengthen their power by concentrating all their force on one single friend who in his turn must be able to understand the ancient rule of politics that those who become our allies must be treated well so they will be devoted to the cause."[31]

We have reached an essential point here as even the patron parties of republican Rome cited by Schabert differ from the political art of friendship as practiced by Kevin White in their approach to *the question of legitimacy*. The patrician-led party of republican Rome had a legitimate base in the relationship between patron and client. It was not based on the evasion of rules about public procurement and conflicts of interest. In the case of the 20th century mayor of Boston, however, re-election did not mean an authorization to pursue politics by a "personal party" for private interests, moreover, to do that in a society which rejects that model. Orbán's rule takes even that model one step further as it does not simply consist in the manipulation of democratic institutions while more or less formally observing the rules, but he consciously resorts to illegitimate government coertion for his own self-interest. This amounts to *criminal state*, a subcategory of which is the mafia state. (We will return to its criminal legal consequences later.)

When describing the system with Schabert's concepts, the ideologues of the Századvég Foundation construe *the legitimacy of the system* in completely different terms than its critics who call the system to account for failing to adhere to the norms of Western liberal democracies. Indeed, this is the distinction between the corresponding descriptive categories of the NER and the mafia state, with the former justifying, the latter rejecting the system. The most important categories are listed in the table below. The system-apologetic description includes terms by Schabert as well as by leading Fidesz politicians and ideologues.

While before the regime change full employment meant that every citizen had their designated place in society, today the idea of *work-based society* means that only those who have a job can be considered part of the nation, members of the household of the political family—even if that job

System-apologetic description	System-critical description
System of National Cooperation, NER The creativity of power transcending fixed relations, unorthodox economic policy, etc.	**Mafia state** The illegitimate extension of the entitlements of the head of the patriarchal family to the whole nation
Nation, political family The reproduction of the private interests of the head of the political family	**Adopted political family** The head of the patriarchal family and his household
Autocrat, patron Head of the political family	**Godfather, chief patron** Head of the adopted political family
Invisible court A "second government," consisting of individuals who are part of the network of power rather than of institutions	**Polipburo** The narrow circle of the supreme decision-makers of the adopted political family, which is not a formal, legitimate body
Personal party From being an interest to being a *political* party; from being a family connection to being a web of widely extended connections	**Vassal party, transmission belt party** Through the mediation of the transmission belt party gives a legitimate form to the adopted political family's will
Patron–client relationship The party uses its political weight to protect its clients	**Patron–client relationship** Eliminating the foundations of personal autonomy and forcing existential situations into an order of dependency
Legitimate Because it was invested with a two-thirds constitutional power by the voting booth revolution	**Illegitimate** Because it was invested with the power of good governance within the system of institutions of liberal democracy rather than the disruption of that system

only means public work. And those who do not even have that—because they are unemployed, sick, homeless, Roma, etc.—are not part of the nation, the adopted political family, the godfather's household: they are excluded from the System of National Cooperation. If they cannot be integrated into the family even as servants, then they are left behind, on the borderline between the nation and the world of aliens. The NER feels and bears no moral or financial responsibility for them. "At least one third of Hungarian society is lost forever; there is no way to bring them back from utter destitution. The society can practically write them off. They don't want to work, and the job market does not want them either (...) it shouldn't come to light that these people must be left behind, because if we do otherwise, then the others will never make it either," a pro-government economist said.[32] The social policy of the NER is neither "conservative," nor "anti-poor" or racist in its ideological intention—it simply ignores those who do not belong to the household. They are not part of the family; they are aliens, so the family bears no responsibility for them. "Those who have nothing are worth just that much," as the minister of the Prime Minister's Office said,[33] and these people have nothing indeed. Nevertheless, this social policy, with overtones of the biblical wisdom "he who does not work neither shall he eat," gives ground to racist feelings as a side-effect of the competition for voters.

And the stakes of this *ideological pyramid scheme* must be raised continually. The *political actor* is not racist in its ideology, but in the *social environment* where it acts it generates and legitimizes massive racist feelings, with ever slighter chances of keeping these feelings in check. Indeed, according to data published by the human rights watchdog NGO, the Hungarian Civil Liberties Union (TASZ), anti-Roma feelings are not necessarily linked to party preference: "46 per cent of [extreme right] Jobbik voters, 33 per cent of Socialist voters and 31 per cent of Fidesz voters are clearly racist, and even within the green party, LMP [Politics Can Be Different] the rate of racist voters is 22 per cent."[34] As for antisemitism, the situation is quite similar. Although the rate of antisemites among Jobbik voters is clearly very high—51 per cent is extremely, a further 19 per cent is moderately antisemitic—their rate is quite high among Fidesz (20% and 19%, respectively), Socialist (13%, and 25%), moderate left Együtt-PM (16%, 13%), and social-liberal DK voters (8%, and 24%) as well.[35]

The *historical union of the "new national middle class," the political family, and those on the periphery of society* who wish to find their way back to society, a union that was declared in Viktor Orbán's Kötcse speech delivered in 2009 means that those who are excluded from the goods and the privileges can at least cherish being part of the emotional community of a deformed national pride and a nation's fight for freedom, hating the European Union, foreign capital, banks, Jews, Gypsies, gay people, communists, and liberals. Just like the community of interest of the adopted political family, the emotional community of losers, conceived in national faith, is a strong cohesive force. And just like the rationality of personal interests overrides the values of the republican idea for the former, the *shared emotional framework* blocks rational judgment and the effect of arguments for the latter. Therefore, their understanding for those who are in a different situation is paralyzed.

And they intend to give less and less to those from whom there is hardly anything to take any more. While in the upper levels of society, they try to squeeze out that part of the *intellectual and economic elite that they consider "alien to the nation,"* in the lower levels they punish *the poor who are not included in the nation.* Why should they care about the poor and the destitute? They do not vote, they are unable to represent their own interests, and they are good targets for the avalanche of disappointment, frustration, and delusion of those who are slightly above them. And then these groups will have it out with each other.

7.4. The national freedom fight

Us and them—the family and those outside the family, aliens, others. As we have seen, many of those who are excluded from the adopted political family are helpless and miserable, but there are others who represent a real danger as "whenever the left was given the chance, they attacked their own nation," as Viktor Orbán said.[36] These aliens outside the family are rival political forces, autonomous civil organizations, competitive entrepreneurs who do not depend on the state, and the independent press. And these must always be fought. *The secular religion of the mafia state is the nation, defended in a national freedom fight.* This is the ideology—complemented with resentment and envy against other social groups—that those in power use to convince those groups which are not beneficiaries of the system to become their adherents. And they are actually doing quite well in that sense.

But what exactly do the three elements of this mobilizing term mean? *National*, as we have said repeatedly, stands for the group with common interests—i.e., "us," the adopted political family. Their identification with the nation amounts to hiding private interest behind what seems like public interest. This is, after all, that "national, communitarian democracy" in which the so-called national goals of the "illiberal state" may override "selfish, individual interests," represented by liberal democracy, based on a respect for human rights. *Freedom* stands for the exemption of the adopted political family from the institutional bonds of liberal democracy; in other words, the institutionalization of arbitrary procedures. This is to be achieved by *fighting*, i.e., suspending the rights of political enemies "resolutely, uncompromisingly, and steadfastly,"[37] and doing that illegitimately, in various ways and to various extents. To those who participate in it, the need to suspend their moral qualms during this fight is justified by the interest of the nation. "Carl Schmitt is probably right in certain ways," Gábor G. Fodor, one of the ideologues of Fidesz's political strategy writes.[38] "He says that the specific distinction to which all political actions and motives can be traced back is the **distinction between friend and enemy**. This is the ultimate and the strongest criterion as it indicates the ultimate degree of connection and separation, integration and disintegration. It is the strongest also because it is capable of transforming all the other oppositions into a political opposition—in the final analysis, even the essentially depoliticizing efforts of liberalism." This is how both politics and the law can be relieved of moral ballasts, and make any political action seem lawful. Elsewhere, G. Fodor argues for the legitimizing effect of communication built on the dichotomy of friend and enemy: "I value authenticity in a different dimension. It is of no interest to people what you think of liberalism now and what you thought of it twelve years ago," he says, alluding to Orbán's volte-face. And he continues, "what really interests them is whether the government will protect them if they face various hardships, or not. The enemies and opponents of ordinary people change with time. If what they see is that the government consistently stands by them in these conflicts, then they will trust it."[39]

Let me quote at length from the book entitled *Boundless Language* by a linguist, Klára Sándor: "The concept of ruling a country is based on the idea of driving a vehicle, especially a ship. The Hungarian words for *lead, control, govern, government, head of government* all have the connotation of steering a ship, and so do some figurative expressions: we will hopefully *avoid whirlpools,* and will not *run aground,* but *reach safe haven,* and *weather political storms,* our economy will not *sink,* and our government will not be *stranded.* If, however, we base the concept of governing a country on metaphors of war rather than sailing, this will have the consequence of making different kinds of actions natural, unquestionable, and acceptable: actions that we do not consider as part of the normal functioning of democratic states in time of peace will be seen as matters of course. If a country is at war, then obviously, there is continuous *struggle,* one *battle* or *campaign* is followed by another. We have *enemies* in a war who must be *defeated,* or perhaps even *eliminated* rather than negotiated with, and it would be downright ridiculous to take notice of their opinion, let alone to try and reach a compromise with them. When people are at war, they have no time for scrupulous deliberation and lengthy debates, as the peacetime rules of lawmaking would have it. In a war, the general staff does not *liaise* with the foot soldiers; they do not *bargain*, they decide without the latter. There is no room for *insubordination*, dissident opinions amount to *betrayal*, and those who are dissatisfied may become *deserters*. As we know, in a war there are *sacrifices, financial and human*; also, there are many who have no choice but to accept living in poverty. At times, there are requisitions—not explicitly, of course, but by way of tax raises or by curbing the income of service providers like banks, phone companies, the media, public utility companies, etc. *War*, however, is not altogether a felicitous choice of metaphor as it calls forth unpleasant associations, so it is important to beef it up—for example, by stressing that the state is not an aggressor: rather, it defends our shared values against all sorts of sly enemies within and without. As the enemy can be an internal enemy as well, the war metaphor is a favorite trick of dictatorships—in the years of socialism and communist dictatorship, the political lingo was a source of irony as it not only talked about *class struggle* and *internal enemies,* but even *peace camp* and *peace fight*."[40]

It is not by chance that autocratic and dictatorial regimes also resort to the rhetoric of war as this is a universal method that is used to stigmatize rivals and temporarily or partially suspend their rights—however slight those may have been to begin with—and thus appropriate the autonomy of their property or status, if they still have any. If the state power massively focuses on such appropriation, in time, in space, or with regard to certain social groups, then this will take the form of various **centrally directed campaigns**. These campaigns have a certain dynamic, an ideological narrative mediated in a propagandistic way, and they are built on one another. However, while in the communist systems the series of campaigns that took the shape of a **permanent revolution** were aimed at the violent elimination of partial social interests, the campaigns of the mafia state that amount to a **permanent national freedom fight** are aimed at the coercive enforcement of the partial interests of the adopted political family.

These campaigns—which have a lot in common in spite of the differences between the various autocratic regimes—can best be defined as an action or series of actions launched by the center of power and directed from above as a political movement rather than as administration. The lawful routine operation of the administrative hierarchy is suspended for the time of the campaign. At such times, the apparatus oversteps its own institutional, legal, and "moral" barriers, and, transgressing even its own declared norms, abuses the chosen institutions, social groups, or individuals. This abuse, however, is far from being a simple violation of law or an incidental, unique blunder or crime of the bureaucratic apparatus or an official—it is a centrally proposed violation of law which is in fact clearly defined and mandatory, and which pertains to certain segments or the whole of the apparatus.[41]

So far, we have been discussing the function of the national freedom fight in fighting "internal enemies." However, to quote David O. Friedrichs, sovereignty claims of autocratic regimes "are now an illusion in terms of their traditional meaning. They are increasingly invoked to justify various forms of state-organized lawbreaking."[42]

NOTES

1 http://2001-2006.orbanviktor.hu/hir.php?aktmenu=3_4&id=2755.
2 This is how Klára Sándor summarizes the ideas of George Lakoff, an active supporter of the Democrats, who is "fairly annoyed by the fact that his ideological protégés do not make full use of the force of the metaphor of the 'nurturant parent model' (...), as opposed to Republicans, whose texts easily activate the thinking scheme of the 'strict father model.'" In Klára Sándor, *Határtalan nyelv* [Boundless language] (Bicske: Szak Kiadó, 2014), 305–6.
3 https://www.youtube.com/watch?v=0s5gzvb87ZY.
4 The questionnaire can be downloaded here in English: http://www.kormany. hu/en/prime-minister-s-office/news/national-consultation-on-immigration-to-begin (Click on 'Related files' to download it in Word format.).
5 http://hungarianspectrum.org/2015/04/26/miklos-haraszti-the-intricacies-of-translation/.
6 http://www.tarki.hu/hu/news/2015/kitekint/20150804_idegen.html.
7 http://www.median.hu/object.c38fa2c9-5bc2-40c9-ae38-bab515a5f172.ivy.
8 http://index.hu/gazdasag/2015/01/29/valaki_boduleteset_kaszal_rogan_otleten/.
9 http://mno.hu/magyar_nemzet_gazdasagi_hirei/otvenmilliardos-uzlet-a-letelepedes-1289722.
10 http://nol.hu/belfold/csak-penz-kerdese-ki-maradhat-1568359.
11 http://www.kormany.hu/hu/belugyminiszterium/parlamenti-allamtitkarsag/hirek/magyarorszagnak-nincs-szuksege-megelhetesi-bevandorlokra.
12 http://tenytar.blog.hu/2015/04/23/ot_ev_alatt_hatszorosara_nott_a_magyarok_kivandorlasa.
13 http://www.theguardian.com/world/2015/apr/29/hungary-pm-death-penalty-work-camps-for-immigrants-viktor-orban.
14 http://www.parlament.hu/irom39/00047/00047_e.pdf.
15 Gyula Tellér, "Született-e Orbán-rendszer 2010 és 2014 között?" http://www.nagyvilag-folyoirat.hu/2014-03_beliv_OK.pdf, 348.

16 Ibid., 356.
17 Ibid., 361.
18 Ibid., 361.
19 András Lánczi, "Mi a tét?" [What are the stakes?] http://valasz.hu/itthon/mi-a-tet-74462.
20 Gábor Bencsik, "Kapitalizmus magyar módra: innen merre van előre?" http://mandiner.hu/cikk/20150422_bencsik_gabor_kapitalizmus_magyar_modra_innen_merre_van_elore.
21 http://index.hu/belfold/2014/08/29/az_orban-rendszer_titkos_bibliaja/.
22 http://magyarnarancs.hu/belpol/a-rendszer-igazsagait-vedem-93802.
23 http://index.hu/belfold/2014/08/29/az_orban-rendszer_titkos_bibliaja/.
24 Tilo Schabert, A politika méltóságáról és jelentőségéről [About the dignity and importance of politics] (Budapest: Századvég, 2013).
25 Tilo Schabert, Boston Politics—The Creativity of Power. De Gruyter Studies on North America 4. (New York: de Gruyter, 1989), 118.
26 Ibid., 128.
27 Ibid., 129–130.
28 Ibid., 112.
29 Ibid., 112.
30 Ibid., 113.
31 http://gfg.blog.hu/.
32 http://kanadaihirlap.com/2013/01/26/ne-higgyetek-a-szemeteknek/; http://valasz.hu/itthon/megszoritjuk-magunkat-59267/.
33 http://index.hu/belfold/2011/03/19/lazar_szerint_akinek_nincs_semmije_az_annyit_is_er/.
34 http://www.hir24.hu/belfold/2013/12/14/nincs-hatara-a-rasszizmusnak-magyarorszagon/.
35 http://www.tarki.hu/adatbank-h/kutjel/pdf/b342.pdf.
36 http://index.hu/belfold/orbiet0723/, http://regi.sofar.hu/hu/node/35163.
37 http://www.parlament.hu/irom39/00047/00047_e.pdf.
38 http://valasz.hu/publi/schmittnek-igaza-van-60296/.
39 http://magyarnarancs.hu/belpol/a-rendszer-igazsagait-vedem-93802.
40 Sándor, Határtalan nyelv, 313–4.
41 Bálint Magyar, Kampányok a falusi térben az ötvenes évek elején, manuscript. [Campaigns in rural areas in the early fifties.] 1986.
42 David O. Friedrichs, "Transnational Crime and Global Criminology: Definitional, Typological, and Contextual Conundrums," Social Justice. Vol. 34, No. 2 (2007): 13–4.; http://www.socialjusticejournal.org/archive/108_34_2/108_02Friedrichs.pdf.

8. The Criminal State

Let us continue with the work of David O. Friedrichs, who, in the field of organizational crime, has systematized criminal acts according to the type of organization that commits them.[1] He makes a differentiation between corporate crimes and state crimes. However, government and business may occasionally collaborate, and even directly encourage and assist each other in committing certain crimes. Three separate categories follow from this: state-facilitated corporate crime, corporate-facilitated state crime, and state-corporate crime, which occurs when the two act together on an equal basis. "**Governmental crime**—or crime that occurs within the context of government—is the principal cognate form of white-collar crime. **State crime** (or crime of the state) is macro-level harm carried out on behalf of the state or its agencies; **political white-collar crime** is crime carried out by individuals or networks of individuals who occupy governmental positions and seek economic or political advantage for themselves or their party."[2]

Yet not only such a thing as **state crime** exists, but also a **criminal state**, which is a state that systematically, deliberately, and perniciously violates and impairs the fundamental rights of its citizens. Within such a state, both the various economic entities that depend on public procurements and tenders, and the civil society organizations—that in reality function as political puppets and serve the interests of power—are interwoven very tightly within the state and government. In such cases, those involved in corrupt activities and those in a repressive regime are connected to each other in manifold ways.[3] Nevertheless, it is worth classifying these potential states according to their main criminal activity. Consequently, one can differentiate between a *"criminal state*, with a central project of a crime against humanity"; a *"repressive state*, with a core project of systematic denial of basic rights to citizens or some group of citizens"; a *"corrupt state*, with systematic looting of the state for the benefit of the leadership and relatives or associates of the leadership"; and finally a *"negligent state*, characterized by a basic failure to alleviate forms of suffering that the state could address."[4] A criminal state, of course, may be characterized by different combinations of the "state projects" listed above.

8.1. Hungarian law on criminal organizations

According the Hungarian Criminal Code, *"criminal organization: a group of three or more people, formed for an extended period of time and acting in concert, with the objective of (...) intentionally perpetrating criminal offenses."*[5] In applying this law, "acting in concert" means that the members of the criminal organization *"share tasks related to criminal activities,"* which *"obviously presumes prior planning, and a certain degree of direction and organization."* A legal harmonizing resolution by the Supreme Court of Justice in 2005[6] also provides guidance on understanding the functioning of a criminal organization for different specific trial situations, as follows:

- a criminal organization is qualitatively different from simply individuals acting together; the *criminal organization itself has to be formed for an extended period of time, and must act in concert*;
- "acting in concert" is a conceptual component of the *criminal organization*, which, in terms of content, is none other than the *mutually-reinforcing effects on those acting in it*; however, the existence of acting in concert does not follow from being in direct contact with actors in a criminal organization, nor specific knowledge of other actions or the identity of other actors; behavior as *a member of a criminal organization* can only be attributed to a perpetrator who has engaged in activities in a criminal organization formed by a division of functions, and in a manner based on superiors and subordinates, with full knowledge of the organization, and collaborated while in constant contact with its members;

- the existing provisions of the Criminal Code do not distinguish among the **hierarchy** (or "posts") **of actions within the criminal organization** in terms of their activity or intensity, as these conditions are only considered during the sentencing phase;
- a person outside of a criminal organization does not become a member of it by receiving a contracted job from the organization, as integration into said organization requires knowledge of the organization's inner workings and active involvement within it; a clear distinction must be made between substantively judging a criminal act committed as a member of a criminal organization, and *a criminal act committed on a contracted job from a criminal organization (or any of its members)*;
- if there is evidence that a criminal offense was linked to the operation of an actual criminal organization, or committed within the context of such, then due to the conditions it was carried out—particularly due to the nature of specific behavior presuming the prior or later **linked actions** of others, and due to events that are necessary and therefore likely to occur, it can be concluded that the action of the occasional perpetrator (participant) is recognized at the time it was carried out as being committed within a criminal organization.

Clear language. Although the legal harmonizing resolution grants a unified interpretation of human trafficking, prostitution, drug trafficking, and other classic activities of a similar nature in the organized underworld, neither the Criminal Code nor the definitions in the resolution exclude the possibility of applying these provisions in cases when a large part of the members of a criminal organization are leaders at the highest levels of public authority institutions. In fact, it does not even exclude this from being the element that moves and defines the criminal organization, which is not the organized underworld, but the organized upperworld itself.

8.2. The Palermo Protocols

The Palermo Protocols against transnational organized crime, adopted in 2000 by the United Nations and ratified by Hungary in 2006,[7] also does not rule out the narrative that the struggle might not only take place between the organized groups in the underworld and representatives of state authority, but that the representatives of the state can themselves form the core of the criminal organization.

Following the Palermo Protocols, the Council of Europe's Group of specialists on organized crime (PC-S-CO) also defined the criteria that, when present, provide evidence of a *criminal organization*. Their definition includes both mandatory and optional criteria. As will be seen, the criteria used by the expert group to define the mafia, or the organized underworld, which also regulates Hungarian criminal law, may also be used to describe the organized upperworld, or the functioning of the mafia state. The Protocols distinguish between mandatory and optional criteria as follows:

Mandatory criteria:
- collaboration of three or more people;
- for a prolonged or indefinite period of time;
- suspected or convicted of committing serious criminal offenses;
- with the objective of pursuing profit and/or power.

Optional criteria:
- having a specific task or role for each participant;
- using some form of internal discipline and control;
- using violence or other coercive means suitable for intimidation;
- exerting influence on politics, the media, public administration, law enforcement, the administration of justice or the economy by corruption or any other means;
- using commercial or business-like structures;
- engaged in money laundering;
- operating on an international level.

8.3. The mafia state as a type of criminal state[8]

It should not be particularly difficult even for the lay reader to see that the mafia state assigns its most suitable persons and events to these criteria. "What is picking a lock compared to buying shares? What is breaking into a bank compared to founding one?" asks Mack the Knife in Brecht's *Threepenny Opera*. In terms of the mafia state, one might ask what law breaking is compared to passing legislation. What is robbery compared to the expropriation of property through laws and decrees? What is abuse committed by one's boss compared to centrally-planned purges? What is hacking a website to illegally depriving someone of their radio frequency? And one can keep going down the list across all areas of life, where it is evident that the institutions of public authority are not the guardians of legality and equality before the law, but just the opposite: institutionalized bodies serving the arbitrariness of personal interests.

The question is no longer how it should be interpreted in a legal sense when "three or more people collaborating"—unlike the presumably original expectations of Hungarian legislators, or the Council of Europe's Group of specialists—does not mean the underworld mafia, but the organized upperworld, sometimes even those with official duties. The question is how the machinery of justice can be put in motion at all in a mafia state, and how society and the immune system of public authority that has not yet paralyzed completely can be activated. The answer to this would naturally go beyond the "descriptive" and "understanding" genre of sociology.

The central figure in the criminal state is not an arbitrarily-structured power elite with an incidental culture, but in the case of the mafia state, as this study has repeatedly stated, it is the adopted political family with powers granted by the patriarchal head of the family, which are then extended to the entire nation through illegitimate means from a supreme, narrow group of decision-makers, working as a non-formalized, non-legitimate body. In this case, the agent of action, *the criminal organization perpetrating criminal offenses, is the "polipburo"* itself, in which some members have senior-level public authority duties at the very top of the branches of power, including all of their key institutions. There are also "advisory" members that have not been incorporated into the institutions of public authority, as well as trusted oligarchs and possibly their stooges as well. Perhaps a dozen or two individuals make up the "polipburo" of the mafia state. The criteria for a criminal organization applies to them: "three or more people," "a group formed for an extended period of time and acting in concert" that has a "hierarchy" and "mutually-reinforcing effects on those acting in it," and includes "the objective of perpetrating criminal offenses," "dividing up tasks" required for this, and if necessary, "contracting" persons outside of the criminal organization.

From amongst isolated violations of the law, the contours of relationships in the mafia state are outlined by the *linked actions* of organized crime. These include acts that are unlawful in and of themselves (such as extortion, fraud and financial fraud, embezzlement, misappropriation, money laundering, insider trading, agreements that limit competition in a public procurement or concession procedure, bribery, bribery of officials, both the active and passive forms of these last two criminal acts, abuse of authority, abuse of a public service position, buying influence, racketeering, etc.) combined with acts that are not unlawful in and of themselves (such as motions submitted by independent Parliamentary representatives, instigating tax audits, etc.).

8.3.1. One example: criminal organizations expropriating property

A linked action may be made up of a wide range of variations on the aforementioned situations. Modeling the actions of a state-sponsored criminal organization and standardizing them in the conceptual framework of criminal law would require a separate study. Therefore, we will only recall the previously-discussed case of outdoor advertising company ESMA in the context of criminal law mentioned above. And so: with ministerial collaboration, an offer to the owner of this particular outdoor advertising company is made to be purchased by a potential new owner belonging to the leading oligarchs of the adopted political family is also named; the business owner does not accept the offer, upon which the tax authorities appear at his door as a means of persuasion through non-physical violence. This still does not convince the owner of the desired company to rid himself of his property, upon which, again as a means of bloodless violence, an ad hoc legal amendment proposed by a parliamentary representative and adopted by the Parliament deprives the company of its concession-based activities. The company's value begins to drop precipitously, and as a final step, a second amendment exempts his rival from any possible negative consequences stemming from the amendment that destroys the business in question. The entire operation takes place within a very short period of time. After the company is starved for several years, the owner sells his hopeless business, at which time the godfather's new, favorite oligarch then makes an offer for it at a moderately-depressed price. And as expected, the discriminatory legal provision that made the business impossible to run is also repealed by the Parliament, so that the new oligarch loyal to the godfather can operate his firm at full capacity. Unlike the traditional mafia, public authority in Hungary uses bloodless means to enforce its will.

This case bears the characteristics of the activities of a mafia state criminal organization. The actions:

- intentionally perpetrating criminal offenses (extortion, abuse of authority, etc.);
- acting in concert, as a wide range of the branches of power (ministerial, governmental control and law enforcement institutions, the legislature) and individuals (see the oligarchs, the chosen beneficiaries who change from time to time) are required to coordinate their actions according to a specific time and sequence;
- the members of the criminal organization constitute a hierarchical group, where those who comprehend the entire operation are isolated from those carrying out the actions, each person just one step lower in the hierarchy (such as public servants conducting tax inspections, or parliamentary representatives submitting legal amendment proposals);
- persons in the criminal organization mutually reinforce the effects of their actions, since they would not be able to reach their desired goal (expropriation of property) by acting independently.

But the multitude of cases described above could also be discussed through a similar framework: starting from the issue of biased leases of state owned land to the concessions on slot machines, casinos or the retail sale of tobacco.

8.4. Classifying criminal organization actions

1. The nature of damage caused by criminal organization actions of the state, broken down by damage caused to either private or public parties:

- *damage to public property and revenue:*
  - ➢ diverting potential state revenue to private parties (e.g., the gas deal between MVM [Hungarian Electricity Company] and MET Holding AG);
  - ➢ forgoing potential tax revenue (e.g., forgiving billions of forints in tax debts without audits by the tax authority);
  - ➢ diverting potential state dues to private parties (e.g., the residency bond—250,000 euro in addition to a 29,000 euro fee, which is collected by some half-dozen firms close to Fidesz that are entitled to deal with it);

> diverting state concessions to private parties (e.g., online gambling);
> expropriating leasing rights (e.g., on the basis of civil law, dispossession of rights to pre-lease state land that is rightfully due to private lessees);
> diverting municipal or government real estate properties to individuals within the political family's sphere of interest at below-market values (e.g., the downtown Budapest real estate racket, which has given rise to alleged misappropriation);
> illegitimately diverting tender funds to overpriced bidders within the political family's sphere of interest (e.g., the series of tenders won by Simicska, Mészáros, Tiborcz);

- damage to private property and income:
  > expropriating property (such as the dispossession of savings accumulated in private pension funds, but also includes the forced nationalization of the savings cooperatives and their subsequent transfer to third parties);
  > expropriating private enterprises (e.g., 300-400 private companies by media estimates, such as the case of ESMA, discussed above);
  > introducing mandatory state concessions for private enterprise activities (e.g., retail and wholesale tobacco sales);
  > expropriating state concessions and leasing rights (e.g., slot machines, allocating state land leasing rights to targeted members of the political family regardless of prior relationships with lessees or producers);

- *causing both public and private damage* (e.g., manipulating the concessions for slot machines and casinos)

2. Connectedness of the actions by a criminal organization:

- *single-staged*: a single-staged corrupt act can be understood as a simple corrupt transaction occurring between two parties that only involves a single deal. These acts fall within the scope of classical corruption with each representing a small amount of value, regardless of how many they are. The mafia state attempts to put these ad-hoc individual actions under its control.
- *multi-staged*: actions with multi-staged connectedness involve many institutions in the legislative and executive branches, and a complex

cooperation between legislative acts and executive bodies may also be possible. This is much more typical of the everyday functioning of the criminal state, since by necessity, only these complex mechanisms are capable of realizing large-scale projects that rewrite market conditions, often fundamentally, implemented through the intertwining of government and business.

3. The institutional scope of managing corrupt transactions by a criminal organization:

- *within one institution:*
  - ➤ at the clerical level: almost without exception, this coincides with single-staged, non-interconnected corrupt actions. Obviously, implementing corrupt plans that are complicated or applicable nationwide simply cannot be conducted at low levels of administration: the vertical structure of the relevant government institution must necessarily be involved;
  - ➤ complete vertical structure within the institution: it is inconceivable that corruption at certain central agencies, such as the suspected corrupt acts of the tax authority, including its well-known tax remissions on the order of billions of forints, would occur without the knowledge and approval of the entire vertical structure of the institution. In these specific cases, "equity," the original purpose of which would be to assist taxpayers in a tight situation with small tax debts, here appears as a means of abuse to increase the profit of the loyal major entrepreneurs;
- *interinstitutional:*
  - ➤ horizontally: when several institutions cooperate with one another, which is considered rare in any event, as in complex transactions require coordination from above;
  - ➤ vertically: due to the functioning of the Hungarian criminal state, as previously outlined, the vertical structure necessarily comes to the fore.

4. Extent of the authority of the institutions involved:

- *local*: areas where the dominions of certain "tax renters" are paid out as actual remuneration—such as the cities of Hódmezővásárhely or Debrecen—are classic examples of relative autonomy from the center, their former mayors being closely linked to top of the political family.

In a certain respect, the real estate racket in downtown Budapest can also be included here.

- *nationwide*: for example, anomalies surrounding the Paks nuclear power plant tender can be included here, as well as MET Holding AG's gas and oil deal with public company MVM that resulted in dividends of around 50 billion forint—most of which went to offshore companies.
- *local and nationwide*: classically included here are the land lease and tobacconist transactions that were centrally directed but carried out primarily at the local level, and without either central or local coordination, they would not have occurred.

5. Type of collaborating institutions according to their branch of power

- *legislative*: during the period 2010–2015, the parliament passed a mass of custom-tailored laws that mostly served as a framework for any subsequent manipulation, as well as laws that generally support the functioning of the mechanisms of state corruption, such as:
  - ➢ raising price limits on public procurements (thereby facilitating the feasibility of a higher degree of corruption in procurements);
  - ➢ facilitating the undue classification of public interest data (under the pretext of national strategy and national security considerations);
  - ➢ the law facilitating money laundering;
  - ➢ eliminating conflicts of interest as an obstacle in applying for tenders and subsidies;
  - ➢ upholding the confidentiality of official asset declarations by the relatives of politicians;
  - ➢ abusive disqualifying applicants from public procurement tenders, on occasion or for longer period.
- *executive* (public administration): the list of collaborating institutions ranges from central bodies (e.g., the tax authority), to municipalities and chamber associations. The use of the Counter Terrorism Centre as a political tool also emerged in the case of WELT 2000, a company that owned software and databases used in applying to EU grants.
- *justice*: selective law enforcement, in which the number of cases prosecuted on corruption-related charges has fallen to an unprecedented extent.
- *any combinations thereof.*

6. Statutory definition of crimes committed by a criminal organization:
- extortion, fraud and financial fraud, embezzlement, misappropriation, money laundering, insider trading, bribery, bribery of officials (both the active and passive forms of these last two), abuse of
  authority, abuse of a public service position, buying influence, racketeering, etc.

Categorization of four cases of criminal organization
acts under the mafia state

Action by the criminal organization	ESMA (Outdoor advertising company)	Land leases	Slot machines, casinos, online betting	Tobacconist concessions
injured party	private sector	private + public sector	private + public sector	private sector
connectedness	multi-staged	multi-staged	multi-staged	multi-staged
institutional scope	interinstitutional (horizontal and vertical)	interinstitutional (horizontal and vertical)	interinstitutional (horizontal)	interinstitutional (horizontal and vertical)
extent of the authority of the collaborating institutions	nationwide	local and nationwide	nationwide	local and nationwide
type of collaborating institutions according to their branch of power	legislative, executive (ministries, tax authority), branches	legislative, executive branches (ministries, National Land Fund Management Organization)	legislative, executive branches (ministries)	legislative, executive branches
applicable statutory definition of crime	extortion, abuse of authority, abuse of a public service position, buying influence, bribery of officials (active and passive)	buying influence, racketeering, bribery of officials (active and passive)	buying influence, racketeering, bribery of officials (active and passive)	abuse of authority, abuse of a public service position, racketeering, bribery of officials (active and passive)

In most cases, there is no need even to run through the entire process,
since the victims understand that the "offer" from the adopted political

family, backed by the full arsenal of state power, "cannot be refused." And so businesses created through threats and extortion take the appearance of being voluntary, which will usually reduce the victim's losses if he can take the hint and is willing to reach an agreement. As with the mafia, in that the proportion of those who suffer physical violence following a "voluntary understanding" is minimal compared to those who pay protection money or offer their services, it is also usually sufficient for the mafia state just to display the range of illegitimate state coercion, accompanied by an offer for a "voluntary" deal. (Needless to say, achieving similar goals in a real dictatorship does not have to be so complicated, or done in a way that imitates the functioning of a democratic institutional system.)

As the institutionalized immune system of liberal democracy is neutralized, the process of socialization of obedience and submission advance forward. If the monitoring power of the public is restricted, if the chances to change the government are reduced by manipulating the electoral system, and if faith is effectively lost in the fair operation of forums for legal redress due to selective enforcement of the law, then the effect will be in the direction of acquiescence and accommodation. One cannot help but notice that the Chief Prosecutor is also a part of the polipburo, a colluding member of the team, and so *there is no means by which the machinery of legal redress or justice can be set in motion against the criminal organization of the polipburo.* (In fact, in the course of selective law-enforcement, it is not only a question of who is not charged with a crime, so that they can be left to run or just continue to "work" obediently according to their instructions in the vassal order, but who is charged merely with criminal intent. Furthermore it is also about who faces a preliminary trial that was initiated by Hungarian prosecutors for protective purposes, so that this person can be "immunized" by the courts, and relieved from having to stand trial in front of international law enforcement agencies.)[9]

As a result of this socialization process, the number of crimes reported between 2010–2013 for three types of criminal activities related to corruption, both active and passive forms of official bribery as well as racketeering, decreased to one-half to one-third of the amount in the preceding four years.[10] One reason for this may be that "citizens were previously more likely to see the value of reporting crimes, or even that they had less fear of reprisals,"[11] meaning that reporting on others for a crime turns into reporting on oneself. But even more telling is that—as an illustration of selective law-enforcement—the number of crimes that were reported but later rejected by the authorities has tripled, and the rate of investigations that were started but then terminated has doubled.

The peaceful enlargement of the political family's assets in spite of the complaints filed against fortunes earned from suspicious sources is served by the amendment of the law on tax authority regulations that states the "Hungarian Tax Authorities will not initiate an investigation of any person based on requests." According to the amendment accepted on 1 December 2015, NAV can only initiate proceedings against a private individual if the authority itself initiates the proceedings on its own account, or if the police already have an investigation underway for suspicion of crimes against property.[12]

NOTES

[1] David O. Friedrichs, *Trusted Criminals* (Belmont: Wadsworth Publishing, 2010).
[2] Friedrichs, "Transnational Crime and Global Criminology," 9.; http://www.socialjusticejournal.org/archive/108_34_2/108_02Friedrichs.pdf.
[3] Friedrichs, *Trusted Criminals*, 132–158.
[4] Friedrichs, "Transnational Crime and Global Criminology," 10.
[5] http://net.jogtar.hu/jr/gen/hjegy_doc.cgi?docid=A1200100.TV, 459. §(1).
[6] http://www.lb.hu/hu/print/joghat/42005-szamu-bje-hatarozat *Resolution 4/2005 by the Criminal Legal Section of the Supreme Court of Justice.*
[7] Act CI of 2006 on the promulgation of the United Nations Convention against transnational organized crime, as established in Palermo on 14 December 2000.
[8] For more on classifying the public legal system as one that stretches the conceptual limits of a criminal organization, see Imre Vörös, "A 'Constitutional' Putsch in Hungary between 2010–2014," forthcoming in: *Twenty-Four Sides of a Post-Communist Mafia State*, edited by Bálint Magyar and Júlia Vásárhelyi.
[9] http://nol.hu/gazdasag/ujabb-botranyos-hangfelvetel-1469927.
"The following is from an audio recording published in the Polish liberal weekly Wprost on Monday. In it, Jacek Krawiec, President of the Polish petroleum company PKN Orlen, is in discussion with Treasury Minister Włodzimierz Karpiński and the latter's deputy, Zdzisław Gawlik. The meeting took place in January 2015 in Sowa and Friends, a restaurant in Warsaw.

Among other things, the petroleum company chief talked about his visit to Budapest and the discussions he conducted with Zsolt Hernádi, President and CEO of MOL, in this passage (quoted): Krawiec: Listen, I'll tell you something that proves how different our situation is from that of the Hungarians. I went to see Hernádi because he can not leave Budapest. I ask him, 'How many years are you going to get?' Relaxed and smiling, he says, 'Y'see, my lawyers realized that if this case goes to trial in any EU country and I am acquitted of the charges, then the verdict has to be recognized by every EU member state, letting me travel around Europe.' I ask him if the case will be tried in Hungary. He tells me it will. So I say, 'But then it may take two or three years.' And he says, 'We'll have a ruling in April.' Sitting next to him is this guy, the head of legal, a real self-important type named Ábel (referring to Ábel Galácz, who is not the legal director but the group-wide sales director). He (Hernádi) turns to him and says, 'Ábel, tell Jacek who the prosecutor is going to be for this trial in Hungary.' He says, 'My wife.' You see? Just imagine such a situation! His wife is the prosecutor, he gets an acquittal, and everything is taken care of. Can you imagine this happening over here?

Zdzisław Gawlik: Maybe it does happen and we just don't know about it.

Włodzimierz Karpiński: This is what Kaczyński dreams about, these are the kind of internal political conditions he would like."

10   Babett Oroszi and Balázs M. Tóth, "Polt Péter kinevezése óta meredeken zuhan a politikai korrupciós ügyekben indított büntetőeljárások száma" ["The Number of Prosecutions for Political Corruption Has Fallen Sharply Since the Appointment of Péter Polt"], *Átlátszó*, February 6, 2015, http://atlatszo.hu/2015/02/06/polt-peter-kinevezese-ota-meredeken-zuhan-a-politikai-korrupcios-ugyekben-inditott-buntetoeljarasok-szama/.

11   Ibid.

12   http://www.origo.hu/gazdasag/20151202-ami-jo-az-embereknek-az-jo-lesz-a-politikusoknak-is.html.

9. Pyramid schemes—the limits of the mafia state

The mafia state's need for legitimization requires pulling the strings of democratic background mechanisms. The latter, however, is only attainable with support from committed believers, coaxed with financial rewards by the regime and forming a spiritual community and a presumably even larger group neutralized with spiritual rewards.

9.1. Economic pyramid scheme

The costs of the reconfiguration of power accompanying the emergence of the mafia state weigh heavily on the economy due to the massive reallocation of income and wealth, rendering it akin to an *oil dictatorship with no oil during times of crisis*. New sources must be sought for the income fueling the power and wealth accumulation of the adopted political family. Domestic sources include the flat tax, cuts in social, healthcare and education spending, the ongoing levies on banks, service providers and other network markets and one-off cases of plunder.

The *flat tax* benefited the top decile of households, saving them an annual 500 billion forints (approximately 1.7 billion euro) in taxes. This social stratum, wielding significant opinion-shaping and interest representation power, was faced with the dilemma of who to vote for, even those not having been wooed into the status of Fidesz clients or sympathizing with the party, for that matter; but the opposition's progressive tax scheme would strip them of significant personal income. While the democratic opposition legitimately criticizes the anti-solidary nature of the flat tax and stresses that the economic stimulus derived from it is in fact negligible, the selfishness and cohesion of the middle class linked to Fidesz are fueled by the derived benefits. Other historical autocratic regimes (corporativist-fascist, communist) had carried out opposing income redistributions, even if the former used the Aryanization of Jewish property and looting, and the latter the expropriation of the capitalist class and levies on peasants and rural areas, labeled as primitive capital accumulation under socialism.

The mafia state uses taxation and budgetary tools, such as **high value added tax and social spending cuts,** to redistribute income to the benefit of wealthier social groups. This is not the manifestation of classic social conservatism, but rather the adopted political family's lack of interest in the social groups outside its own circles and the resignation regarding these groups. Many can be grateful for even having a job, despite being short-changed by the tax regime. In this **economic pyramid game, there are three losers to each winner.** The central power field's resignation of citizens regarding them of no value creates an even deeper division of society, economic stagnation and a dead-end in terms of development. The question is how long can the operators of the mafia state use the refined tools of repression and brainwashing to maintain the political passivity of those struggling to get by, in other words, to isolate and demobilize them?

The regime has mobilized domestic resources to fuel its ruling needs with the 27% value added tax rate, record-high by European standards, and the aforementioned sector-specific taxes, coupled with spending cuts. Both channels were subject to the communication need to prevent "the people" from directly perceiving the burdens: benefits should appear as direct donations from the state, while withdrawals should appear as the work of hostile forces. Thus

- either impersonal market mechanisms should work for the government (through the salient value added tax), or
- tax levies on multinational companies should feed the budget, with any attempts by them to pass on these costs met with hostile rhetoric or even punitive measures by the government, or
- the murky deterioration of the services of large redistribution systems (social, healthcare and education) should provide the resources to be reallocated within the sluggish economy.

But these resources cannot be increased any further, and certain public services are on the brink of collapse. Moreover, faced with pressure from the EU, certain sector-specific taxes had to be abolished. In the wake of these events, the government is now going after the bits and bobs, which may counter its communication objectives. Two of these measures have sparked sudden mobilization fuelled by social dissatisfaction: one was the seizure of 200 billion forints in savings still held in private pension funds, and the other was an attempt to tax internet traffic. The former affected 60,000 middle class citizens, with a firm belief in individual responsibility and who were willing to staunchly oppose state coercion, while the latter affected young generations who had formerly steered clear of politics but were sensitive to this attack on their personal freedom. These measures prompted tens of thousands of citizens to take to the streets in protest in the late 2014. Of course, payback time was not long in coming for members of the private pension funds who showed resistance: due to the "delay" in government passing the necessary decree the funds have not been able to pay dues to their members who have reached pension age. "This is no better than mugging by means of legal tools," the socialist deputy chairman of the Parliamentary Committee for Social Affairs said.[1]

Although falling oil prices and the forint conversion of foreign currency denominated loans, accompanied by forcing the banks to pay compensation for the unfair credit contracts to those indebted in foreign currencies, increased the purchasing power of the slipping middle class (by 1–1.5 billion euro) and provided a temporary boost to the economy, the fact remains that Hungary has been unable to narrow its lag behind the founding EU member states over the past 25 years. In addition, Hungary's lag compared to the Eastern region of the European Union, in particular the sustained dynamism of Poland and Slovakia, is becoming drastic.

9.1.1. Autocracy and autarchy

The right economic context for *autocracy*—even for Orbán—would be *autarchy*. If he could have his way, he would not tolerate any deviation by the economy from the logic of his dictate. This is the motive behind the string of campaigns aimed at regulating and taxing ideologically criminalized economic players. One of the real limits to the autocratic political turn carried out with the two-thirds parliamentary majority is that contrary to the public sector, the disobedience of stock markets cannot be handled with orders or magic spells. Global market institutions extend beyond the authority of autocratic legislators: no matter how many holes the autocratic measures of state coercion attempt to patch up, no matter what obstacles are raised to market logic, market forces are always able to burst through the dams built by non-market coercive measures. And if the market does not function in accordance with autocratic "unorthodox" arbitrary will, it sees the emergence of paranoid conspiracy theories and the anthropomorphized national freedom fight emerging on its soil, and a host of new administrative coercive measures.

However, political coercion exercised in the economy has shown its limitations even in large, isolated regimes, such as Stalin's attempt to establish "socialism in one country." Hungary, with its post-Trianon dimensions, has become an integral part of globalized markets. While communist regimes were able to close their borders to prevent their citizens from voting with their feet regarding the system, today, in the European Union, no political intervention in the economy is capable of preventing firms from diverting their capital and citizens from diverting their savings abroad or emigrating in response to such attempts.

Because the available domestic resources are insufficient for the regime's ruling needs, and also because their utilization is largely restricted by institutional obligations, economic isolation is not an option. Paradoxically, the freedom allowing the enrichment of the adopted political family is mainly fuelled by *European Union funding*, ranging from the agricultural single area payment scheme to large infrastructural developments. The effort to decouple the utilization of EU funds from EU norms and oversight has exacerbated the conflict with Brussels. Large donor countries will sooner or later have to face the sensitive political issue of how much longer their taxpayers will be willing to finance the personal enrichment of the beneficiaries of the Hungarian mafia state, definitely not figuring among the objectives of European Union funding.

9.2. Foreign policy pyramid scheme—"peacock dance" and Hungarian-style cunning

The ongoing mobilization and demobilization in the name of the national freedom fight has repercussions that extend beyond national borders. Beyond the ideological and economic pyramid scheme, there is also a *political pyramid scheme playing out at the international level, with increased bidding,* dubbed by Miklós Haraszti as a strategy of *"sailing in a western boat propelled by eastern winds."* While the national freedom fight is a cold civil war aimed at subjecting Hungary's own citizens in internal politics, in external relations a "peacock dance"[2] is being performed, swaying between transatlantic and eastern obligations. In the context of this external policy "peacock dance," to quote Orbán, "must combine the elements of understanding, agreement, rejection and opposition in the context of a highly complex series of actions" in its relationship with the European Union.[3] One step of this dance consists of statements such as "no one can dictate to us, neither from Brussels nor Moscow"[4] and "we will not be a colony, Hungarians will not live according to the dictate of foreigners,"[5] while the other step consists of statements such as "there is naturally no doubt that the community of countries forming part of the European Union will remain a key partner for us."[6] The peacock dance aims to maintain this external policy balance, giving Hungary access to European Union funding while maintaining sufficient leeway for the adopted political family to use these funds arbitrarily for private purposes and to cement the mafia state's position serving this objective.

Hungary's relationship with the European Union is therefore also a question of identity: **what is the relationship between Hungarian and European identity** for a citizen? If the former constitutes the exclusive basis of comparison overriding every other value, the European Union remains nothing more than an opportunity for free-riding, something to milk to the greatest extent possible while only giving the bare minimum in return. This is Fidesz's policy of placing profitable "national interests" above considerations of value. This is the **set of values of the unique criminal code of honor** that only recognizes moral obligations in respect of the adopted political family. The others are not "us"—they are the "them," "outsiders," "aliens," so we must wring out the most we can from every situation. Hungarian cunning serves this purpose, lacking the capacity for brute force. The forest of national flags serving as a backdrop for the Hungarian prime minister's public appearances—with not one single European Union flag to be found among them—clearly reflects the current ruling power's position on identity.

9.2.1. Dilemmas faced by the European Union

It has slowly become clear for the European Union that its geopolitical objectives cannot be attained purely on the basis of shared values, which may give rise to the creation of a buffer zone within the EU, but largely outside the eurozone.[7] In this context, it must turn a blind eye to the eastern ruling tactics applied by the regimes violating the norms of liberal democracy in a variety of ways. The EU aimed to achieve its geopolitical objectives through support granted to buffer states and the long-term acknowledgment of the democratic deficits that were previously just tolerated. The insolent aggressiveness of Orbán's regime, with its open declaration to set up an illiberal state and the risks stemming from the policy of opening towards the East, has created a fait accompli for the EU: Orbán has forced western democracies into a situation where they cannot avoid to regard him as a committed opponent of liberal democracies rather than a politician committing the occasional faux pas.

Orbán's regime is unique in the sense that his effort to reshape the system is taking place within the European Union. Hungary is slipping back from a liberal democracy to a fully-fledged autocratic system, *"back to the future."* Even the external political and economic constraints on the emergence and consolidation of the mafia state—the values shared by the European Union and Hungary's embeddedness in the global economy—are unable to achieve a change in policy of autocratic governance where morale and democratic values do not restrict the concentration of power and the adopted political family's will and techniques to accumulate wealth. Fidesz's governance had lacked all self-restraint even in 1998–2002, but lacking a two-thirds parliamentary majority prevented it from showing its true colors.

At the same time, the European Union is unable and unwilling to intervene in Hungary's day-to-day government politics. As it is increasing pressure in the wake of the government's measures chipping away at democracy, it is apparent how limited its tools for restoring democratic norms are. It is forced into debates on specific topics, while struggling in vain to legitimately criticize the broader autocratic context. The EU is equipped for addressing ad hoc violations of the common European values through mediation, persuasion or judicial avenues, however it lacks the tools for preventing the systematic erosion of liberal democracy. It is going on the assumption that the countries that have been admitted to the club will not act up, or at least not frequently, and thus it lacks the tools for addressing these new behaviors. Meanwhile, Fidesz adroitly implements a few corrections for show, its prestige slightly tarnished, but the spirit of the new regime remains unchanged. The example of Hungary sheds light on the

European Union's weakness lying in the fact that without a common legal framework wielding sufficient powers to apply effective sanctions to breaches of its values, there is no real community constituting a force to reckon with. This restricts the EU's leeway to take action in response to measures that violate the democratic institutional system. At the same time, the limits of the political community restrict the development of future economic cooperation in Europe.

The anticorruption action taken by international bodies addresses day-to-day forms of corruption, focusing on fighting one-off breaches even if they occur en mass. For example, criticism is directed towards the quality and practice of public procurement legislation, a typical source of risk in western democracies. The EU might be aware of the other type of corruption committed by oligarchs rising from the underworld and gaining mainstream influence, but with the exception of international matters such as drug trafficking, illegal migration or prostitution—these go largely ignored. The third type, the regime led by mafia state politics and built using arbitrary non-market tools, has gone entirely unnoticed so far, because it would require these international bodies to classify Hungary among the autocratic regimes functioning outside the European Union. There is no way of knowing whether sensory or political illusion explains the fact that they are *unable to see the forest for the trees, the mafia state for the corruption*. Even the adequate terminology is lacking.

The governments of the more advanced EU countries may feel some degree of frustration as they look on, powerless, while the adopted political family accumulates wealth at the expense of their taxpayers. "Nearly 88% of the hundreds of billions of forints in public procurements won by companies linked to Lajos Simicska consist of EU projects. Although this figure does not necessarily reflect the proportion of the company's revenue fuelled by EU funding, it does give some indication of the vast portion of its activities that are made up by EU-funded projects. This ratio is even higher for the billions in contracts awarded to the companies of István Tiborcz [Orbán's son-in-law] and Lőrinc Mészáros [mayor or Felcsút]. Over 94% of public contracts won by energy firm Elios Innovatív Zrt., partially owned by Tiborcz, consist of European Union projects, and this ratio stands at over 99% for Mészáros's construction firm Mészáros és Mészáros Kft."[8]

In 2013, the European Parliament took action against the methodical erosion of the political institutional system of liberal democracy in the context of the heated debates on the Hungarian situation. The core document was a report by the European Parliament's Committee on Civil Liberties, Justice and Home Affairs authored by Rui Tavares.[9] This document goes beyond formulating ad hoc critiques and is a *critique of the regime*, calling on the Commission to "focus not only on specific infringements of EU law (...) but to respond appropriately to a systemic change in the constitutional and legal system and practice of a Member State where multiple and recurrent infringements unfortunately result in a state of legal uncertainty."[10] Alas, the implementation of this approach is restricted by the European Union's sluggishness in creating institutions and procedures. Beyond the interest-neutral bureaucratic hurdle, actual opposing interests also prevent an effective response to illiberal attempts: for one, the *"dirty party solidarity"* (characteristic of both the political right and left), secondly, *coalition-related interests within the EU*, and thirdly, *conflict-minimalization efforts* in an attempt to protect the economic interests operating in the criticized countries, and finally, broader *geopolitical considerations*.

The EU has *three options* in the long run. The first is to *remain a victim of the system of blackmail* where national interest is a right superseding everything else, while international and European Union solidarity is an obligation expected under all circumstances. The second is for the leading political and economic powers of the European Union to *opt for a two-speed Europe*, where the unruly children are left on their own to play, while serious matters are discussed in their absence—*nicht vor dem Kind*. The third is a firm shift towards *a federal Europe*, substantially expanding the scope of community legislation. However, this would require European citizens to harbor equal feelings of national and European identity.

However, the contradictions between the wishes of the value community and geopolitical realities—the most likely scenario—can only be resolved in a two-gear Europe. All political constraints point in this direction. A manifesto recognizing this was published by Emmanuel Macron and Sigmar Gabriel, the ministers of economy for France and Germany, prompting for economic action:[11] a eurozone-level budget with its own revenues; social and tax regulation convergence; bringing the debt crisis resolution mechanism under community law and the establishment of a proper monetary institutional structure; exemption of both from national dependency, in other words, elevating them to a European level. This calls for the establishment of the right political institutional environment, with a common parliament, legislative and control mechanisms.

One of the gears of a two-gear Europe, the Western one, is the eurozone itself. The post-communist states, irreversibly embedded in the European Union, are either part of the eurozone or their governments, irrespective of political belonging, are firmly prompting accession to the eurozone in the years to come. Some however, including Hungary, are fabricating state ideology for remaining outside the eurozone in the long run. The need for independence concealed within the rhetoric of the national freedom fight is in fact the euphemistic demand for exemption from liberal democratic norms. For these countries, the "Europe of nations" refers to their need to set up and maintain their autocratic regimes. Only their own citizens can take effective action against this effort. Without this or in the event of the failure of such action, the efforts of national autocracies to stabilize themselves will be more or less successful. At the same time, the European Union's geopolitical considerations cannot allow the Russian empire to spread to the Leitha, i.e., to the western borders of Hungary. The political elite of Western Europe, abandoning its romantic faith and original mission that had accompanied the fall of the Berlin wall, now regards the lagging part of Eastern Europe increasingly less as a cultural partner, and more as an economic zone of influence. Today's Eastern European political elite aims to bolster the eastern-like values prevailing in their countries through national and social populism in an effort to establish and conserve their own autocratic or semi-autocratic power. The consequences for us are quite ominous: solidarity with Eastern Europe and the policy of convergence will be replaced by a policy of simple pacification. This will be much cheaper for the eurozone countries and more palatable for their citizens than the futile integration effort that has only managed to trigger responses in Eastern Europe such as the corrupt System of National Cooperation (NER). In other words, instead of consolidating democracies in this buffer zone at a high cost, they will pacify semi-autocratic regimes at a minimal cost.

9.2.2. Opening towards the East

Hungarian foreign policy, going against the grain of European Union and transatlantic obligations, consists of the search for legitimization and begging for financial favors from eastern autocrats. This is nothing more but the expansion of the adopted political family's leeway, that is, of their power and wealth accumulation through the tools of foreign policy. But "why would autocrats like Orbán want to lead their countries out of the EU, if in these buffer zones they can cement themselves while 'taxing two empires': the structural and cohesion funds from the EU, and the energy agreements with the Russian empire ensure a supply of funds," writes Attila Ara-Kovács. The former has to pay with its civilized political manners and the appearance of the ideals of freedom, while the latter, by succumbing to eastern dependency. (...) Foreign policy truly became an extension of the arm of domestic policy. Just as the national freedom fight signified the self-serving freedom of government opposing the norms of liberal democracy in domestic policy, so the sole purpose of foreign policy became the political and financial protection of this autocratic freedom."[12]

Foreign policy and foreign trade policy have been replaced by family business, and the multiple-phase transformation of the institutional system of foreign policy was also carried out in view of this objective. While foreign policy was led by the ministry for foreign affairs, mainly staffed with career diplomats, the foreign trade policy was overseen by the ministry for economy. The appointment of former Fidesz spokesman and later head of Orbán's cabinet and press, international and organizational staff Péter Szijjártó as secretary of state for foreign affairs and the foreign trade policy within the prime minister's office in 2012 was a sign of the change to come in the role of foreign policy. As the godfather's direct delegate, Szijjártó was tasked with visiting a host of autocratic regimes, from Saudi Arabia to Azerbaijan, from Moscow to Beijing, forging special relationships serving the interests of the adopted political family. This activity was subject to the interests of "family business" instead of the professional requirements of national diplomacy. Since September 2014, he is not only the dedicated ambassador/businessman of the adopted political family, but also minister of foreign affairs and trade. This, however, required the quasi-total disbanding of the ministry's multi-generational team of experts, going beyond what usually accompanies changes of government. This was more than the replacement of the diplomats of the previous government with ones loyal to the new government, but a complete change of genre, replacing loyal diplomats with lay vassals. A never before seen *wave of cleansing* had already swept through the diplomatic corps in 2010–2011, resulting in nearly forty ambassadors being sent into retirement or dismissed. But while prior to 2014, "fidelity to the right and/or Fidesz party membership were sufficient, these are no longer enough today: stable positions of leadership are assigned to those who have no qualms about using *tools outside the realm of diplomacy*. (...) Within one year of the Orbán administration regaining power, 100 of the 112 head of mission positions were reassigned, with 30 fideszniks parachuted to these positions."[13]

The absurdity of fathoming Hungary as the "eastern gate of the EU," "Central and Eastern Europe's financial and logistics center" or other similar dreams, and the failure of its attempts to replace IMF loans with resources from Middle Eastern autocracies or China have narrowed down Hungary's options of opening towards the East to Russia or a handful of ex-Soviet republics of Eastern Asia (Azerbaijan, Kazakhstan, Turkmenistan). The increasingly stronger relationships of autocrats are psychologically fed by their desire to quench their own international legitimacy deficit through mutual recognition.

If we look at the business aspect of these relationships, however, clearly the other members of the Visegrad Group—comprising the Czech Republic, Poland, Hungary, and Slovakia—have managed to achieve a more dynamic trade growth with eastern countries without the propagandistic policy of "opening towards the East."[14] What is growing in Hungary is the proportion of foreign trade deals linked to the adopted political family. Hungary, however, **has little in the way of solvent goods than disloyalty towards the EU and NATO,** besides the petty family dealings. As a bonus, Hungary has also let an Azeri officer, convicted of murder in Hungary and welcomed as a national hero in his home country, off the hook; the Hungarian Post has issued a commemorative stamp for a former KGB general and later Azeri autocrat, and has published the memoir of his successor son. Another significant legitimization gesture towards the authoritarian Kazakh regime, ranked 132 of the 167 countries listed on the Economist's Democracy Index, and a clear message to Brussels was Orbán's declaration during his visit to Kazakhstan, proclaiming that "it is with great pleasure that we come to Kazakhstan. The European Union treats us as an equal partner in political terms, but we do not belong there based on our origin. When in Brussels, we have no relatives. But when we come to Kazakhstan, we have relatives here. It is strange that one has to travel east to feel at home."[15] Hungary's critique of western sanctions, describing them as an ineffective measure not conducive to a solution amidst the Ukraine conflict, was show of loyalty towards Putin and a gesture aimed to bolster legitimization, alongside the lifting of Putin's diplomatic quarantine and his warm welcome in Budapest in February 2015.

The real danger lies in the fact that while the Hungarian government is carrying on its freedom fight with Brussels, it is becoming a useful tool for

Лoscow's offensive energy diplomacy designed to gain influence: not only does it do nothing for reducing Hungary's eastern energy dependency, it even exacerbates it. This is how the gas-oil-nuclear energy Bermuda triangle works, where the leeway of affected countries' energy policy disappears but the personal interests of the ruling elite are prevailing.

The government:

- has committed itself to the professionally questionable expansion of the Paks nuclear power plant, to be funded for the most part by a 10 billion euro Russian loan. The documents of the transaction have been classified for 30 years. Not by chance, as the few documents that were leaked "clearly show that the feasibility studies written are of extremely poor standard and fail to cover vital topics, but what they do contain presage a catastrophic impact of the Paks2 project for the Hungarian energy sector, the profitability of Paks1 and the Danube's temperature regulation alike," writes Benedek Jávor, member of European Parliament on his blog.[16] According to estimates, construction costs granted with no public tendering and thus going straight to the pockets of the adopted political family account for approximately 40% of the total budget. The European Commission finally did take steps on the issue of the large investment at the end of 2015, and "opened infringement procedure against Hungary for lack of compliance of the Paks nuclear power plant project with EU public procurement rules. And yet it is not this procedure for lack of compliance that is most important. For this is only one of three Brussels investigations in process with regard to the Paks extension. The issue of state subsidy, and the acceptance of the Unions energy policies form the basis of separate investigations."[17] The commission has called upon the government to suspend further procurements related to this investment, though this is not legally binding.
- Hungary staunchly supported plans for the **South Stream pipeline** despite opposition from the EU, until the Russians abandoned the project. In October 2014, by adopting the lex South Stream (which enables the construction of gas pipelines even for gas companies that do not hold a transportation and system operation license), it even ensured that the development could be implemented despite disapproval from the EU or other international bodies.[18]

- repurchased the companies owning E.ON's gas reservoirs at prices unjustifiable under market logic. Meanwhile, selling off part of Hungarian gas reservoir capacities (e.g., creating a transit nationalization or a bargain chip nationalization), which "could only mean that Hungary would sell off its capacities bought from the German E.ON to Russian energy firm Gazprom, as no other company is seeking such capacities in Europe at present."[19]
- Since 2011, the public Hungarian electricity company Magyar Villamos Művek (MVM) concluded a host of new contracts with energy trader MET Holding AG, partly owned by offshore companies. The model of the centrally operated cash pump—with participation of parliament, the government, a public mammoth company and the private offshore company—in a nutshell:[20]
  - ➢ In the context of a utility price cut campaign, the state granted exclusive access to a large portion of the pipeline capacities located along the Austrian-Hungarian border to energy company MVM (covering the import of an annual 2.2 billion initially, to be later increased to 2.9 billion cubic meters). Without the state's authorization, use of the pipeline would have been awarded through a tender.
  - ➢ The pipeline is key because gas can be procured by Hungary more cheaply from Austria than from the East. MVM had used the pipelines lying along the border by purchasing cheaper gas from MET on the Austrian side, bringing it across the border and returning it on the same day on the Hungarian side.
  - ➢ The opportunity granted by the state to MVM did not generate profits for the public company or cut utility costs for citizens, but did boost MET's bottom line. While in 2012, MVM, a public company, closed its gas trading business with a loss of 0.5 billion forints, the owners of MET (including quite a few prominent oligarchs indirectly linked to Orbán, through ties independent of Simicska) distributed dividends of 55 billion forints.[21] This carries special significance because the "primitive capital accumulation" independent of Simicska and his interests is what gave financial independence for the godfather in favor of Simicska's demotion and containment that played out in 2014.

Online news site Index reported[22] that the documents of public interest—obtained through judicial avenues in June 2015—reveal that there is no information on why

- the state did not hold an auction for allocating capacity and why no open tender was held find subsequent suppliers and partners for MVM;
- the public company was entrusted with a task that it was, by its own admission, unable to complete alone;
- MVM Partner struck a deal with the offshore MET without having knowledge of its actual owner;
- MET International AG (METI) sold gas to MVM at a higher price compared to the commodity market and similar competitors;
- MVM Partner consistently purchased the largest quantities of gas from METI if it had cheaper alternative sources;
- METI supplied gas to MVM Partner at cheaper prices outside the main deal;
- MVM sold gas at a cheaper price to MET than the price at which they purchased it from METI.

By autumn of 2015 it also became clear—on the basis of documents on the procurement of a billion cubic meters of gas made available through court order—that "between 2011 and 2014 the MMV could by gas in the West without the MET, even for less than the price the MET could achieve."[23]

Economic policy objectives are superseded by the desire to procure funds that can then be spent with no public oversight and to operate short and long-term money pumps. The price that the polipburo has to pay for this is covered by the budget, that is, taxpayers. But the price that Hungary pays for such businesses has a political nature as well: increasing dependency on Russia. Chairman of Gazprom "Alexey Miller's visit on September 22, 2014 was a memorable one. After the talks held on Monday, MOL's Gas Transmission firm suddenly declared on Thursday evening that it would cut off gas transmission to the Ukraine, right before the tripartite summit scheduled for the following Saturday morning between the EU, Russia and the Ukraine. Diplomatic sources say that the occasion gave the impression beyond any doubt that Hungary was acting out Russia's agenda. According to one source, a similar scenario would be if the Slovakian-Hungarian interconnector (the equipment allowing gas to flow in both directions), built with EU funding, were used to secure a better position for Gazprom within the EU."[24]

Gazprom, Rosneft, Rosatom are not run-of-the-mill corporations with mere economic interests, but also the instruments of Russian imperial interests supported by their secret services, extensions of the rekindled Russian imperial influence. They fit snugly into these ambitions—their motive is not merely profit maximization, but also serving national interests. The fact that they foster their objectives by corruptly serving private interests is almost self-evident. It should be noted that Russian corruption of the political elite that it wishes to draw into its circle of influence through the energy sector is not an exclusively Hungarian phenomenon. "Hungary, the Czech Republic and Slovakia have become Russia's Trojan horses within the European Union over the past years."[25]

Parading as Gazprom's happiest barrack could only be a successful tactic during times when the great rival powers are at peace; in a Cold War context, however, it could prove a catastrophic strategy. While during times of peaceful coexistence, it can be dressed up to appear as a linking bridge, during a Cold War, it merges into the role of a double agent mistrusted by both sides. One side regards it as the betrayal in the legitimately undertaken role of transatlantic and European ally, the other regards it as nothing more than a paid vassal. "According to Rasmussen, Russia is engaging in a 'hybrid war' with Europe, adopting a mix of very well-known conventional warfare and new, more sophisticated propaganda and disinformation campaigns including Russian efforts to influence public opinion through financial links with political parties within NATO and engagement in NGOs. 'We know the nationalistic right-wing parties have expressed a clear sympathy for Russia, so have some of the extreme left. We have such parties in Greece, Hungary, Bulgaria and France', said Rasmussen."[26]

Hungary currently represents a ***security policy risk*** for both the EU and NATO within the Western alliance system. The diplomatic rumors that the German and French embassies in Moscow are refraining from sharing any sensitive information with their Hungarian peers testify to this. The string of sharp critiques voiced by Bill Clinton, John McCain, and Barack Obama clearly attest to the fact that the Hungarian government has been repeatedly mentioned along with other autocratic regimes when brought up as examples. Assistant secretary of state for European and Eurasian Affairs at the US Department of State Victoria Nuland explicitly stated that Eastern Europe is affected by "twin cancers of democratic backsliding and corruption."[27]

9.2.3. The disparate logic of EU and US sanctions

We have reason to fear that the Hungarian mafia state will not be a unique phenomenon among the ex-communist member states of the European Union. Although a constellation of unfortunate circumstances is needed for its emergence, the temptation is also present elsewhere. The European Community **lacks not only the effective tools for expulsion, but even for the disciplining** of countries conducting themselves this way.

It is worth looking at the disparate logic of EU and US sanctions, their underlying assumptions and mechanism of action.

European sanctions are mainly applied in two areas. One avenue for taking action in a more broadly interpreted European context is the **European Court of Human Rights** located in Strasbourg and operating in the context of the Council of Europe, while the other consists of sanctions applied specifically by the EU.

The former can be sought out in individual cases once all national judicial options have been exhausted. In these cases however, the institution of actio popularis cannot be applied, in other words the court's case law only allows for entities other than the victim of the state infringement to seek the court in a very small number of scenarios. This means that the victims of a national law violating European norms have to seek out the court individually, and taking into account the national-level procedure, the process may stretch on for several years. The underlying assumption of the procedure is that the demonstrated effects of individual cases will compel the affected national institutions and authorities to implement broader changes while also compensating the injured party. This, however, only works if the violation of internationally endorsed norms is not the result of a conscious government effort.

The other main, specifically European set of tools (EU sanctions in the strict sense) consist of restricting or suspending member state funding. Minor breaches are addressed by the European Union with an infringement procedure, which consists of the European Commission examining the breach committed by the member state, and if it considers the outcome of its discussion proceedings unsatisfactory, it can refer the case to the European Court of Justice based in Luxembourg. As a last resort, the affected member state may face financial sanctions imposed by the court. The other tool frequently applied by the European Union addresses the contentious utilization of **EU funding,** and consists of the **suspension, non-payment or claim for the reimbursement of funding.** This, however, is restricted by various foreign policy considerations. Thus so far, despite the broad-ranging symptoms of corruption, these have only been applied to a fraction of EU funds. By spring of 2015, the recognition of Orbán's announcement of the illiberal state, the national security risks of opening towards the East and the systemic money pump operated by the mafia state, feeding private interests, has superseded the considerations of EU-level dirty party solidarity, and the more intense application of sanctions was undertaken. In April 2015, the European Commission suspended 708 billion forints in payments to Hungary's Economic Development Operational Program, and Hungary is expected to pay the equivalent of 10% of the allocation in fines. Brussels identified severe breaches in the 2012 and 2013 tender procedures in the areas of innovation, economic and business infrastructure development, as the tenders were regularly tailored to specific companies.[28]

These EU sanctions are akin to the military tactic of *carpet bombing,* where the victims are mostly civilians. The underlying logic of these sanctions is that the suspension or withdrawal of funding will prevent key developments for citizens from being completed, resulting in growing dissatisfaction; governments will strive to avoid losing popularity, and will thus change their policies, avoiding the need for further sanctions. Brussels imagines these events as being part of the democratic learning curve, where those doing the learning are themselves interested in passing the exam. But the reality is starkly different. As more severe sanctions are held back by numerous political and bureaucratic factors, and even if a procedure is launched, it is aimed against impersonal institutions, allowing the government to avert any direct responsibility. It even seizes the opportunity to interpret the events in the context of its national freedom fight and to portray Hungarians, and thus Orbán himself as the victim to foster EU-hostile sentiment.

External constraints are, by nature, passive: they are not active policy-shapers, and are at most the signposts of policies violating democratic values or voluntarist economic actions. The EU, assuming a fundamental community of values, builds on the mechanism of warnings, and thus persuasion. In places where the community of values is lacking, it is unable to prevent the emergence of an autocratic regime. International organizations are easily ensnared in the usual trap of action against the dictatorships, with sanctions dealing a heavy blow to citizens while leaving the political regime unscathed. Moreover, external warnings and sanctions also risk prompting those holding the power to turn even more to unlawful, coercive measures to maintain equilibrium, and are able to mobilize their followers in the name of national self-defense.

As the most conspicuous of *US sanctions*, in October 2014 a right-wing daily reported that members of the Hungarian government had been listed among the persons denied travel visas by US authorities pursuant to Presidential Proclamation 7750 To Suspend Entry as Immigrants or Nonimmigrants of Persons Engaged in or Benefiting from Corruption. A few days later, president of the National Tax and Customs Administration (NAV) Ildikó Vida alone publicly announced that she was one of the officials affected. The grounds for her banning were, according to Dávid Jancsics,[29] that "two independent sources claim that protagonists linked to the Hungarian government claimed kickbacks from two American firms in exchange for a tax break and a change in the VAT rate. The kickbacks would have been channeled through a foundation linked to the government in the form of orders for research and study work, allegedly in the amount of roughly 2 billion forints. Under the offer, the tax authority would have also allegedly imposed hefty fines in the ballpark of billions of forints on the rivals of the implicated companies, substantially weakening competition and putting the US firms at a great competitive advantage. As the blackmailed firms failed to yield to the offer, the tax authority started pressuring them, and the firms ended up reporting the bribery attempts. The fact that the top NAV officials are on the US ban list corroborates this version." But as the US authorities did not initiate criminal proceedings, merely issuing an administrative decision barring entry to the US, the details of the case cannot be ascertained.

Contrary to the EU's practice, **US sanctions** are similar to **GPS-led missiles**, presuming that infringements are not ad hoc, dispersed acts of corruption committed against the regime, but conversely, actions centrally orchestrated or at least endorsed by the regime. Accordingly, they do not presume that the self-correcting methods of democracy will resolve the situation, and instead target the initiators of the infringements, attempting to penalize the breaches and perpetrators of corruption with laser-like accuracy. So despite the government's attempts, it is difficult to portray these actions propagandistically against the US, as they do not impinge on the interests of Hungarian citizens, instead reinforcing their dim view of their country's political leaders.

The banning of NAV president, Ildikó Vida clearly signals a critique of the regime, as the case it involves illustrates the systemic operation of the mafia state. Namely that the matter is one of blackmail performed using tools of public authority and an attempt to extort and launder money because:

- the initiative does not come from below, from market players;
- it is not a corrupt transaction between a presumed market player initiator and a public official;
- as centrally organized money laundering in the context of which tax breaks would have been converted to private benefit, it would have needed to go beyond
  - ➤ both the lower administrative echelons, as the top officials of the organization needed to be involved in the deal;
  - ➤ the institution, as some of the services rendered in the context of the deal would have extended beyond the organization of NAV itself, and the consideration paid by the corruption players involved would have also required the involvement of entities outside the organization or its representatives;
  - ➤ the degree of ordinary bribery, as the corruption transaction involved in the deal would have reached ballpark of billions of forints;
- as the head of the tax authority, Vida was not only a high-ranking government official, but also a key figure of the adopted political family, a stooge wielding both the power to dole out favors and engage in blackmail.

The US sanctions applied after a few preliminary warnings struck the mafia state's Achilles' heel: the essence of the mafia state consists of the adopted political family protecting the executors of the infringements, endorsed or even ordered by the polipburo, positioned at the various public organizations. Without this capacity, the mafia state would not be able to use illegitimate coercive tools of public authority. The fragility and constraints of this protection and immunity are reflected in the denial of visas and in the potential freezing of foreign bank accounts.

Both types of sanctions share the common trait of only wielding the power of persuasion to address the contested actions (such as corruption), to set the self-protecting mechanisms of democracy into action, led by the judicial system, to take the action expected in a democracy. But this is a futile expectation when dealing with the mafia state.

It is therefore a pivotal question whether, as a member of the European Union, national level judicial institutions can be prompted to take action with the cooperation of the EU's institutions. The NGOs grouped

	US sanctions	EU sanctions
launch of sanction proceedings	partly based on political considerations, but the reporting obligation of the companies approached entails the mandatory launch of proceedings	bureaucratic, cumbersome, may be subject to political bargaining
suspension of sanction proceedings	the proceedings cannot be suspended; once they are launched, they are no longer within the reach of political bargaining	may be subject to political bargaining
targets of sanction proceedings	persons committing the presumed infringements, allowing the personification of narratives	institutions committing the presumed infringements, making the link between the perpetrator and the crime more difficult to personify and communicate
underlying message of the selection of targets	erosion of the integrity of the adopted political family and the protection provided by the godfather, dissuading mafia state's public servants from participating in infringing procedures	it does not address the matter of personal liability, enabling the mafia state's public servants to continue taking part in operating unlawful coercive mechanisms; the godfather still has the unscathed capacity to guarantee exemption from criminal law consequences
criticism horizon of the sanctions	target the regime	target the government

under the New Hungarian Republic movement presented a proposal to this effect at their rally held in February 2015 prior to Angela Merkel's visit to Hungary. Tamás Lattmann, associate professor at the National University of Public Service and Eötvös Loránd University, presented proposals in three areas for reforms to EU-level oversight and judicial mechanisms to give them the legal tools to assist the self-healing of the autocratic democracies emerging within the European Union:

- *Setting up the public prosecutor's office for the European Union and passing European laws on the persecution under penal law of the mismanagement and misuse of European Union funding.* Although a European Public Prosecutor's Office can be established pursuant to Article 86 of the Treaty on the Functioning of the European Union, the European Council must support the pertaining European Commission proposal. Although the current model grants oversight powers to

European institutions (such as OLAF), it passes on the power to hold perpetrators accountable to member state authorities. But this does not work when member state authorities fail to take action. This issue could be effectively remedied if this task were allocated to a European institution vested with the necessary powers. The judicial process would remain in the hands of member state courts, respecting member state sovereignty, based on the principle of the independence of courts. Under the current rules, member state courts may pass a preliminary ruling if they have any questions linked to European Union in the context of proceedings, and member state proceedings remain under the supervision of the Strasbourg-based European Court of Human Rights. Though the founding treaties of the EU allow for the **creation of a Union-level prosecutor's office**, the Commission's proposals for establishing one have been rejected by certain governments of the European council so far. A way to compel the dissenting states would be for the net contributing states to stop the flow of EU funds— on grounds of their responsibility to their tax payers—to those states, which reject the competency of the Union-level prosecutor's office in overseeing the way these funds are spent.

- Establishing the **institution of actio popularis** on a European level i.e., reinforcing the European Court of Human Rights for taking action against mass and systemic violations of human rights and incorporating their outcomes into the European Union's rule of law procedures.
- If EU funds are misused by member states, that is used corruptly, on a mass and systemic scale, **international juries should be applied in the member states' tender procedures**.

No matter how widespread the Hungarian autocratic regime's measures to tear down the rule of law, it has so far been unable to eradicate all the elements of the rule of law to the degree of an open dictatorship. Just like the erosion of the media landscape remains incomplete, the subjection of judges also remains partial. The rule of law no longer applies broadly speaking and lies in shambles, but a few holds still remain for the critics of the mafia state. Reinforcing these remaining holds is imperative if Hungary is to return to a path leading to the realm of Western liberal democracies. At the same time, the EU's dilemma will be how to address the autocratic regimes within its own community, where it is no longer possible to restore liberal democracy while maintaining legal continuity. Although this question does not beg for immediate response, it must nonetheless be posed. Because while EU has no need to legitimize or delegitimize the orange or rainbow revolutions or regime changes disrupting legal continuity in regimes outside the EU, should such events occur within the community, there is a need to address the problem of legitimacy of democracy restoring actions not having a legal continuity. It would thus be simpler to foster the creation of such legal holds by bolstering community law and guarantee institutions that could support the strategy of democratic self-healing to be effective while maintaining legal continuity. In other words, they should actively contribute to making the *"technique of holding on to the law"*[30] an effective tool for Hungarian human rights activists for eradicating the autocratic regime. The aforementioned proposals addressed to the EU in the spring of 2015 are geared towards this very objective.

9.3. The precarious equilibrium of the mafia state: the spiral of delegitimization and the constraints on use of coercion or violence

The various pyramid schemes have come to a breaking point, and their aggregate impact has disrupted the regime's state of equilibrium, creating a *spiral of delegitimization*:

- The limited number of remaining sources for applying new levies concealing their ultimate targets—where it remains hidden who are really paying for them—signals a *failure of the economic pyramid scheme*. Hurried efforts to find new sources for taxation (the Internet tax, the plan to siphon off remaining private pension fund savings, or the rollout of new highway fees) have sparked open opposition. Some of the tasks of collecting funds have been delegated to local governments in the context of a unique "pick-your-own movement," prompting them to apply local taxes to fund their social expenditures. This is a cynical policy, as settlements with higher demand for social subsidies are generally coupled with lower taxpaying capacity.
- New recommendations for supporting the *"national middle-class"* keep emerging (such as the single-digit flat personal income tax, or other tax breaks geared towards higher-income large families), their source of funding uncertain. These could only be granted if even more sectoral

taxes were levied, which would be met with greater organized resistance from market players.

- At the same time, the ***ideologized interventions in private life***, serving presumed national Christian middle-class values, no longer yield any political benefit, and not only vex broader general opinion, but also create discord among Fidesz's own followers. These measures were mainly intended to be communication diversions to deflect public attention—such as the entry-exit systems installed in schools or the mandatory drug tests for certain social groups and job categories, including journalists—, although they would have also served to increase arbitrary state control of citizens. Then there are the ideologically-tinged measures serving the adopted political family's economic interests, such as the mandatory Sunday closure of stores, shopping malls and plazas, which two-thirds of citizens oppose. This measure has caused upheaval in the weekend plans of millions, who regard the measure as an aggression against their lifestyle and has managed to spark hostility towards the government among the formerly apolitical.
- The growing number of those short-changed by the regime has rendered public opinion susceptible to seeing the essence of the "politics of friendship" in the ***quasi-legitimized open corruption of the adopted political family***: the mafia state. The collapse of brokerage firms linked to government figures through multiple ties (such as Quaestor) in spring of 2015 and the method for bailing out the remaining assets and for selectively compensating the injured parties is also a revealing illustration of systemic corruption.
- Meanwhile, the ***gang war between Orbán and Simicska*** is also chipping away at the adopted political family's power. Although the godfather has the power to turn off the sources supplying the faucets feeding Simicska's companies and can begin drying out his empire, on one hand the latter's accumulated reserves require a long-term approach for achieving this objective, and on the other hand, Orbán is also limited in pushing Simicska aside using legitimate tools of coercion.
- By abandoning a key ***identity-shaping element*** with this policy of opening towards the East from 2010 onwards, Orbán has broken the tradition of politics conducted since 1993: the anti-Russian sentiment linked to anticommunism. It is the first time the adopted political family has resorted to destroying an identity-shaping symbol in the hopes of gaining an economic and political advantage. But not even

his believers can be reprogrammed so radically. Although he might believe that politics is the art of moderately dosing inconsistencies, this latest step is more than a mere inconsistency, undermining the emotional consistency of his politics: Fidesz cannot be both anti-Communist and friendly with Russia, especially amidst Russia's growing imperial ambitions.

- The Orbán administration's **international isolation**, the US and EU sanctions not only to narrow the regime's leeway, but also reveal its status of pariah.

- Up until 2014 only a small group of media outlets was critical towards the government. But since the biggest commercial television station **RTL Klub**—which had withstood a hostile takeover attempt and was later hit with a hefty advertising tax—became the main mouthpiece of government criticism. While the adopted political family gained control of TV2, the other major commercial TV station, the attempted takeover of RTL Klub was unsuccessful. The latter's daily news segment has abandoned its past tabloid journalism, replacing it with political news strongly critical of the government, while seeing its ratings double. The station is now revealing to viewers that their daily experiences are not isolated cases, but the general, day-to-day traits of the system. Simicska's alternative media empire is also chipping away at the government's position, creating doubt in the minds of Fidesz's core audience with its moderate but cunning criticism.

- As another consequence of the **ideological pyramid scheme**, Fidesz has eroded the moral boundary preventing its disillusioned sympathizers from being drawn in by the extreme right as Fidesz continues to lose popularity.

The string of electoral defeats at municipal government and parliamentary by-elections since the fall of 2014 testify to the intertwined, mutually reinforcing impact of the elements of the delegitimization spiral. Fidesz's candidates were defeated by a socialist candidate in Újpest, by an independent candidate supported by NGOs and the democratic opposition parties in Veszprém, and the extreme right Jobbik candidate in Tapolca, fracturing the two-thirds parliamentary majority ruling power.

The ruling power could only **break this delegitimization spiral exerting a downward pull** by expanding its tools of lawful and unlawful coercion, and **establishing a new equilibrium for its rule, albeit with decreased legiti-**

mization. However, the adopted political family is unable to do this due to the *coercion threshold.* The escalation of coercive tools comes up against other obstacles in Hungary—a member of the EU and NATO—than in countries that are not part of these organizations, such as Russia or the ex-Soviet republics of Central Asia. Although the regime's internal logic stemming from the loss of legitimization would be to move towards the more openly coercive forms of autocratic regimes, this is restricted by *geopolitical position that sets different thresholds on the coercion or violence that can be used.*

The Hungarian mafia state can manipulate democratic institutions, threaten and blackmail market players, subjugate various social groups, assisted by parliament, fidesznik municipal governments, the tax authority, the Government Control Office, the public prosecutor's office or even the Counter-Terrorism Center special ops unit, but Hungary's geopolitical position and EU and NATO membership prevents or restricts the regime from using *tools of open violence,* contrary to its Eastern relatives. We have previously discussed in depth how the mafia state uses the nonviolent tools of illegitimate coercion to reach its objectives. Why would it do otherwise if the tools of public authority coercion with no real social oversight are at its disposal? More aggressive measures are only needed against those who are not part of the patron-client structure of subordination, who disobey or fail to acknowledge the regime. No surprise that in Russia, journalists critical of the regime are victims of assassinations from time to time. Hungary cannot be compared to Russia or the ex-Soviet republics of Central Asia in terms of the degree of open repression, nonetheless the nature of mafia state is similar across these regimes. The sole difference is the threshold on the coercion or violence used. The difference between these regimes is no greater than between the single party communist dictatorships of the past built on the monopoly of state ownership, such as Hungary or Romania, and the Soviet Union. The question that appeared in the press, reflecting public sentiment, enquiring as to whether "Is Simicska afraid because of them? Mysterious deaths, unbelievable explanations..." signals the possibility of violence exceeding bloodless public coercion "if needed." The common trait shared by three of the four cases of death scrutinized in a piece by investigative journalist Antónia Rádi is that the victims were in possession of compromising information or databases that the adopted political family went through great pains to get its hands on.[31]

Due to the coercion or violence threshold, Orbán has no choice, in an effort to slow the delegitimization spiral, but to switch to top gear in applying the manipulative ideological pyramid scheme aimed at mobilizing the dark side of citizens: elements of homophobia, xenophobia, religious fundamentalism, the national freedom fight and of the opening towards the East are added to an increasingly inflammable mix featured in his core communication. Accordingly, at a Friends of Hungary event held in May 2015, initially hiding behind a quotation, Orbán said: "The energy that can be found in the international system today stems from the great autocratic powers. They are the ones taking action, while democracies only react. The world today consists of Europe arguing while the East is working. One sometimes feels that on our continent, debate is held in higher esteem than work. (...) At present, those who believe that Europe should go further towards expanding freedom are in majority, and this currently means three things. We would have greater freedom for instance, they say, if we could rid ourselves of our gender identity. They also think that we would have greater freedom if we could rid ourselves, say, of our national identity. And more progress could be made if we could rid ourselves of our God-given thoughts, freeing ourselves of the shackles of creation to decide more freely about our lives. We do not agree with this. It is better to state this openly. So in our view, what makes a person free is not ridding himself of the limitations stemming from his created nature. We do not think that we need to rid ourselves of our gender identity or our national identity, and we will not yield in these matters. We would rather have a bad reputation, but in these matters, we will not feign agreement. The truth is that we do not agree with the school of thought that calls itself progressive that has gained traction in Europe."[32]

This book has attempted to convince readers that when Orbán's actions seem irrational, inconsistent, random or even chaotic according to most analysts, it stems from the fact that they presume different underlying motives than the ones we attribute to him based on the illegitimate power of the patriarch. We regard Orbán's actions and words as calculatedly and consistently rational. Nonetheless when his power structure is shaken, his consistency compels him to take steps that are irrational even in light of his power. But in fact, what appears as irrational, impossible, crazy or even demented is none other than the unsustainability of his situation. It only shows that he has not escaped the fate of autocrats.

* * *

Although the mask has fallen from System of National Cooperation (NER), the mafia state, it has not lost any of its power, only losing some of its magic at best. What is in store: erosion, agony, and the fall....but this is a whole other story.

NOTES

1. http://nol.hu/belfold/a-kormany-ezzel-bosszut-all-a-magannyugdijpenztarban-maradt-embereken-1553061.
2. Viktor Orbán, Pávatánc, avagy hogyan verjük át az EU-t (Peacock dance, or how to fool the EU) - 31.05.2012; https://www.youtube.com/watch?v=0s5gzvb87ZY.
3. Ibid.
4. Viktor Orbán's speech given on March 15, 2011; http://www.origo.hu/itthon/percrolpercre/20110315-tudositas-a-marcius-15i-unnepsegekrol.html?pIdx=1.
5. Viktor Orbán's speech given on 15 March 2012; http://www.origo.hu/itthon/20120315-orban-viktor-miniszterelnok-marcius-15i-unnepi-beszede.html.
6. Orbán, Pávatánc.
7. It is no coincidence that Greece's situation within the eurozone is doubtful in light of its unorthodox economic wishes and its political environment slowly adapting to these wishes.
8. http://444.hu/2015/02/26/orban-ot-eve-harcol-az-eu-val-legszukebb-kore-addig-gazdagodott-belole/.
9. http://www.europarl.europa.eu/sides/getDoc.do?pubRef=-//EP//TEXT+REPORT+A7-2013-0229+0+DOC+XML+V0//HU.
10. Ibid.
11. Europe cannot wait any longer: France and Germany must drive ahead, *The Guardian*, June 3, 2015. http://www.theguardian.com/commentisfree/2015/jun/03/europe-france-germany-eu-eurozone-future-integrate.
12. Attila Ara-Kovács, "The Diplomacy of the Orbán System," forthcoming in: *Twenty-Four Sides of a Post-Communist Mafia State*, edited by Bálint Magyar and Júlia Vásárhelyi.
13. Ibid.
14. http://indavideo.hu/video/InfoRadio_-_Arena_-_Tolgyessy_Peter_-_1resz_1.
15. http://index.hu/belfold/2015/04/01/orban_kazahsztan_idegenek/.
16. http://javorbenedek.blog.hu/2015/06/22/vannak_tanulmanyok_paks2-rol_de_nem_veletlenul_titkosak.
17. http://hvg.hu/gazdasag/20151119_Brusszelben_elmeszeltek_Paks_IIot.
18. http://hvg.hu/gazdasag/20141022_Roganek_modositoja_Dorgolozzunk_meg_jobba.
19. http://vs.hu/kozelet/osszes/ujabb-nagy-biznisszel-tehet-szivesseget-az-oroszoknak-magyarorszag-1222#is15.
20. http://444.hu/215/02/10/a-met-és-az-mvm-menedzserei-atultek-egymas-szekebe/.

[21] http://tldr.444.hu/2015/01/14/a-legtobb-penzt-most-igy-lehet-csinalni-magyarorszagon/.

[22] http://index.hu/gazdasag/2015/06/22/met_mvm/; http://mszp.hu/hirek/a_nagy_gazlopas.

[23] http://444.hu/2015/11/05/nem-stimmel-a-met-mvm-uzlet-miniszteri-magyarazata

[24] http://vs.hu/kozelet/osszes/ujabb-nagy-biznisszel-tehet-szivesseget-az-oroszoknak-magyarorszag-1222#!s16.

[25] http://vilagterkep.atlatszo.hu/2015/02/17/igy-foglalta-el-putin-csehorszagot-hogyan-haloztak-be-az-oroszok-a-cseh-politikai-elitet/.

[26] http://444.hu/2015/04/16/oroszorszag-hibrid-haborut-inditott-europa-ellen/.

[27] https://euobserver.com/foreign/125881.

[28] http://444.hu/2015/04/16/sorra-buknak-brusszelben-a-magyar-penzek/.

[29] http://blog.atlatszo.hu/2014/10/a-rejtelyes-7750-diszkret-es-drasztikus/.

[30] Emil Kürthy (Bálint Magyar), *Polgárrá válni* [Becoming bourgeois], *Beszélő* Szamizdat, issue 4, September 1982; (http://beszelo.c3.hu/epublish/3/v1n2).

[31] http://atlatszo.hu/2015/02/13/miattuk-retteg-simicska-rejtelyes-halalesetek-hihetetlen-magyarazatok/.

[32] http://hvg.hu/itthon/20150509_Orban_Az_autokratikus_rendszerek_cseleked.

Annexes

Annex 1

Fidesz-affiliated persons at the head of sports associations

Sports Association	Name	"Related experience"
Hungarian Table Tennis Association	Roland Nátrán	State Secretary for the Finance under the ministership of Matolcsy, presently the CEO of Exim logo Hungarian Export-Import Bank Plc. and Hungarian Export Credit Insurance Plc.
Hungarian Wrestling Federation	Szilárd Németh	Representative of Fidesz for the "utility price cuts" campaign
Hungarian Ice Hockey Federation	Miklós Németh	CEO of Közgép Zrt.
Hungarian Handball Federation	Iván Vetési	Ministerial commissioner when appointed in 2011
Hungarian National Skating Federation	Lajos Kósa	Fidesz MP
Hungarian Basketball Federation	Ferenc Szalay	Fidesz Mayor of Szolnok since 2010
Hungarian Volleyball Federation	Csaba Poór	Founder of CME Hungary Zrt. marketing and communications company, helped the Fidesz candidates in Szeged for the 2010 elections, purportedly close to Gábor Kubatov
Hungarian Chess Federation	Miklós Seszták	MP since 2010. Minister of National Development in the third Orbán government since 2014
Hungarian Ski Association	Gábor Kálomista	One of the main suppliers of state media, with over a billion HUF (3.2 million euro) from the Hungarian National Film Fund under Andy Vajna for productions headed by him
Hungarian Tennis Association	Lajos Szűcs	Fidesz MP
Hungarian Rambler's Association (Friends of Nature)	István Garancsi	President of Videoton FC and close friend of Viktor Orbán
Hungarian Triathlon Union	Béla Bátorfi	Dentist of the Orbán family, developer of dental care tourism to Hungary
Hungarian Fencing Federation	Zsolt Csampa	Former MDF politician, joined Fidesz, Deputy State Secretary for the Ministry of the Interior

Source: 444.hu and atlatszo.hu
Based on http://tenytar.blog.hu/2015/02/27/fideszes_uradalmak_lettek_a_magyar_sportszovetsegek
    At the helm of the Hungarian Handball Federation Iván Vetési has since been replaced by Máté Kocsis, communications chief of Fidesz.

Annex 2

Special taxes on specific sectors in Hungary after 2010 (bn forint)

	2010	2011	2012	2013	2014E	2015 target
Special tax on financial institutions	182.3	168.5	84.9	139.1	148.4	144.2
Credit institutions' contribution	10.0	9.4	9.7	17.5	21.6	15.4
Special levy on select sectors	151.7	171.9	165.6	9.8	0.0	0.0
Income tax on energy suppliers	17.0	16.9	5.6	54.1	35.6	44.7
Telecom tax	0.0	0.0	12.2	47.0	56.4	56.4
Public health product fee	0.0	0.0	0.0	13.0	19.0	26.4
Accident tax	0.0	0.0	0.0	20.0	23.4	23.6
Financial transaction tax	0.0	0.0	0.0	259.6	269.4	206.2
Insurance tax	0.0	0.0	0.0	26.2	28.0	28.6
E-toll	0.0	0.0	0.0	45.0	127.7	150.0
Public utility infrastructure tax	0.0	0.0	0.0	60.0	54.0	54.0
Advertising tax	0.0	0.0	0.0	0.0	2.4	6.6
Supervision fee for food retail chains	0.0	0.0	0.0	0.0	0.0	30.0
Special tax on tobacco companies	0.0	0.0	0.0	0.0	0.0	10.0
Total	**361.0**	**388.0**	**278.1**	**721.3**	**815.9**	**825.1**
Stricter rules on the base for the local business tax	0.0	0.0	0.0	30.0	30.0	30.0
Grand total	**361.0**	**388.0**	**278.1**	**751.3**	**845.9**	**855.1**

timate (deductability of COGS changed)

Source: State Audit Office and own data of the online financial journal Portfolio,
http://www.portfolio.hu/en/economy/two_charts_that_reveal_the_mindset_of_the_hungarian_government.28805.html

Annex 3

Bank taxes in selected countries

Country	Amount of the bank tax (million euro)	Use of the revenue	Year
Sweden	250	Special fund for the help of banks	2009
United Kingdom	2300	Income for the budget	2011
Germany	1200	Special fund for the help of banks	2011
France	500	Special fund for the help of banks	2011
Austria	500	Income for the budget	2011/2012
Hungary	695	Income for the budget	2010
Poland	380	Income for the budget	2011
Croatia	—	Income for the budget	—

Source: http://www.politicalcapital.hu/blog/?p=1937739

Annex 4

Oligarchs' share of proceeds from agricultural development grants and size of areas receiving support

Agricultural holdings (corp. group) / Person (owner)	Agricultural development support (in billion forint)				Size of area funded		
	2011	2013	Total	Growth in %	2011	2013	Growth in %
1. Zsolt Nyerges – Lajos Simicska (Mezort Group)	3.739	5.186	8.925	38.7	14.7	23.17	57.6
2. Sándor Csányi (Bonafarm Group)	3.969	4.997	8.966	25.9	16.84	20.73	23.1
3. Tamás Leisztinger (Forrás Group)	2.676	3.139	5.815	17.3	11.97	23.75	98.4
4. István Mádl (Agroprodukt Group)	1.479	2.475	3.954	67.3	5.1	11.3	115.7
5. Árpád Dorogi – Helmut Gsuk – Tibor Zászlós (GSD Group)	1.15	1.813	2.963	57.7	7.66	13.96	82.2
6. László Kárpáti – Zsolt Harsányi – József Délity (KHD Group, Hód Mezőgazda Zrt.)	0.927	1.613	2.54	74.0	2.1	10.13	382.3
Total	13.94	19.223	33.163	37.9	58.37	103.04	76.5

Source: VS.hu

Annex 5

Distribution of state advertising revenues in media channels over two government cycles

Share of state advertising revenues among daily newspapers (May 2006–April 2014)

Gyurcsány–Bajnai governments (May 2006–April 2010)   Second Orbán government (May 2010–April 2014)

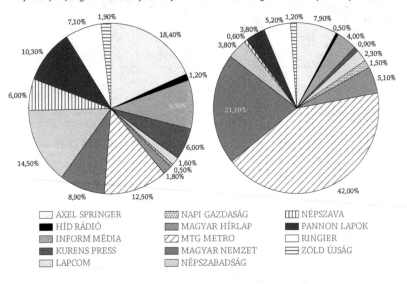

AXEL SPRINGER	NAPI GAZDASÁG	NÉPSZAVA
HÍD RÁDIÓ	MAGYAR HÍRLAP	PANNON LAPOK
INFORM MÉDIA	MTG METRO	RINGIER
KURENS PRESS	MAGYAR NEMZET	ZÖLD ÚJSÁG
LAPCOM	NÉPSZABADSÁG	

Share of state advertising revenues among social-political weeklies (May 2006–April 2014)

Gyurcsány-Bajnai governments (May 2006–April 2010)   Second Orbán government (May 2010–April 2014)

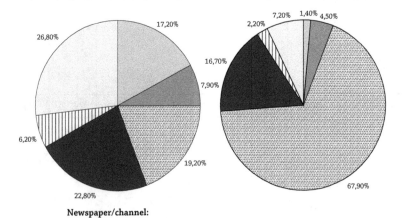

Newspaper/channel:

168 ÓRA	HETI VÁLASZ	MAGYAR NARANCS
FIGYELŐ	HVG	SZABAD FÖLD

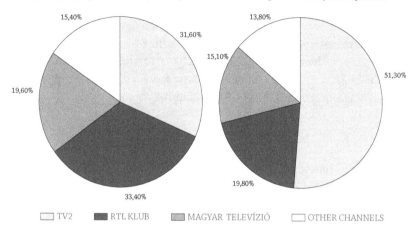

Share of state advertising revenues among televisions (May 2006–April 2014)

Gyurcsány-Bajnai governments (May 2006–April 2010)   Second Orbán government (May 2010–April 2014)

☐ TV2   ■ RTL KLUB   ▨ MAGYAR TELEVÍZIÓ   ☐ OTHER CHANNELS

Permission for the use of the diagrams was granted by Attila Bátorfy, journalist at kreatív.hu. (See also under the following link: http://www.kreativ.hu/databanya/cikk/ hogyan_mukodott_orban_es_simicska_mediabirodalma.)

List of accompanying studies

The following studies are a selection from studies from *Magyar polip – A posztkommunista maffiaállam* 1. és 2. [Hungarian octopus—The post-communist mafia state vols. 1 and 2, edited by Bálint Magyar and Júlia Vásárhelyi] (Budapest: Noran Libro, 2013 and 2014), forthcoming under the title *Twenty-Four Sides of a Post-Communist Mafia State*, edited by Bálint Magyar and Júlia Vásárhelyi, CEU Press – Noran Libro.

I.

1. Balázs Trencsényi: How shall I Call you?
2. György Csepeli: The Mafia State's Second-hand Clothes
3. Imre Vörös: A "Constitutional" Putsch in Hungary between 2010–2014
4. Zoltán Fleck: Law under the Mafia State
5. András Becker: Orbán's Wealth and Oligarchs
6. Dávid Jancsics: From Local Cliques to Mafia State: The Evolution of Network Corruption
7. Zoltán Lakner: Links in the Chain. Patron-Client Relationships in the Mafia State
8. Balázs Krémer: The Social Policy of the Mafia State and Its Effect on the Transformation of the Social Structure

II.

9. László Békesi: The Economic Policy of the Mafia State
10. Attila Károly Sós: Tribute Payments through Special Taxes: Income Generation, Populism and the Displacement of "Foreigners"
11. István Csillag: Mission: Get Rich. Exchange of Elites on a Family Basis
12. Éva Várhegyi: The Banks of the Mafia State
13. Iván Major: Utility Price Cuts and Sector-specific Taxes in Network Industries
14. András Deák: The Expansion of the Paks Nuclear Plant – A Captive to Policy and Power Dilemmas
15. Pál Juhász: Historic Incompetence in Agricultural Matters and Competitiveness

III.

Former Publications

This volume is an updated version of the Hungarian original, *A magyar maffiaállam anatómiája* (Budapest: Noran Libro), 2015. Both versions are based on, and often quoting from the following former publications of the author – studies, articles, interviews, and statements – without specific references in the text:

- Bálint Magyar, "Európai Magyarország—Liberális Ajánlat (programalkotási vázlat)," [European Hungary—Liberal proposal] in: *Egy leendő program elé*, SZDSZ, November 1999.
- Bálint Magyar, Egy liberális választási és kormányzati program vázlata [Outline of a liberal election and government program] *A Korszakváltás Programja*, SZDSZ, November 2000.
- Bálint Magyar, "Magyar polip – a szervezett felvilág" [Hungarian octopus—the organized upperworld], *Magyar Hírlap*, 21 February, 2001.
- Bálint Magyar, "Maffia-fejlesztési bank," *Népszabadság*, 7 March, 2001.
- Bálint Magyar, "A visszautasíthatatlan kétharmados ajánlat," *Népszabadság*, 12 March, 2011.
- Márton Kozák and Bálint Magyar, "Szürkeségből sötétségbe" [From twilight to darkness], *Népszabadság*, 4 June, 2011.
- "A hatalmi logika Mengyelejev-táblája – Magyar Bálint volt oktatási miniszterrel Rádai Eszter készített interjút." *Élet és Irodalom*, 28 October, 2011.
- *A demokrácia alkonyán, a diktatúra hajnalán. Az egykori magyar demokratikus ellenzék tagjainak újévi üzenete.* 2 January, 2012.
- Bálint Magyar, "Az új nemzeti középosztály. Szolgáló nemesek és udvari beszállítók rendje" [The new national middle class], *Élet és Irodalom*, 9 March, 2012.
- István Csillag and Bálint Magyar, "Az európai válságkezelés válsága" [The crisis of European crisis management], *Heti Világgazdaság*, 16 June, 2012.
- Bálint Magyar and Iván Pető, *Profi amatőrök – amatőr profik. Szociológiai csapdák és az SZDSZ*, part 10. Manuscript.
- "Ki játszik ilyet, majd megmondom, milyet" – Rádai Eszter interjúja Magyar Bálinttal [Eszter Rádai's interview with Bálint Magyar], *Mozgó Világ*, 39, no. 5 (2013): 19–32.

- Eszter Rádai, "A posztkommunista maffiaállam. Interjú Magyar Bálinttal" [Post-communist mafia state – Interview with Bálint Magyar], *Élet és Irodalom*, 14 June, 2013, 5–9.
- Bálint Magyar, "Magyar polip – A posztkommunista maffiaállam" [Hungarian octopus—Post-communist mafia state], in: *Magyar polip – A posztkommunista maffiaállam*, ed. Magyar Bálint és Vásárhelyi Júlia (Budapest: Noran Libro Kiadó), 2013.
- Bálint Magyar, "A posztkommunista maffiaállam rendszerképző sajátossága," in: *Magyar polip – A posztkommunista maffiaállam*, ed. Magyar Bálint és Vásárhelyi Júlia (Budapest: Noran Libro Kiadó), 2014.

Index of Names